Deep France

Celia Brayfield is the author of nine novels, including *Wild Weekend*, *Mister Fabulous and Friends*, *Heartswap* and the international bestseller *Pearls*, as well as a non-fiction guide to storytelling in popular fiction, *Bestseller*. She was born in north London and was educated at St Paul's Girls' School and Grenoble University. Before becoming a full-time novelist, she wrote for the *Evening Standard* and *The Times*. She has one daughter, with whom she now lives in West London.

Also by Celia Brayfield

FICTION

Pearls

The Prince

White Ice

Harvest

Getting Home

Sunset

Heartswap

Mister Fabulous and Friends

Wild Weekend

NON-FICTION

Bestseller

Glitter

Celia Brayfield

DEEP FRANCE

*A writer's year in
the Béarn*

PAN BOOKS

In memory of Glynn Boyd Harte

First published 2004 by Pan Books
an imprint of Pan Macmillan Ltd
Pan Macmillan, 20 New Wharf Road, London N1 9RR
Basingstoke and Oxford
Associated companies throughout the world
www.panmacmillan.com

ISBN 0 330 41182 9

Typeset by Intype Libra Ltd
Printed and bound in Great Britain by
Mackays of Chatham plc, Chatham, Kent

All Pan Macmillan titles are available from
www.panmacmillan.com
or from Bookpost by telephoning 01624 677237

Acknowledgements

Whenever I come to write this page of a book, I'm acutely and guiltily aware of how much a writer depends on her friends, who innocently carry on their existence, doing all the living that she's too chicken to do, and never really appreciating that their lives will become her raw material. This book more than any I've ever written has been inspired and created by my friends. It is in many ways a celebration of friendship and with all my skill and all my gifts I can't really express how grateful I am to the people who have made it possible.

First of all, I have to thank Willow and Tony Schulte, for introducing me to the corner of France which they have made theirs, for inspiring me, going travelling with me, welcoming me into their home, checking my facts, enlightening my ignorance and in turn introducing me to many of the people, places and experiences that made my year so memorable.

I'm also more grateful than I can say to Annabel and Gerald Marvin, for being the best of all possible neighbours, and for their gaiety, wisdom and generosity, without which the best bits would have been much less wonderful and the worst bits so much worse.

Without Andrew Downs and Geoffrey Wilkins it wouldn't have been nearly so exciting; nor would it have been so much fun without Gordon and Fiona Reid, not to mention Cam and Margot. The kindness of Margaret Grieve and the irrepressible spirit of Roger Hallett were as warm as all the sunshine we didn't have that summer. I'm also grateful to Mary Graham,

Acknowledgements

the owner of Maison Bergez, and Alexander and Annie Mill, who introduced us.

Marie-Pierre Moine was kind enough to read my manuscript and save me from looking too much like a complete fool. Denise Spencer accepted the challenge of translating some French rugby songs and Zoe Gelis cast a critical eye over my attempts to translate French poetry. Michael Barker generously shared his knowledge of art history. At Pan, Nicholas Blake, Senior Desk Editor, was a merciless exterminator of inaccuracies. Notwithstanding the best efforts of these experts, I accept full responsibility for any errors, misunderstandings, lurid overstatements, sloppy elisions of historical events, excessively free translations or economies with the *actualité* which may remain to offend the reader. Short extracts from the text have already appeared in *The Times* and the *New Statesman*, and I am most grateful to the editors of these publications for permission to reproduce this material.

Sometimes, when my agent, who is Jonathan Lloyd, the Managing Director of Curtis Brown, gives me a ring and I say, 'How are you?' he answers, 'Extraordinary,' which seems a fair description, particularly over this demanding year when his client was off doing more enviable things than mere writing. I'm also grateful to Tara Lawrence, my editor at Time Warner Books, for keeping her meticulous eye on *Mister Fabulous and Friends* and commissioning *Wild Weekend*.

I am immensely grateful to Imogen Taylor, for being clever enough to commission this book and for the continuing faith in my writing, which has been the best inspiration any author could possibly have. Above all, of course, I would like to thank Chloe, for saying, 'Go for it, Mum.'

Contents

Introduction

On the Road

It's after 2 a.m. and I'm driving through the Landes. And driving through the Landes. And driving through the Landes. And driving through . . .

Sometimes I think the Béarnais arranged the creation of this wilderness to make sure that northerners would despair, turn back and leave them alone. If it wasn't dark, the landscape would be putting me in a trance. Flat, covered in pine trees, ferns and heather, a dark forest stretching away to infinity all around us. The Sleeping Beauty's best defence.

My daughter Chloe is dozing in the passenger seat. About an hour ago, I missed our turning off the ring road and we went round Bordeaux twice. She woke up long enough to point out that we'd driven off the Pont François Mitterrand before. The first time I said improving parentlike things, like: 'See, the French are happy to name a big public monument after a politician. You can't imagine anyone in Manchester wanting to name a bridge after a Prime Minister, can you?' She's gone back to sleep now. She's taken a few days off from university to help me start this adventure.

On the back seat are our three cats. They stopped yowling about six hundred miles ago, but they are not happy. Tarmac – well, guess what, he's the black one – is sitting on top of the cat boxes keeping watch; he knows he's the only being in the household with a decent sense of responsibility. Piglet, the long-haired tabby, is sitting in his box with outrage on his whiskers. His mother, the Duchess, has crammed herself under the seat. She's a James Bond cat, a white Persian. Long pedigree, no brains. Everybody warned me not to have one.

Behind the cats is the rest of my life. A box of books, the computer, the duvet, a bag of clothes. You're a writer, you can work anywhere. Can I really? People have been saying that to me for years. Now I'm going to find out if they're right. Nobody, but nobody, warned me not to do this except a writer friend of far greater distinction, whose eyes widened in horror when I said I was taking off without a contract for my next book. Apart from him, the hardest part of the last few weeks has been dealing with the universal envy which I provoked every time I said, 'I'm going to live in France for a year.'

Friends, family, neighbours, colleagues. The bank manager, my accountant, the estate agents who've rented out our house, the lady in the dry cleaners, the guys in the garage. They gave me back my elderly Daihatsu jeep with a card: *Have a good time in France. Easy on the wine.* That's how the average Brit thinks of France. A place to have a good time. With wine.

I could be having a better time. I'm tired. I've driven hundreds of miles and I don't actually like driving. I've packed our possessions into a container and turned our home into a neutrally decorated wood-floored rental property. I've said tearful goodbyes to my friends, a whole ocean of emotion poured into the few stress-free moments we could find in our diaries.

I've lived on the same page of the London *A–Z* since I was twenty. Page 73, with a few short excursions to Page 74. I used to love living in London. Now I'm tired of the crackheads and the chewing gum on the pavements. I've been a writer since I was twenty; I still love writing but after eight novels and a mountain of non-fiction, a girl gets cabin fever. And I've brought up Chloe alone for twenty-two years. From the tooth fairy to the tuition fees, and beyond – that's a long time to do two people's jobs. 'I've been thinking,' I said to her about six months ago. 'I could rent our house out and go and live in France for a year. What do you think?' 'Go for it, Mum,' she said at once. Now maybe she's not so sure.

The guys in the garage, bless 'em, have buggered the electrics so the stereo doesn't work. Somewhere in Portsmouth I bought a blue plastic battery radio that looks like a foetal Dalek. It's hissing at me on the dashboard while it tries to pick up a French station. I don't think I'm starry-eyed, but that's something you never know about yourself until it's too late. Will I be able to live with French radio for a year?

I'm driving south, south, south. My destination is almost as far south as you can go in France. Just half a valley away from the Basque Country, an hour's drive from the Spanish border. Deep France in the geographical sense and Deep France in the cultural sense. *La France profonde*, the France of fields and farms, of little villages and ruined castles, of vineyards, of cows and sheep, chickens and ducks, corn and cabbages. Actually, the Béarn is not noted for its cabbages, but for garlic and Jurançon wine, the national symbols.

What am I looking for? What everyone, French or otherwise, has always looked for in Deep France: a simpler, more authentic life. I'm a modern Marie Antoinette, I want to play at being a shepherdess with freshly washed sheep in my model village. Well, it would be nice to grow artichokes and keep chickens, anyway. The key to my new home is heavy in my bag, a great iron key about eight inches long. A real key to a real life.

I am also looking for the spirit of the land. For ten years I've been visiting this small and overlooked corner and it seems as if I've never been here long enough. The mountains always call me. Of course, when you get into the mountains, the peaks beyond them are still calling. Already, I'm ten years older than when I first saw the snow shining in the far distance beyond the green hills, and if I don't set off now, maybe I'll never get there.

Finally, the never-ending Landes gives way to the undulating hills of the Chalosse. Outside Dax, we pass the statue of the *écarteur*, the cruelty-free Landais matador who stands weaponless in the path of a charging bull. The road from here is a Roman road, leading straight as a die into the darkness. I turn off and drive through the sleeping village of Ossages, with its commanding church spire and the house of the friends who introduced me here, but they're away now so we're on our own.

Between the Chalosse and the Béarn is the valley of the Gave de Pau, a broad green river that rises in the Pyrenees, above Lourdes. The river has been joined by the motorway and the Route Nationale 117, which we cross at a village called Puyoo, built a hundred years ago as a railhead and dormitory for the rope-making industry. The rope-works sign, *Tressage de Puyoo*, is still painted on a wall by the side of the bridge.

Now we're in the Béarn, though it hardly shows. Thick patches of mist lie across the road as it sweeps up a steeper hill, then descends to the roundabout with a fountain outside Saliès-de-Béarn. Nobody about. No police running a stake-out for ETA terrorists or drunk drivers, no customs officers hoping to catch a foreign truck importing drugs from Morocco. It's November, thank God, so the begonias on the roundabout have been removed. The roundabouts of France, the nadir of municipal art, the proof that not all the clichés are right, that everything French is not automatically more stylish than everything not-French.

Chloe is awake now. I turn off, and we pass an avenue of plane trees. They look too young to have been planted to shade Napoleon's army, about the same size as those painted more than a hundred years ago, by Monet and Pisarro, up in the north, safely close to Paris. No Impressionist ever ventured this far, not even Van Gogh.

Three deer leap across the road in front of us. The road starts wavering, pottering, winding, climbing, twisting. I can feel that it's running along the spine of the hills, following an old shepherd path chosen for the best sight of the sheep. The night is now absolutely dark and starless.

Suddenly the Dalek radio bursts into life and the joyful voice of a Basque singer resonates through the crammed body of the car. Somewhere out there are the mountains, and somewhere in the mountains is a lone DJ, getting ready to talk to his compatriots in the oldest language in Europe. All five of us revive instantly. We're nearly there.

At the crossroads, turn right past the one-time *auberge*, then left by the pollarded plane trees outside the ex-bar, then right where the signpost says 'ORRIULE'. That will be our village. Or rather, my village. I'm out of 'our' now, I'm into 'my'. After twenty-one – well, twenty-two really – years, Chloe and I are taking different paths.

The gate is on the right, past the bamboo. The gate is open. To be truthful, the gate is half off its hinges and looks like it's been in an open condition for several decades. Through the gate lies the house.

It is a tradition of the English-abroad genre of writing that somebody falls in love with a house. I did not fall in love with Maison Bergez. This is an arranged marriage. I've seen the house only once before, on a sulking day last August. All I can remember are small dark rooms crammed with crazy furniture, and my friends telling me that it'll be fine, I'll be able to make it nice, and anyway, it's the only house to rent for miles around.

The door is massive and studded, and the key won't open

it, but I've been warned about this, and given a tutorial in key jiggling. After some minutes, the lock reluctantly turns and the door opens. A beamed ceiling. A tiled floor. A light switch. The staircase.

I remember the staircase, a handsome little feature of polished oak. The house has a lot of modest status symbols like this, two stone steps to the front door, a false balcony at the landing window, the pollarded catalpa trees outside; the date carved over the front door: 1897; small embellishments to emphasize that this is not a peasant hovel.

It's not a traditional Béarnais house, either. The Béarnais style is a tall, narrow stone-walled building with a steep brown-tiled roof whose hipped ridges run down to drooping eaves. It's the house you know from fairy-story illustrations, as owned by Cinderella's father. Maison Bergez isn't typical. Its roof shape is low-pitched, like the Landais or the Basque houses, and it boasts the plastered walls and the double-fronted layout of a nineteenth-century town house. Only the dark green shutters are of the region.

Inside, half the wall in one of the front rooms is taken up with a magnificent stone fireplace, with a massive iron basket and a chain to suspend your cauldron from. A full-on peasant-style *cheminée*, no pretensions here. Upstairs is some of the original furniture, *lits-bateaux* in oak and mahogany, huge armoires, one with a key labelled, in tiny writing, *chambre de maman*. This *maman* chooses the smallest bedroom, for the ease of heating.

It's the beginning of November and deadly cold. The house's guardians have left a vase of red canna lilies, a welcome card and a bottle of wine. We carry in our bags, shut the doors and open the cat boxes. We make the beds and Chloe sleeps, but I can't. I am as wide-eyed as the night after childbirth. A new life starts here.

In the morning, we give the cats the run of the house.

Obese metropolitan that he is, it takes Piglet about five seconds to realize that there are mice in the kitchen, and to jam himself under the hot-water tank in pursuit of them. We hear squeaking and scuffling, then the bulk of our youngest reappears, cobwebby and elated. Just like us.

We go outside to stand on the steps and look at the mountains. The house faces south, with the two catalpa trees in front of it. The fields slope down to the valley from the far side of the road, and the Pyrenees fill all the horizon, a 180 degree kaleidoscope. Foothills, blue and purple ranges, snow-capped peaks. As the clouds race up from the Atlantic, the air changes constantly, and the view with it. One minute you can see the grey crags of the middle ranges as clear as a photograph, the next there are only the peaks, sparkling in the sun.

'Are you in my dream or am I in yours?' asks Chloe.

We could watch forever but there is work to do. The owner of Maison Bergez has left in situ a vast quantity of knick-knacks which would shame a car-boot sale: dozens of postcards with curly corners, metres of dog-eared romance novels, malevolently bad paintings, ugly lamps, a sinister doll in a blue velvet dress with a rabbit-fur hat who flops like Coppelia on a bedside table.

From the beams hang macramé plant-pot holders dripping with sad spider plants. The sofa is in the dining room, the table and chairs in front of the hearth. It takes two days to move the basics into position.

There is some urgency, not only because a writer has to keep cheerful and my mood tends to crash in ugly surroundings, but because our first house guests are expected for Christmas. 'You are still going, aren't you?' asked Glynn, the painter. 'Of course I'm still going,' I replied. 'Oh, good. Because I've got an exhibition of paintings of France and the gallery got *tremendously* excited when I promised them some of Biarritz. Only thing is, I've got to be back in London by January the sixth.'

We shop, briefly, to fill the fridge, and I cook some of our favourite things, pumpkin gratin and *poulet basquaise*, recipes from the region which we love and have put in the family cookbook. I want to convince both of us that the basic things in life aren't going to change. When I realized that I was to be a single mother, I vowed to make an extra effort to prepare good meals and serve them with proper ceremony, realizing that our home was to be the centre of our social life and afraid that one day Chloe would be judged inferior if she wasn't used to napkins and home cooking. Besides, my mother was a cook by profession. She taught me to stir sauces as soon as I was old enough to hold a wooden spoon, and it seemed the right thing for me to do in my turn with my daughter.

So there will be recipes in this book – how could there not be? The South-West is the breadbasket of France. Farming is the bedrock of the regional economy. The rolling hills are perpetually changing colour with what they are producing, gold with corn, white with flocks of ducks or sheep, brown with kiwi fruit, russet with vines, red with apples, grey with melon vines, black with the plastic that brings on the straw-berries. Every week throughout the summer a different town puts out the flags and opens the bars for the festival of whichever harvest it claims – the peppers, the beans, the ham, even the salt.

People eat what's grown and raised around them, which seems to me the way things should be. Amazingly, even though I grew up in a desolate London suburb, only a few streets away from the neighbourhood where Zadie Smith's *White Teeth* was set, our family grew their own fruit and vegetables, and kept chickens. We had Hitler to thank. My parents had lived through World War II and obeyed the government's exhortation to 'Dig for Victory' and turned their suburban plot into a market garden. Food was rationed in Britain for years after the war was over, so they kept on gardening and never completely lost the habit.

With childhood memories of collecting eggs and picking raspberries, I have always felt uncomfortable living in a greedy, ignorant metropolis, and being tempted by invisible food chemists to live off the labour of harvesters in another continent. I am that woman who causes a trolley jam in a London supermarket as she stands rooted to the spot by the fruit chillers, trying to calculate the food-miles per grape in a bunch labelled 'Country of Origin: Guatemala'. I was also that mother who grew tomatoes on the balcony and runner beans on the patio and took her daughter fishing. If I have to be the last link in the food chain, I'd like to be at least partly conscious.

Besides, this is also one of the great gastronomic regions of France. Food is its past, its present and its future. And its politics. Its greatest king, Henri IV, started out as plain Henri of Navarre and won the heart of his people by promising that in his reign every peasant would have a chicken in the pot every Sunday. Many dishes that ordinary people from here have cooked and eaten for centuries were eventually reinvented in Paris and became the basis of classic French cuisine. Many others – for me, the better ones – remained the keynotes of French country cooking. And if Alexandre Dumas, the supreme mythologist of all Gascony, could travel round Europe writing cook books, I think I'm allowed a few recipes.

After two days, Chloe went back to university. She had just begun her second year of a degree in literature and film studies, and she was anxious to do well. On our last evening we drove to St-Palais, a little Basque market town about half an hour to the south, to have dinner at the cheap and cheerful Auberge du Foirail on the main square. It was packed with beefy young men having a piss-up after the kiwi harvest. For the coming year, for me, there will be no more heaving bars, no more slumping girls with pierced navels, no more slobbering lads going on about the footy, no more irony, no more vodka-with-everything and no more getting mugged for your mobile on the way home.

Chloe hates flying, so next morning she took the TGV from Dax to Paris, then the Eurostar to Ashford in Kent, which is handily near her university in Canterbury. It was a slow and hair-raising drive, because a thick white fog came down overnight. Maison Bergez is on a hill. Actually, half of the Béarn is made up of steep little hills, laced about with hedges and copses, the hollows filled with woodland. It is the landscape of a medieval tapestry, full of flourishes and short perspectives, embroidered with oak trees and mythical beasts. When a fog gathers, however, you can't see a thing.

I waved goodbye to her on Dax station. She sent me a text. 'Don't be sad, Mum. It'll soon be Christmas.' I saved it, next to the clever message featuring a semaphoring stick person made of letters, saying:

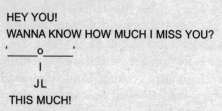

HEY YOU!
WANNA KNOW HOW MUCH I MISS YOU?
‘_____o_____’
           l
           JL
THIS MUCH!

The fog was melting away and the sun rising over the invisible mountains as I drove back. The tops of the hills were clear in the sun, but where the mist still filled the valleys it looked as if someone had poured milk into them. I'm on my own now, for the first time for twenty-one years.

November

Orriule – Maison Bergez is behind
the trees at the top of the hill

The First Week

I've been here almost seven complete days. I'm so tired I can hardly type. Yesterday I almost fell asleep at the wheel of the car. My bum aches, my quadriceps are screaming and at the end of the day a gin and tonic goes down really easily. I'm too tired to feel lonely, which is just as well, since I have met only several cheeky dogs, who run in and out of the open gateway as if they own the place.

It is possible that Orriule is actually run by the dogs. They are all outrageous mongrels, from a tiny genetic absurdity with a shaggy coat, a curled tail and legs two inches long to things that look almost, but not quite, like pointers. They meet every morning on the corner of the lane opposite Maison Bergez, have a lively discussion about their affairs then disperse in self-important groups to patrol different parts of the village.

The few humans I pass on the roads around the village stare at me with open curiosity, but nobody says hello, although they must know who I am. There are very few British here. The Béarn is a wild frontier for ex-pats; previously, I've met two kinds of foreigners in this region: those who have settled here for the love of it, and the rest — which includes the broke, the crazy and the people who got in their car in Sheffield and drove blindly south until they ran out of money. I called a couple whose names I had been given, and got the husband on the phone. 'Come over any time, we're pissed as newts here,' he slurred. Was I going to turn into a sodden ex-pat? It seems to be a real danger.

Will I miss friendly old London? Or will I only miss the filthy streets, the dismal shopping mall and my mad neighbours? Every metropolis has a high quota of roaming maniacs. On our street we have our share of items, including a character, who calls the blossom from his neighbour's apple tree 'filth'.

I have set up the computer, bought a French modem cable and connected up the technology. The day is starting to get a rhythm. Writing needs a rhythm. There are days when rhythm doesn't happen and everything slides into a pleasant sequence of pottering, which you rationalize by explaining to yourself that it is more creative to dawdle back from Rymans via the junk shop on the corner, or that you really *really* need to tidy up that box of handy old nails and screws *right now*.

The days which slide are pleasant but they weigh heavy on my conscience. Worse, much worse, are the days when the rhythm gets choppy then breaks into something agonizingly and disgustingly chaotic, which is like that moment when you know you're going to throw up, but extended for an entire morning. This is not a good feeling. My theory – get a rhythm and keep it. The day starts with the sound of the dogs barking and my neighbour's tractor roaring past. When the school bus, actually a luxury coach, comes by I know I should be through with the coffee and heading for my desk

It snowed this morning, big fluffy flakes whirling in from the north. At first I thought they were falling leaves. They didn't settle. This afternoon the sky cleared – meaning huge grey and white clouds came surging over the intense heavenly blue above them – and when I went into Sauveterre to get my *Times* the landscape was bathed in rich golden sunlight. The trees are redder and browner every day, burnished by the sinking sun. The mountains are clear in the distance, snow-capped now. I arrange the room which is to be my office so that I can see the Pyrenees from the desk. My neighbours, I notice, have all their shutters firmly closed.

Sauveterre is my nearest town. It is a jewel. The name means 'safe ground', describing it in the lawless early Middle Ages, when its huge grey-stone fortress was impregnable and guarded the road south to Spain. What's left of the fortress is a grey-stone battlement, sweeping along the top of a cliff that overlooks the river, and a mighty, half-ruined tower. Huge magnolia trees grow wild along the bottom of the cliff, and half a medieval bridge spans the water. Behind the tower of the Romanesque church the main square opens out, in front of a gracious seventeenth-century Hôtel de Ville.

Sauveterre's fate has always been to under-achieve its own magnificence. There are two beautiful hotels overlooking the river; one, the Hostellerie du Château, was shut because the original owner has died and so many cousins have inherited the business that they can't decide what to do with it. The other is also shut.

A la Maison

The house is sorted now, and ready for my books, plus clothes and the household stuff I couldn't live without, which will come in a container next month. The workshop is stuffed to its beams with macramé plant-pot holders and fringed lampshades. The French beds are against the wall as they were intended to be, the floorboards gleaming, the walls bare. I can see our friends in the place. I have a little white bedroom with a dressing table and my clothes folded on shelves. This feels like my home now.

I've put our family photographs on the wall, together with a couple of fine paintings by Glynn, and the framed cover of *Variety*, the American show-business newspaper, on which my name appears. I am very, very proud of having been on the front page of *Variety*. The story refers to Tom Cruise, whose production company bought an option on my last novel last year. They bought it to turn into a film starring Nicole Kidman. Then Tom Cruise and Nicole Kidman got divorced. The option is still current, but I suspect that all I will have to show for it is my name in *Variety* and the memory of being briefly brushed by stardust from Tinseltown.

On Sunday, somebody spoke to me at last. There had been a hard frost, overnight temperatures down to $-3°$, followed by a glorious sunny morning. I set off to walk around the village with my camera. My neighbour over the road smiled at me as he passed in his car.

All the countryside is white with frost, every bramble leaf dusted with diamonds. Everywhere the noise of falling leaves, pattering on the branches on their way down. The hedges are foaming with yellow-green mistletoe.

I met a woman on the road, a farmer walking down with her dog to move her cows to another field. We chatted for a few minutes about the weather. She'd found an icicle as long as that (three centimetres) on her tap and was glad she'd taken her flowers in or they would have been dead this morning. I'm amazed that I can remember enough French to get through this conversation. The dog's fur was hanging in dun-coloured dreadlocks.

Orriule

The village is scattered over two small hills, and divides into the realms of body and spirit, or church and state. Maison Bergez is near the top of the temporal zone. There are two houses above it, one just over the brow of the hill, which I can hardly see, and my immediate neighbour at the end of the field above the garden, a large, handsome farmhouse with palm trees and oleanders outside.

Downhill from Maison Bergez is a pottery, with a showroom full of blue-and-white plates decorated with a cherry pattern and stoneware bowls glazed in a brilliant metallic turquoise, the signature style of the potter. Behind the pottery is another business that is dependent on the natural deposit of clay in the hillside, a factory whose speciality is medieval-style roof tiles. About twenty people seem to work here, judging by the cars, but it is well hidden by pines and cypress trees, so when you look back at Orriule from the next hill, you can hardly see the factory and the warehouse at all.

Opposite the pottery is the *mairie*, a new building, clean-walled and grey-shuttered, plus the post box, the phone box, and the new village hall, the *salle multiactivités*, essential in every small village because the national budget for rural regeneration has to be spent on something. The hall is one storey, connecting at right angles to the village school, with the *fronton*, the court on which pelota is played, filling the open space between them.

The noise of a ball being knocked about the pelota court by an idle boy was to become one of the most evocative sounds of Orriule in the months to come. The slow, echoing *ka-pok*, *ka-pok* is to the Béarn what the smack of leather on willow is to an English village. Pelota is a Basque game which exists in many different variations, most of which are like squash played with wicker scoops instead of racquets. Orriule is not a Basque village, of course, but pelota, like many other Basque institutions, seems to offer an enhanced sense of identity to the entire region, so when the hall was built the pelota court was considered an absolute necessity.

Beyond these buildings are the farms, their barns spilling down the hillsides in attitudes of dilapidation. Every old building is crowned with a Béarnais roof, ending in fantastic pointed eaves: Gothic, fanciful, the roofs of the tumbledown cottages of the poor woodcutters in the stories of Europe's childhood. The house walls are of the local white limestone, rendered with *crépi* which, after several centuries of weather, mud and cow shit, takes on a pale beige hue, the colour which people in Notting Hill pay fortunes to paint mixers to achieve.

You can work out the organic evolution of a Béarnais farm. First, somebody builds a fine stone farmhouse, usually on the shoulder of a hill where he will have a good view of his cows, and plants a handsome pair of palm trees outside the front door. Then he builds a fine stone barn, usually at right angles, and then a second barn a bit later, usually of a different size and in different materials. Then the next generation inherit the place, ambitions of grandeur trickle away, and they chuck up the add-ons, the pig sties and the poultry house, with maybe another barn, or a smaller house for the younger brother, then perhaps a nice concrete all-purpose building, and a tin-roofed lean-to and wood store. After the first hundred years, the whole complex starts to surrender to gravity, rain, wind and the occasional earthquake, all of which encourage the walls to crumble downhill a few centimetres more each year. The result is chaotic, dilapidated, picturesque and nothing like the super-neat farms of Normandy, with their matching stable blocks and semicircular gravel drives.

As you keep walking downhill, the next thing you pass is the fish pond and/or reservoir, created by damming a stream

in a hollow of the hillside. There is a small pine wood behind
it on one side, and the rest of the land around it is marshy
and covered with tufts of that spiky grass that's half a reed and
always grows where there is underground water. The stream
itself trickles out of a pipe at the foot of the dam, but picks
up momentum from ditches feeding into it at the bottom of
the valley, and rushes happily away to the south, overhung
with alders. It will eventually hit the bottom of the big valley
and run into the big river, the Gave d'Oloron.

Then the road climbs again, up the next hill, which belongs
to the church and the spirit. The church looks like not much
more than a pile of rocks, a building with vastly thick walls
but so tiny that it is dwarfed by the slabs of porphyry marking the family graves in the minute churchyard. It too stands
on the hilltop. I paced out the walls to measure them, allowing for the massive stone buttress on the downhill side.
Twenty-five metres long, with an immaculate tiled roof.

The interior is beautifully plain, white walls rising to
a dome over the altar, which is an oak chest carved with
Maltese crosses. The pine pews are recent. Against the back
wall, in the shadow of the wooden balcony, stands a line of
prie-dieu chairs, every one different, carved in country style
from different woods. The copper cover of the font is highly
polished, and by the door a bowl from my neighbour the
potter holds the holy water.

Across the road from the church is a very old and largely
dead oak tree, its gnarled roots rising clear of the tarmac.
The oak was a sacred tree to the Basques, and to the Celts,
and the fact that nobody has tidied up this hulk and turned it
into firewood suggests that the tradition has lingered. A half-
rotten notice board, with nothing on it, is nailed to the trunk.

I walked down through the village then turned up the hill
to Orion, joining the road from Sauveterre that runs along a
ridge of hills. We are on the pilgrim route to Compostela, and

just outside Orion is a medieval hostel for the faithful who've set out to walk over the Pyrenees to the shrine of St James in Compostela, in Spain.

As I passed through a wood I heard birds calling. The notes were rounded and expressive, but much deeper than the call of the doves. I didn't recognize the sound and wondered what silly species would advertise itself to predators so noisily. Then a line of birds flew low overhead, about fifty of them, a long ribbon of silhouettes, wing tip to wing tip, rippling across the clear blue sky above the bare tree tops and calling to each other as they went. The cranes were flying south for the winter.

Not all the wildlife is so majestic, or so far off. Something brown scuttled into the bamboo thicket by the front gate yesterday. Something black shot out of the woodpile into the undergrowth this morning. It was a rat – there are half-gnawed walnut shells in all the gaps between the logs. I'm not a woman to freak over domestic rodents. I think mice are rather sweet, but only outside my own living space. Rats really aren't my style. I decided it was time to let the cats out for a stroll.

Tarmac, old and stiff as he was, was still a deadly hunter. He stalked down the front steps and investigated the garden systematically, spending a lot of time sniffing around the kitchen window. He made the other two look like amateurs, and they watched him gratefully.

Maison Bergez seemed to have a terrifying case of subsidence. There were huge cracks in all the walls, and the floors sloped in all directions. By local standards, none of this was cause for concern. However, I was so unused to uneven floors that the first time I got out of the bath I nearly fell over.

My spiritual friend Adrienne had given me her feng shui guide, from which I diagnosed the house as a major disaster zone. The front door jammed and wouldn't open, nor would the door to the room that was now my office. Instructed by Adrienne, I had packed away the clutter from the hall and the landing, but feng shui divides a home into areas bringing good luck to various specific aspects of life, and it seemed that the wealth zone of this house contained the loos, the drains and, worst of all, the septic tank, all guaranteed to bring ruin on the occupants. When I worked it out, the bathroom has been in the wealth area of every house I've ever owned.

Adrienne advised a mirror or several to attract the right chi. I moved a mirror into position and the pin holding it fell out of the wall immediately. On the phone, Adrienne cackles with laughter. 'That's what happens,' she says, 'houses fight back.'

Where Are You, Exactly?

People are calling, people are emailing, and this is the question everybody asks. I'm in the Béarn, I say. They're confused. They ask: Er – where *is* the Béarn? Between Pau and Biarritz, I say briskly, having worked out that a lot of people have heard of Biarritz, the big seaside resort on the Basque coast, and some have also heard of Pau, which is not only the Béarnais regional capital but also one of those towns to which the English, in the past century or so, have taken a particular fancy. Pau is also the setting for *Aspects of Love*, the story by David Garnett which inspired the Lloyd-Webber musical. So the Pau–Biarritz formula seems to have the highest recognition factor.

Not a high recognition factor, however. People say, 'Is that near the Dordogne? Is that near the Lot? Is that near Béziers/Foix/Cahors/the Aveyron?' No, no, no, no and no. I'm south of the Dordogne, where the British are so well established that some have even become village mayors. I'm

south of the Lot, with its hard-baked fields of sunflowers.
I'm even south of the Gers, which the British property finders
are pushing as the new Dordogne.

I'm hundreds of kilometres west of Béziers and the rest.
They're on the Mediterranean side and I'm near the Atlantic
coast. Oh, people say, groping for geography, you must be
near . . . er . . . Bordeaux? Not really. Two and a half hours
south of Bordeaux.

Then there is silence. People run out of map references. I'm
in the south, I say. The deep south. As far south as you can go
without getting to the Basque Country. Mystification can
be heard. Isn't the Basque Country in Spain? Not entirely.
There are seven Basque provinces. Four in Spain and three
in France – Soule, Labourd and Basse-Navarre. The Soule is
nearest to us, it starts on the other side of the big river down
in the valley here. Then people say, 'Oh.' Then they say, 'And
when are you back in London?'

It doesn't help that there are at least four perfectly accur-
ate ways to describe this location. First, the departmental.
Orriule is in Département 64, the Pyrénées-Atlantiques.
When I want the weather report from the *Figaro*'s telephone
weather service, I key in 64. Simple.

Second, there is the provincial. On some maps, such as
that used by the electricity board, Orriule is in Aquitaine.
Everything south of Bordeaux and west of Toulouse gets
lumped into Aquitaine at times. British people with a taste for
history can usually relate to Aquitaine, because the English
used to think they owned it. Maybe we were tempted by the
description of a medieval writer called Heriger of Lobbes:
'Opulent Aquitaine, sweet as nectar thanks to its vineyards,
dotted about with forests, overflowing with fruit of every kind
and endowed with a superabundance of pasture land.'

For a while, England had a right to Aquitaine. This came
with a queen, a beautiful red-head, in her day the richest

heiress in Europe – Eleanor of Aquitaine. She was thirty-one, the ex-wife of the King of France, when she ran off and married a nineteen-year-old, Henri, Duke of Normandy, in Poitiers. By way of a honeymoon, the young power couple travelled through Aquitaine to recruit some troops, and with the help of this army, Henry became King Henry II of England two years later, in 1154.

Although Henry owed a lot to his French soldiers, forging a kingdom out of England and Aquitaine was straining the logic of geography, at a time when it would take a month to travel the length of the realm, most of which was still a collection of small feudal states with ever-changing borders and ever-shifting alliances. The dynamic Henry and the astute Eleanor kept their dual kingdom together in their lifetimes, but after both were dead much blood was spilled by later English kings trying to pursue their claim to this lush French province. After the Hundred Years War, Crécy, Poitiers, Henry V at Agincourt and finally Joan of Arc, the French reclaimed Bordeaux and everything south of it in 1453.

There are traces of England all over the land that Eleanor and Henry ruled together, which includes most of the west of France. The stained-glass window they commissioned to commemorate their wedding is still in Poitiers Cathedral, while the cathedral in Bayonne is rampant with three-lion emblems. The pretty little town of Mauléon, half an hour south of here, is overlooked by the ruins of the massive castle built by the most appealing of Henry and Eleanor's sons, Richard I of England, Cœur de Lion. There are also places called Hastingues and Commingues, and families called Smith and Richardeson, and liking for bacon sandwiches, and a passion for rugby. Also, there is a folk song in the repertoire of the local bands which shares almost everything with the Cockney classic, 'Roll Out the Barrel'. Then there is the question of the Gascon sense of humour.

The third possible way to describe my location is to say that it's in Gascony. I wouldn't attempt this in front of a hard-line Béarnais, because the Béarn has always claimed the status of a state separate from its larger neighbour in the South-West of France, even though at times they've been ruled by the same person. Nor would I talk about Gascony to Parisians, because they would just snigger. Nor would I mention Gascony in the hearing of one of my French friends in London, who sniffs that only the English talk about Gascony. However, my bank account comes under the Gascony department of the Crédit Agricole and the bit of the Atlantic off the coast by Biarritz is called the Golfe du Gascogne on my Michelin map, so it seems that the French also recognize the name.

Besides, Gascony is as much a state of mind as a region. A twelfth-century travel guide written for the pilgrims to Compostela describes the Gascons as poor but generous people, but warns that they can also be frivolous, talkative, cynical and promiscuous. No wonder I like them so much.

By the time of the Three Musketeers, the Gascons were also known as swashbuckling meat-heads, all mouth and trousers, always looking for a fight. Edmond Rostand, the author of Cyrano de Bergerac, made his hero one of the Gascony cadets, under a commander called Castel-Jaloux, and this is how Cyrano introduced his regiment:

> These are the Gascony cadets –
> Captain Castel-Jaloux is their chief –
> Braggers of brags, layers of bets,
> They are the Gascony cadets.
> Barons who scorn mere baronets,
> Their lines are long and tempers brief –
> They are the Gascony cadets,
> With Castel-Jaloux as their chief.
> They're lithe as cats or marmosets,
> But never cherish the belief

They can be stroked like household pets
Or fed on what a lapdog gets.
Their hats are fopped up with aigrettes
Because the fabric's come to grief.
These are the Gascony cadets.
They scorn the scented handkerchief,
They dance no jigs or minuets.
They cook their enemies on brochettes,
With blood as their aperitif.
These are the Gascony cadets,
Compact of brain and blood and beef,
Contracting pregnancies and debts
With equal lack of black regrets.

Thanks to the mythology of the Musketeers, the word
'*panache*' came to be associated with the Gascons. Literally,
panache means a plume. As a personal quality, Rostand tried
to define it for the Académie française in 1901: 'It's not greatness, but something which can attach itself to greatness, and
which moves underneath it. It's something fluttering, excessive and a bit decorative . . . panache is often in a sacrifice you
make, a consolation of attitude you allow yourself. At bit
frivolous, perhaps, a bit theatrical, probably; panache is just a
grace – but what a grace.'

The Three Musketeers came from all over the region, while
Bergerac is some way north of it. This is how outsiders have
seen the Gascons. There is also the question of how they
define themselves. There are tastes, pursuits and customs
which bind this region together, for all its citizens like to
protest their differences. All Gascony, and the Béarn, plays
rugby, enjoys the music of the *bandas*, the village brass bands,
and tucks into hearty meals based on the traditional dishes of
the region, confit of duck or *poule au pot Henri IV*. Nothing
succeeds like excess, for the Gascon, and it is almost possible
to enjoy all these pursuits at the same time, by singing the

rugby song in which every verse is about a different dish in the local cuisine.

All Gascony, and the Béarn, shares a folklore featuring the man-headed monsters that live in the mountains and the pot-bellied guzzler San Pansard who is ritually burned in effigy at carnival time for the crime of feasting in Lent. There are the old languages, too, a cluster of the Occitan dialects which are still spoken in this region. All these ties bind Gascony together.

None of them, however, quite holds the spirit of the Béarn. Strictly speaking, the Béarn is the wedge of land south of Gascony proper, an ancient province which only became a full part of France after the Revolution of 1789, and remains a distinct region, with its own language, its own music, its own history, its own heroes, its own face, its own voice, its own wines, its own flag – red and yellow – and its own coat of arms, featuring two cows of its own breed.

The boundary of the Béarn in our corner of it is the Gave de Pau, running from Lourdes, through Pau, through the nearby town of Orthez and on to join the Gave d'Oloron near the town of Peyrehorade, forty minutes west of here. 'Gave' is a Béarnais word, meaning a torrent that runs down from the mountains. Orriule is the French name for our village; in Béarnais, it would be called Aurriula. Confusing, isn't it?

French as a Foreign Language

I set off for Orthez, where I had been told that there was a class in French as a foreign language every Thursday, because I can sure as hell stand to improve my French, and I like being a pupil; it's a role with such tiny responsibilities and easy to play well.

Once, I got a good-grade French O-level, but that didn't go far, although I learned to love France as I learned the language at school. I had begun to study French when I started secondary school at the age of twelve, and the three women who taught me – tall, white-haired Miss Bareham, rounded, witty Miss Drewe and the glamorous Mlle Béal – all delivered their lessons with elan – a unique sense of excitement and superiority. This, they taught us, as they coaxed us patiently through Alphonse Daudet's *Lettres de mon Moulin* and the thrillingly macabre short stories of Guy de Maupassant, was the study of an extraordinary people, an extraordinary place, an extraordinary culture. One day, if we were incredibly lucky, we might be able to actually visit France.

They also gave me the priceless gift of some French conjugation – the different forms of verbs, which we learned by heart. I'm largely unaware of this amazing heritage until I find myself struggling to say something that's tense-dense, such as: 'I used to think that learning verbs was boring, but now I'm in France I'm really glad I did it.' Suddenly, like swamp gas bubbling to the surface, the right words can just pop up out of my memory. Today's GCSE candidates have a much worse time, being deprived of so much formal grammar teaching that they cannot master their own language, let alone French. Institutionalized barbarism, if you ask me.

Later, I spent the best part of a year on a language course at a French university, in the eastern industrial town of Grenoble, where my ear was attuned to the inflexions of spoken French, but my grammar did not improve because our lecturer was an adorable man who looked like a New Wave film star and it seemed silly to pass tests to move up into the advanced class, which was taught by two sadistic women.

On this basis, with years of visiting France and reading the original *Marie-Claire*, I've reached what you might call a working knowledge of French. This means that I can read *Le Figaro*, but I can't read *Le Monde* without a dictionary, or understand the rugby reports in any medium. I can understand people, as long as they don't talk too fast, and talk to them, as long as they're patient with me. In my first week at Maison Bergez, I discovered that I could also read instructions for operating an answering machine in French, something I find challenging even in English.

Orriule is only ten minutes by car from three gorgeous medieval towns – sleepy Sauveterre-de-Béarn, where I buy my *Times*, half-timbered Saliès-de-Béarn, always conscious of its status as a royal spa, and Orthez, which has such pretensions to urbanization as pay and display parking (20 centimes (2 p) for two hours) and an underpass in which the graffiti art has been commissioned by the municipality.

Above the exit from this underpass is a former school building, probably dating from the Sixties, now the home of the Centre Socio-Culturel, a voluntary organization whose aim is promoting the well-being of society. Here I enrol for the year for FFr 60 (£6), which entitles me to learn sewing, painting, patchwork, yoga, hip-hop or household budgeting as well.

The class is taught by Renée, a classic Béarnaise beauty with dark hair waving vigorously back from her forehead, a fine-bridged aquiline nose and a humorous mouth. Her colleague, Dominique, teaches the beginners' class, and they are both unpaid volunteers. I have treated myself to something I've always wanted to own, a French school book, with the pages elaborately ruled to make sure that the handwriting upon them will be of exactly the right breadth, depth and height for classic French script.

My normal handwriting is terrible. It looks like the tracks of a stoned centipede dancing the macarena. Had I been forced to write by hand, I would never have written a single book. Now perhaps some French discipline will improve things.

Around the table are people from all over the world: an Argentinian exchange student, a Brazilian au pair, a German grandmother, three Australians, a New Zealander, a Palestinean, two Moroccans, one Thai, two Vietnamese, three or four English.

The Christmas party, Renée informs us, will be on 20 December, and each student is invited to contribute a dish from his or her country. This naturally brought out competitive nationalism among the pupils. The English went for mince pies and smoked salmon. The South-East Asian faction brought a stupendous dish of green curry and fragrant rice, but the outright winners were the Moroccans, with a plate of incredibly light and creamy pastries called Gazelles' Horns. Renée and Dominique brought plates of Béarnais black pudding and *charcuterie*.

Local Media

I needed news. As a journalist, I was trained on the stories of the press baron Lord Beaverbrook giving spot quizzes on the day's paper to any young journalist he met in the corridors of his Fleet Street flagship and sacking any hapless cub who passed on an answer. They had left me in permanent terror of losing touch.

Mad fantasy number one was that I would be able to read the London newspapers on the Internet. My first browse revealed that the online editions were cut down to skeletons for the barely literate. French television was no help, because the news programmes were fixated, not with the action in the war in Afghanistan, but with the part that French aid workers and doctors were planning to play in the peace.

Mad fantasy number two was that I would cycle into Sauveterre every morning, buy newspapers at the Maison de la Presse and read them in one of the cafes over a leisurely *grand crème*. The cafes didn't open until almost lunch time and the road would have been challenging if I had been twenty years younger and three stone lighter. I took the car, and slotted the trip into the day's schedule after lunch.

In the Maison de la Presse, the proprietor offered to keep a *Times* for me every day. 'Le Time,' he called it. The editions were a day old, and the *Sunday Times* came with all its pointless supplements except the one you really wanted.

Just before I left London, a new editor had arrived at *The Times*. A new editor means that dead wood will be cut out, heads will roll, budgets will be slashed, sorrows will be drowned, new brooms will sweep clean and wheels will be reinvented. I had been writing regular features for *The Times*, but with all this agony going on in Wapping, burying myself in France seemed like a smart move. All the same, the paper was still part of my identity. As things turned out, they did not lose my phone number. Every now and then, when I was in the car park at Leclerc or out feeding Annabel's donkeys, my mobile would be called by a newly promoted editor eager to commission a feature.

I decided that I would also buy a French national paper, *Le Monde* if I was feeling strong enough for the tiny grey type and advanced vocabulary or *Le Figaro* if I was feeling weak. Then there were the three local papers: *Le Sud-Ouest* (Béarn edition), *La République* (Béarn-et-Soule edition) and *Le Pyrénéen*. And I had ordered from the UK the weekly *Guardian*, which proved to be a caricature of the bad old *Guardian* written exclusively for social workers in Africa, and the inestimable news digest *The Week*, an absolute mustread, even in London.

These packages intrigued the post lady. She was also besotted with the Duchess. Homage is this cat's favourite conversation, and she took to waiting by the door in the morning to receive her daily fix. I apologized to the post lady for the extra work I was making for her, explaining that I was a writer and I needed my newspapers. The is proved to be my introduction to my neighbours.

The White Van Men

There are a lot of white vans about. They are parked in odd places, nosed with intent into field gateways and little patches of woodland. They seem to be empty most of the time. Occasionally, the soft pop of guns somewhere in the hills tells you where the action is.

In London, a white van is traditionally driven by a skinhead with a bad case of road rage. Around Orriule, the white vans belong to the hunters. A beat-up old van is perfect for setting out before dawn with your dogs and transporting your kill to the railway station in the late morning, in time to be loaded onto the train for Paris for the wholesale meat market in the wee small hours. The vans then rattle back to the shelter on the edge of Orion, a barnlike building at the crossroads. Here at weekends the hunters gathered from noon, and set up long tables for their lunch, which lasted until well into the afternoon.

I once dropped in on some French friends to find one of their hunting neighbours already in the parlour, dipping his long nose into his aperitif, well satisfied with the dead deer lolling from the rear doors of his elderly Renault. He wore an old green anorak and well-worn boots. Unlike the Italians, for whom hunting is an excuse to pose around in brand-new camouflage jackets festooned with bandoliers, the Béarnais enjoy their sport without making a fashion statement.

The hunters are gifted, skilled and experienced men, and at this time of year they are after the big game, the deer and the wild boar. There is no dispute that the main motive is the pleasure of the chase, but also acknowledgement, formal and informal, that controlling these species is necessary for the ecological balance of the farmland. Though the argument gets a little strained sometimes.

'Deer are swarming all over the region!' warned the Orthez edition of *La République*, reporting at least two hundred and fifty animals causing crop damage, breaking down the hedges and alarming passing motorists. One driver counted seventeen animals in a field next to the Route Nationale 117. 'Only the panel beaters are going to be happy if people stop hunting,' he predicted grimly.

Hunting is, of course, licensed and controlled. The local clubs are called the ACCA, Association Communale de Chasse Agréée. On the notice board outside the *mairie*, a memo from the Fédération de Chasse and the Direction Départmentale de l'Agriculture confirms that the village's annual quota for deer has been raised to eight.

The regulation is that no more than 30 per cent of the estimated local population may be shot in a year. This is enough to keep the ACCA Gaston Fébus, around Orthez, busy with a shoot every fortnight, beginning in late October after the final maize harvest and ending in late March with a hunting supper to which everyone is invited, and three different venison dishes are served. The ACCA Gaston Fébus was also authorized for three fox-shoots a year, but foxes are thought of as low-status vermin.

Since the boar and the deer have no predators other than man, plus a benign climate and an abundance of food, they breed fast – some does giving birth every six months. It is forbidden, the notice sternly reminds the hunters, to transport a dead animal any distance at all, even from the ground where it has fallen to the white van which awaits it, without first attaching a bracelet provided by the Fédération confirming that it is part of the quota.

The hunt club in Orthez was named Gaston Fébus after

one of the romantic personalities from the Béarn's history, whose presence is still so vivid you half expect them to come riding into the market square any day. This is partly because they are remembered as much for embodying the spirit of the people as for their historical achievements.

Fébus is just a vernacular spelling of Phoebus, and the Viscount Gaston, who ruled the Béarn from 1343 to 1391, was given this nickname because of his blazing red hair. Long before the Renaissance, he was a perfect Renaissance man, writing poetry, playing music, addicted to hunting and the creator of a brilliant court to which troubadours flocked from all over the Pays d'Oc, the pleasure-loving, sun-kissed southern provinces.

The manuscripts kept in the Bibliothèque de France witness that Gaston Fébus wrote very well, particularly when he was writing about one of his favourite subjects, hunting. 'War, love and hunting are enough to fill a man's life', he believed. 'In the field, the hunter lives joyously, because he is in communion with Nature. He gets up early and sees the blush of the dawn on the branches, and learns to recognize the songs of the birds, which bring great joy to the heart of the hunter. The hunt is at the same time an apprenticeship for war which is essential to a horseman. The hunter has to understand his territory, to analyse all the possibilities of the ground which the hunt will cover, and all the tricks of the quarry. This makes him a cunning warrior who never makes a move without thinking.'

Gaston Fébus was not only a brilliant military commander but also a wily statesman. From his postage stamp of a principality he intimidated and manipulated his predatory neighbours so successfully that his subjects enjoyed peace and prosperity for decades, protected by his majestic castles, which still dominate the skylines of Pau, Orthez and Sauveterre. Fébus thus gave his subjects the maximum opportunities for enjoying their lives and the minimum need to involve themselves with the rest of the world, although the French and English armies were fighting all over Aquitaine during his time.

The modern novice hunter can read a whole portfolio of hunting magazines for tips on buying a gun, choosing cartridges, training your dog and stalking, not to mention exotic hunting topics from abroad, such as the grouse shooting in Scotland or falconry in Pakistan. My favourite magazine was entitled *Wild Boar Passion*. 'Step One. Gently move your gun 20 to 30cm away from you, holding it almost vertical. Step Two. In taking aim at the game, turn the weapon gently towards the horizontal. Keep the gun well clear of your jacket. Step Three. Position the sight a few centimetres higher than the desired point of contact on the boar's shoulder. Tips: when you raise your gun, the game will run off. You must stay calm. Hold your breath before you pull the trigger. You will soon be able to control your emotions and, in achieving serenity, you will be more efficient.'

First Contact

One dark evening, just as I was logging off and shutting down the computer, the doorbell rang for the first time. On the doorstep outside was a woman with blonde hair and bright eyes, looking a little nervous. 'I've just come from feeding our donkeys,' she said in English. 'The post lady told me you were here. I think she's told the whole village.'

Her name was Annabel. She was my neighbour, the owner of the donkeys in the field opposite, and of the imposing house which is half hidden by the fall of the land at the brow of the hill. Anywhere else in France a house of this stature would be called a chateau, but they are resolutely down-to-earth in the Béarn, so it's simply called a *manoir*, and given the dialect name for a house, La Maysou.

I made tea for us, and she sat curiously at the table, eyeing the mess of papers which had already covered it. 'What are you working on?' she asked.

'Nothing major,' I told her. 'I finished a novel before I left England, and I'll have to do some revisions on it at some point. I've proposed a new novel back in July. Now I'm just fiddling about with odd book reviews and an entry on another writer for the *Dictionary of National Biography*.'

I showed her the pages I'd printed out and the proofs from the *DNB*. An expression of alarm crossed her face. At this point, I had not realized that many of the English abroad are living complete fantasy lives. Even if an ex-pat is not trying to pass him- or herself off as a former SAS hero, a millionaire, a brain surgeon, an aristocrat, a high-class call-girl or an international sustainable agriculture consultant, the neighbours may still prefer to think of them as a far more glamorous character than they really are. With this Walter Mitty spirit abroad, it is unusual for someone to produce concrete proof of their profession.

Annabel is an interior designer and lives with her husband, who is retired from a colourful career as a marketing entrepreneur. They've been in France for fourteen years, first in a big house in the Gers and for the last four years in the Béarn. She keeps the donkeys, she tells me, because her family have always kept horses and they are good therapy for the children who come to visit them in the summer, the pupils at the leading London prep school where her daughter teaches French. 'These poor children,' she says, 'are so deprived that some of them have never actually touched an animal before.'

The idea of feeling sorry for a young Belgravia trustafarian was touching. She seemed like a nice person. I was invited over for a drink the next evening. Her husband, Gerald, is a veteran of World War II, in which he flew Spitfires, and of major surgery the previous year, in which the triple bypass was just for starters. He immediately revealed himself as one of the most charming men I've ever met, even if he began our relationship with the words a writer never wants to hear: 'I'm going to write a novel,' he said. 'I've got a great idea. Why don't you write it for me and we can make lots of money?'

I told him how this works. 'You have to write your own book,' I said. 'And there are no lots of money.' He didn't believe it. Nobody ever believes it.

Recipes

Poulet Basquaise

This is our family favourite, and the first dish mentioned in that rugby song. Any dish called 'Basquaise' will feature peppers and be distinctly spicy. The richness of *Poulet Basquaise* is achieved by slow-cooking the chicken and peppers together, rather than just making a pepper sauce. The classic combination is red and green bell peppers and *espelette*, the hot pepper which is the number-one keynote of Basque cooking.

There are more species of pepper grown in the Basque Country than there are variations on pelota, because Basques were great sailors and navigators. Most of Christopher Columbus's sailors were Basques. As they got to America early, they had a head start in growing exotic New World vegetables in their own country. They brought back maize, tomatoes and chocolate, not to mention the peppers.

Espelette is the favourite pepper in the Basque Country. It has a warm, generous heat, said to be somewhere between paprika and chilli, and the peppers are very dark red and of medium size. The full name is *piment d'espelette*, after the village of Espelette around which it is grown in such abundance that every building virtually disappears under a mountain of peppers when they are threaded on strings and hung outside to dry at harvest time.

Espelette also comes as a dry powder or a paste. Go easy with

it at first and, if you're crumbling the whole pepper, do not
on any account rub your eyes during the process or you'll have
to put your head under a cold shower until the agony ceases.
If you have to make this dish without *espelette*, you can use a
combination of warm paprika and a dash of chilli.

> a seriously decent chicken, organic, free range, say about
>   1.8 kg (4 lb)
> 3 tbsp olive oil
> 60 g (2 oz) lardons, preferably of Bayonne ham
> 1 large onion, chopped
> 6 red bell peppers, or 3 red and 3 yellow, seeded and sliced
>   or chopped
> 3 cloves of garlic
> 450 g (1 lb) fresh ripe tomatoes, or 2 tins chopped tomatoes
> 1 tbsp chopped dried tomato paste
> a pinch of sugar
> 1 glass dry white wine
> a pinch of *espelette* pepper
> sprigs of thyme
> a bay leaf
> a piece of orange peel, pared carefully without any pith

Elizabeth David suggests adding about 6 of the spicy Basque
sausages called *loukenkas* as well. I've never tried this, but it
seems like an excellent idea, particularly if you have to stretch
the dish at the last moment for unexpected guests.

Wash and dry the chicken, and cut into large pieces, carcass and all. Most domestic French cooks would do this with
a cleaver or poultry shears, and plan on a chicken feeding 10
to 12 people.

Put the oil in a sauté pan over medium heat and brown the
chicken pieces. When they're sealed on all sides, take them
out of the pan while you turn down the heat and sweat the
lardons and onion until the onion is almost transparent. Add

the bell peppers and garlic, and continue cooking for another 5 minutes.

Add the tomatoes, the tomato paste, the sugar, the wine, the *espelette*, the herbs and the orange peel and mix well. Then put the chicken pieces back, make sure they are well buried (add a little water if you need to), put the lid on the pan and leave to simmer very gently for at least 40 minutes, by which time the peppers and tomatoes should be melting into a rich red sauce.

Poulet Basquaise is usually served with sauté potatoes or plain rice, but it would be delicious, and perfectly authentic (as we shall see later), to serve it with polenta. I usually serve it straight from the cooking pan, after checking the seasoning, cutting the breast and thigh portions in half and picking out the less attractive bony bits.

Pumpkin Gratin

This is a lovely and simple recipe from my all-time favourite cook book, *Memories of Gascony* by Pierre Koffmann, the founder of London's Gascon cooking tradition, who grew up in the Béarn, in the town of Tarbes, but spent his summers with his grandparents on their small farm in the Gers, near Lectoure.

The gratin by itself is a deliciously creamy vegetarian dish. It's a great solution to the post-Halloween pumpkin problem, and a good side dish to serve with a roast.

2 tbsp duck fat, or olive oil if you want the vegetarian version
800 g (1¾ lb) pumpkin flesh, cut into cubes
120 g (4 oz) cooked round-grain rice
100 ml (4 fl oz) double cream or crème fraiche

salt and pepper
60 g (2 oz) grated hard cheese – ideally Ossau-Iraty
    ewe's-milk cheese, but Gruyère, Parmesan or Cheddar
    would be fine

Melt the fat or heat the oil in a thick-bottomed saucepan over a medium flame, then tip in the pumpkin cubes, put on the lid and let them cook gently in their own water until they can be mashed easily – 30 to 40 minutes. Shake the pan occasionally, though if the pumpkin catches and browns in places it won't be the end of the world.

If you haven't already cooked the rice, you can do that at the same time. Preheat the oven to 220°C/425°F/Gas 7.

Mix the rice roughly into the mashed pumpkin and bind with the cream. Season with salt and pepper and pack into a greased gratin dish. Sprinkle the cheese over the top, and brown for about 15 minutes, then serve at once.

December

HENRY IV
Roi de France et de Navarre

Henry IV of France — *nouste Henric*

A Moving Experience

A call from a mobile phone. A trip out to the front gate with the largest piece of paper I can find bearing the words THIS IS IT, which I fix to the hedge with clothes pegs. Soon a massive lorry lurches into the lane outside the house, bringing the container stuffed with my books, my clothes and the rest of the things I think I need or can't expect my tenant in London to tolerate, the bookcases, the bicycle, the work table, the photographs, the souvenirs, Chloe's old toys and the little bag of her baby shoes.

Oh, and the No. 1 family heirloom, a mahogany four-post bed that my father bought in an auction in Dorset, now known to be from the time of William IV. For Chloe, the bed is all about fun and romance, and climbing up onto the billowing mattress is a nightly adventure. Our heirloom has passed to her with no argument. Luckily for all of us, the bed is a fine example of early self-assembly furniture, and can easily be taken apart for transport.

In fact, two lorries arrived, having come in convoy from England, the younger driver leading, the older one complaining and calling his colleague on his mobile with navigation tips. The younger driver was on only his second trip abroad, but the road to the South was extremely familiar to the older one, who has spent the past six years of his life helping the British to emigrate.

They had slept overnight at a truck stop in Castets, on the motorway near Biarritz where there had been no coffee available, so they were grateful for mine. Everything was carried in, and the bed squeezed into the largest bedroom, by lunch time, when they drove off to Spain to make another nine deliveries among the vast British diaspora.

There aren't any reliable figures for the number of British people who've chosen to live in mainland Europe. Maybe the government just can't face knowing how uncongenial the country has become to its citizens. There are only official European statistics, which suggest that Spain is the least popular place for Brits to settle, with a mere seven thousand expatriates. Wrong, obviously.

Unofficially, the Foreign Office thinks there are about half a million British ex-pats in France. Many of them take care to be invisible, of course, but many more have been happy to notify themselves to their local *mairie*, fill up their tax returns annually and apply for the *carte de séjour*, which gives them certain temporary rights to French state benefits.

There are certainly enough British abroad to keep dozens of international removal firms in business, not to mention hundreds of international estate agencies, scores of property finders and fixers, companies who will export and assemble an Aga for you, two Web sites from which British delicacies such as Marmite can be ordered and an ex-pat newspaper, the *News*, in which all these industries advertise.

I've found many back numbers of the *News* in the kindling basket. Among many other gems of reportage, I read a story from Charente-Maritime headlined 'No Rural Post Offices To Close', fundraising appeals for animal sanctuaries run by various dotty English ladies, a feature on tea and the report of the tenth official championships mounted at Abjat-sur-Bandiat by La Fédération Française de Conkers, at which the defending champion was a Frenchman, Claude Bernard.

There hadn't been a British-born conker champion in France for six years.

There's nothing like moving house to make you want to be a Buddhist nun, with no possessions except a robe and a begging bowl. To heighten my sense of death by over-consumption, it was clear that most of the things I thought I couldn't live without were actually French: the table I intend to work on was knocked up somewhere in Normandy from an oak plank and cherry-wood legs. It has the great virtue of being so 'distressed' (the antique dealer's word for bashed) that no coffee spill or maladroit move with scissors can do anything but add to its charm.

The clothes, of course, the Robert Clergerie shoes, the Agnès B skirt, the underwear by Chantelle and Lejaby, the myriad T-shirts and beach bags emblazoned with the logo 'Elle'. I left in a hurry, so there was no time to do sensible things with the kitchen. Thus the moving men scooped out the cupboards wholesale and I found myself repatriating a cornucopia of French items: the tart tins, the steak knives, the coffee bowls, the jar of duck fat, the apricot jam, the bottles of walnut oil, cassis syrup and Crème de Mûres.

Finally, I got to the plates. The plates are symbolic as well as beautiful. I bought them when my first novel was a best-seller, to make up for all the wedding presents I'd never had. It had been a little hard to look on while my relatives and friends got married and were deluged with food mixers and matching china that they never used because they hate cooking, while I, who love to cook, was still single and therefore denied such equipment. The plates are wavy-edged Provençal pottery, glazed a beautiful rich green. I put the big ones up on the mantelpiece over the fireplace.

Tea at la Maysou

Annabel, I realized pretty soon, is the queen of the international community hereabouts. She is the vice-president of the Club International de Saliès-de-Béarn, which is currently homeless and in crisis since the Mayor of Saliès has withdrawn the privilege of an official meeting room. Sessions have to take place in the pool room of the Café du Temple, under the inhospitable eye of the proprietor.

She speaks very pretty and absolutely fearless French, which is a considerable asset in integrating with the community, and essential in her career as an interior decorator. She also has a lovely soprano voice, which has allowed her to join a choir in Pau.

Annabel's most recent clients were a South African couple, for whom she has decorated a grand chateau in the nearby village of Andrien. She invited me to tea to meet them.

'Tea' proves to be the total English tea-time experience, complete with cucumber sandwiches and scones. I remember from my student days how living in another country suddenly moves you into a whole new area of national consciousness, so that experiences you might have passed on in England are suddenly infused with a nostalgic glamour. The tea is served in the primrose drawing room, which has an Aubusson carpet, a grand piano for Gerald and six pairs of French doors leading onto the terrace, with a full-on 180-degree view of the Pyrenees.

The South Africans are planning their Christmas party, and talking about fish to a Frenchman, Christian, whose major profession is angling. Could Christian get lobsters for them? Certainly. And prawns? Of course. And display them all magnificently in a buffet? Understood. Christian's wife, a Russian who he met when she was his translator on a fishing trip to her country, sits beside him and smiles shyly.

The other guests are a young Dutch couple, lawyers in their mid-thirties, who maximized their earnings for ten years in Amsterdam then sold up everything and bought a farmhouse not far away. They keep a lot of chickens and are very happy. Also in the party are my neighbours, the potters, an elderly couple, and their son, Benoit, a slim, large-eyed man also in his early thirties.

I have been warned that nobody else in the village talks to the potters, because they are supposed to be *pieds-noirs*, French colonists who returned to the mother country from Algeria after the war of independence in the Sixties. They obviously know that their reputation precedes them, because the old man launches into an elaborate definition of *pied-noir*, which, he explains, cannot possibly include him because he merely attended university in Morocco during the war. Not that he approves of all these Arabs over here, marrying nice blonde French girls. Benoit, who attended university in New York State, hears his father with a fixed half-smile.

Goodbye to Tarmac

Tarmac died suddenly. One morning, instead of grabbing a quick breakfast before going out to patrol his new territory, he refused food and drink and went to sit on the sofa with the decisive look of a cat who knows he is seriously ill. Having lived with Tarmac for twelve years, I respected the opinion of a noble animal with superior street-smarts who has often judged situations far better than the rest of us. Annabel told me where to find the vet in Sauveterre.

The practice was a suite of rooms in a building on one of the main streets. I took a seat in the corridor, and read the announcements on the notice board while we waited. Puppies offered to a good home. Animal refuge has kittens. A two-page letter written in biro on blue paper, from a farmer thanking the vet from the bottom of his heart for saving one of his cows.

The vet was a middle-aged man, taciturn but reactive, who took the cat box off me as if it was a heavy burden I shouldn't be carrying. Being completely unaccustomed to small acts of consideration from strangers, I nearly burst into tears at that point.

He looked at Tarmac's eyes and mouth, felt his stomach, which made him squeal, and told me that there was a big lump in his abdomen and he wanted to take an X-ray. The X-ray revealed the white mass of a tumour the shape of a cuttlefish under his ribs. This, said the vet, was almost certainly in his liver, since he was very anaemic. As Tarmac was already too ill to survive a general anaesthetic, he proposed giving him shots of saline solution, vitamins and stimulants and hoping for the best – if he survived, he'd operate on Friday.

Tarmac died that night. I sat up with him, though he didn't want company, but lay on the rug, panting, with his eyes wide open but not responding. At eleven, he was just about fit for a last cuddle. I watched him go, telling him how much we loved him, which I had been telling him for more than a year, ever since he'd been looking thinner and his coat had lost its gloss. He died just after midnight. I phoned Chloe to tell her, ruining her night's clubbing, and then stayed up, drinking whisky, until four. Among the many splendid cats who have lived with me, he was the best.

Next day, crying my eyes out in a howling storm, I dug a hole in the garden, under the hedge but within sight of the kitchen window, and buried him with a big chunk of white stone to mark the grave. When I went to pay the vet, I stretched my French to say that Tarmac had been the master of the house. So who will replace him? he asked, flirting in the good-natured way that Englishmen can never manage. I said I'd see. I sent the X-ray to the vet in London, who had passed Tarmac fit to travel only a month ago.

Mistletoe: in French *gui*, in Latin, *Viscum laxum*

I took the axe from the woodshed and cut us our very own mistletoe bough. Now I understood how mistletoe came by its sacred reputation. In the depth of winter, when all the trees are brown and leafless, the huge bunches of yellow-green mistletoe that bristle from their branches do indeed look as if they've been given life by some supernatural force. Some of the great spherical bunches are as much as six feet across.

Mistletoe won't grow where the air is polluted, which means you don't find it for miles around London, and nowhere in England have I seen it in the abundance that I found it in Orriule. There is a grove of trees, mostly acacias and oaks, between my garden and the tile factory, and every one is crowned with great bunches of mistletoe. It has also infested the hazel bushes, the apple tree and the blackthorn in the hedge.

Mistletoe is a semi-parasitic plant. Instead of sending its own roots into the earth, it grows on a bigger and stronger host which holds it up in the light and lets it toss in the winter storms and scatter its sticky poisonous white berries around to find new homes on nearby branches. Being the image of life-in-death, and having healing properties, it was sacred to the Celts, and could only be gathered by the druids, as fans of the Asterix cartoons will have learned from the character of Getafix, the druid, forever bustling about with his sickle looking for the holy plant to harvest and stuff in his cauldron. Getafix is, of course, the English version of his name; in French he is called Panoramix. His wisdom is probably well founded, since herbalists use a tincture of young mistletoe stems to treat heart and artery problems, and as a stimulant to the immune system.

The Road to Emmaus

Sandy and Annie, the friends who found Maison Bergez for me, took me to Pau for a day of brocanting. Known as 'les Écossais', since they're Scottish, they own a house in a village in the valley, which, between Annie's colour sense and eye for furniture and Sandy's talents as a builder, they have made very lovely. They are fugitives from the London design industry who moved to France over twenty years ago, and their profession is really creating the international French country-living fantasy for their more timid compatriots. In the summer, they move out into another property which they are restoring, and rent their home to tourists. This gives them just enough to live on, frugally. They can't afford a TV, so on most long winter evenings, they sit on their bentwood dining chairs at their farmhouse table, each with a paperback in one hand and a fork in the other, and share a budget meal. Now it's time to sell on the house, and organize their finances to make their lives more comfortable. All they need is a handful of extra accessories to set the rooms off to perfection.

Brocanting is their passion as well as part of their business. They are always ready to add to the collection of bentwood chairs, or the trunks full of gorgeous textiles which Annie keeps in their attic. One of their happiest hunting grounds is on the outskirts of Pau, at the vast recycling centre run by an organization called Emmaus.

Emmaus is possession Armageddon. The unwanted things of half the department are brought here, sorted by the workers in the morning, priced and arrayed neatly to wait for the buyers, who will be queuing outside the doors when they open for business in the afternoon. It is the bottom of the food chain for the *brocante* industry, and the dealers are usually first in the queue, followed by the poor, the thrifty and the opportunistic, such as us. In the gloom of the warehouses, young couples setting up home come to look for fridges and washing machines, immigrant families turn over the pillows and blankets, DIY fanatics measure old window frames and amateur collectors cruise the shelves with roaming eyes, searching for art deco, art nouveau or earlier.

This time, Sandy and Annie found a chair, a discarded Le Creuset casserole and a chandelier for their hall. I treated myself to some fluted glass plates for 1 franc each, a 1950s red-ringed glass bowl and a bolster in black-and-white striped ticking. Our sales were processed by the workers, who are mostly prisoners at the end of their sentences, for whom the centre is a halfway house to the community.

Emmaus is far more than a convenience. It is a movement, which was founded in 1951 by Abbé Pierre, a priest and MP. Abbé Pierre is now in his nineties and the best-loved public figure in France, on a par with the footballer Zidane. During the Second World War, Pierre worked for the French Resistance, helping Jewish families escape the Nazis. After the war, he became a priest in Paris and was persuaded by General De Gaulle to stand for parliament, representing a poor mining constituency in Moselle.

Always devoted to the poor and the marginalized, Abbé Pierre took up the cause of the refugees, displaced persons and beggars who still crowded the Paris streets in the post-war chaos. He turned his presbytery, and his own rambling house in the suburbs, into hostels, hoping to foster reconciliation among the post-war generation. Then, with another former Resistance worker, Lucie Coutaz, he established the first Community, who became known as Les Chiffonniers d'Emmaus (the rag pickers of Emmaus) and who began to support themselves by recycling, refurbishing and re-circulating other people's rubbish.

Emmaus now has a hundred and thirteen communities in France, which help four thousand vulnerable people at a time to find their feet in the material world. In line with the Abbé's founding principles, they are completely self-supporting and receive no state aid. Any profit the Communities make is sent to partner villages in Africa. Their mission statement is written out on a hoarding by the compound gate: 'When you choose Emmaus at Lescar-Pau, you are acting in solidarity with us in France and Africa; you give us work; you contribute to helping hundreds of people, men, women, couples and families; you enrich a spirit of sharing rather than a profit-making business; you keep people off welfare and you help us to help others. It's easy to do. All you have to do is bring us your bric-a-brac or telephone for free collection from your home.'

Christmas

Did I miss the round of parties in London? Unexpectedly, no. The French do Christmas differently. Between the religious and agricultural calendars, there is an excuse for at least one festival every month, and Christmas is just another one. There is no frantic round of festivity, with friends and lovers desperate to connect before family duties pull them apart. Nor do whole towns disappear under tinsel and fairy lights. The municipalities stick kitsch little bows on their Christmas trees, the shops discreetly apply fake snow to their windows, and a few send the undermanager out abseiling from the roof to fix an effigy of Father Christmas, in his red suit and boots, carrying a sack-full of presents, to the exterior of the building. At great risk to life and limb, these life-size figures are posed in the act of climbing towards the chimney. The *mairie* in Sauveterre went for a particularly convincing Santa, shinning up a drainpipe.

The main event in most French families is on Christmas Eve, when the presents are exchanged and a big family meal, which may well be centred on a turkey stuffed with chestnuts, is shared. This fortifies the children for the lighting of the bonfires in the garden which will show Father Christmas the way to their house. The fires will still be smouldering enough to add a touch of magic to the car ride to midnight mass afterwards. In the Béarn, they often leave the feast until after the mass, when a warming daube comes out of the oven to feed the famished faithful.

By the time Chloe returned by TGV, I had bought a tree of the perfect size at the trusty Leclerc supermarket in Orthez. The Christmas decorations were waiting for her, having arrived in the container. Dressing the tree is her job, buying it is mine. Family traditions are important, even in a family of two. We installed the tree on the front window sill of the sitting room. It isn't really a window sill at all, but the old kitchen range, surfaced with the traditional blue and white tiles. I also bought some little glass balls, red and silver, to put in the bushes by the front door. The rat immediately mistook them for an enticing new kind of nut and tried to eat them. When I came out the next morning, I found broken red glass all over the doorstep.

We were entering the coldest winter the region had seen for thirty years. 'You're so unlucky,' said everyone apologetically. 'Normally you can eat outside on Christmas Day.'

Indeed, we had done just that the year before at Sandy and Annie's house, listening to the happy sound of strong men opening oysters in the kitchen.

Now an armour of hard, gleaming frost covered the fields and in Saliès all the fountains were frozen into icebergs. Maison Bergez, being built on a slope, has an air space under the ground floor, which made it a relatively easy house to heat, if you were wasteful with wood and kept the fire in all day. Friends with houses in the valley, and stone flags laid directly on the bare earth, found their floors turning into skating rinks over night, when the walls exhaled enough condensation to freeze into a skin of ice. Our floors are quite cold enough, however.

In the special Christmas market at St-Palais, while hundreds of ducks and their festive livers were traded in the main hall, I bought Chloe a pair of goatskin slippers, with shaggy cuffs of silky white fleece, from a young Basque woman who kept mohair goats. The Auberge du Foirail was packed, and a group of young Basque musicians came in to entertain the diners. A violin, a clarinet and three of them played the *txistu*, a simple pipe with three holes, which the pipers played with one hand while keeping time on a small drum with the other.

Hospitably, the South Africans had invited us to the party at their chateau. Annabel regards giving directions to other drivers as a rather despicable branch of witchcraft, and prefers to lead a caravan of fellow-guests from her house. In the freezing fog, the man who was said to be a former SAS commando managed to drive into a ditch.

In the high-living north of France every farmhouse tends to be a chateau, embellished symmetrically with turrets, French doors and *œil-de-bœuf* windows, and every village seems to have several of them. Down here a farmhouse is a farmhouse and a chateau a rare luxury. The South Africans, however, had the real thing, an imposing grey stone edifice

with towers at each corner, surrounded, at a respectful distance, by stables and outbuildings in red Toulouse brick.

Inside we found a Versailles set-dressed by Visconti, room
after room of museum-quality paintings, mostly nineteenth-
century still-lifes and landscapes, plus blazing chandeliers,
massive encrustations of ormolu and curtains fit for a small
opera house.

Our hosts greeted us in the wood-panelled hall, accompanied by three large dogs of the kind usually kept to deter a
Zulu army. The guests of honour from Africa, their grown-up
children and teenage grandchildren, were in the art zone,
looking tanned, golden-haired and bewildered. 'Don't tell my
mother,' said the son of the chateau, 'but my business was
robbed by gunmen just before we came away.'

'And our car was stolen five times last year,' his wife added.

Around them were a modest throng of international
guests, at least two of whom were French – Babi and Thiérry,
who, with the help of their six children, had a small concert
hall in the hills. Among the remaining Anglophones, I recognized several faces from our French class in Orthez.

Buffet may be a French word, but as an entertaining
concept it is understood completely differently in France and
England. At an English buffet supper, guests are expected to
eat standing up, or perch on chairs, sofa arms or the stairs
with their plates on their knees. The food offered is usually in
pieces small enough to manage with a fork.

The French regard this as madness, and need to sit down
at a table with a knife and fork to eat anything more than a
few peanuts. Thus a French buffet will offer man-sized portions. This cultural dissonance meant that although Christian
had been true to his word, and supplied dozens of lobsters,
these had been neatly chopped in half lengthways, then
reassembled, pinned together with cocktail sticks and draped

over the stainless-steel stands used in restaurants to raise a *plateau de fruits de mer* above the tabletop.

The guests were at first baffled and shunned the display of lobsters in favour of the humbler dishes below them. After an hour or so, a few diners figured out how they were actually real lobsters, not plastic decoration, and that we were supposed to eat them. Some of the crustaceans were tentatively disassembled and the bravest guests went on to the next challenge – figuring out how to eat a half-lobster from a plate balanced on your knees, without the use of claw-crackers and without making a mess of the surrounding silk-damask cushions.

'Do you know Fay Weldon?' asked a fine-looking man whose white hair waved strongly off his forehead. We were at another party by then. It wasn't the first question I'd expected to be asked in Deep France. 'Not really,' I said, 'I've met her once or twice. She's been awfully kind about my books.'

The speaker turned out to be a painter, the artist whose panorama of Saliès-de-Béarn was then one of the must-sees of the town. Roger came to Saliès ten years ago, with his wife. She didn't like living in France and returned to England, where Fay Weldon waas one of their friends. So he had a tenuous link to the world of books.

Roger lived more or less alone, in an eccentrically spiky modern house in a beautiful valley on the outskirts of the town, and could often be seen driving around in one of his cars – a vast cream-coloured Mercedes for formal occasions, or a dilapidated Mini Moke for every day. His fox terrier, Fanny, sat on the seat beside him, enjoying the wind in her ears.

It was, I discovered, hard on a marriage when a couple decided to make a new life in a new country. It seemed to be rare for both partners to feel equally happy, and common for one spouse to suddenly develop a social disability which kept the other one reassuringly enslaved. Often a husband wouldn't learn French. Often a wife would declare she couldn't possibly drive on French roads. Annie, who refused either to drive or to learn French, had clearly gone for the belt-and-braces approach to anchoring her mate.

On Boxing Day, I was determined to drive up into the mountains, where the snow was lying deep and white and magical. My goal was the forest of Iraty, halfway to Pamplona, not from the pass of Roncesvalles where Roland, commander of the Franks, supposedly blew his horn to call his uncle Charlemagne to help him after he had been attacked.

According to the eleventh-century epic poem *The Song of Roland*, he was attacked by the invading Moors. According to history, however, Charlemagne's army, retreating from the invasion of Catalonia, roused the enmity of the Basques in August 778 by sacking Pamplona. In revenge, a small number of Basque fighters let the Frankish army march into the narrow pass, then ambushed and massacred them.

I wanted Chloe to see this real primeval woodland, the largest oak forest in Europe. Iraty is awesomely lovely under the snow and a perfect place to watch showers of tiny crystals fall upon the bottomless drifts as some rare Pyrenean bird hops from twig to twig.

The trouble with trying to get in the mountains, as I had discovered before, is all the stuff you come across on the way. This time plans were derailed as early as St-Palais, where we found a horse fair in progress. Or, more accurately, a donkey and pony fair. Including baby donkeys. Irresistible. We parked the car and went to investigate.

Only one horse was on offer, a skinny young bay, whose owner, following the tradition of the fair, was dressed for the animal's work and carried the tools of its trade. Which meant that she was got up in her best dressage jacket and carried the saddle in her arms. She stood shyly apart from the farmers, who chatted in small groups, their Basque berets pulled low over their long noses, leaning on the yokes or the panniers belonging to their donkeys.

The donkeys were mostly of the Pyrenean breed, relatively large animals with chocolate-brown coats and markings like a panda in negative, with pale rings around the eyes and muzzle. The ponies had shaggy golden manes and chestnut coats, typical of those seen in the fields in the Basque Country. Their colouring suggested they shared some ancestry with the *pottocks*, the wild ponies who must once have roamed the whole of south-west France, since drawings of them exist in prehistoric caves as far north as the Dordogne.

Their phenomenal strength and tiny stature – a *pottock* is never more than 120 centimetres at the shoulder – made them useful pit ponies and some were exported to Britain in the last century to work in the mines; their chunky build also made them good eating, though, since France had its own BSE scare, the *bouchers chevalines* buy 95 per cent of their meat from Argentina.

The demands of these two trades nearly drove the breed to extinction, but the mayor of the small Basque town of Sare stepped in and saved them. There are still wild *pottocks* in the Pyrenees, most of them now in protected reserves. The ponies in the square in St-Palais, however, with their gentle faces and big dark eyes, looked safe enough and, judging from the number of small girls pulling their indulgent fathers in their direction, were destined to be pampered pets.

In the end, we got no further than the next town in the general direction of the mountains, an elegant and prosperous little place called Mauléon, which seems to have got rich on espadrilles, since its only industry is the manufacture of these rope-soled sandals. The day was almost as warm as an English summer, and we ate a picnic under the walls of Richard Cœur de Lion's castle, watching a shepherd check over his flock, some of whom had just begun lambing.

Our Good King Henry

On a bitterly cold morning, I went out to retrieve the post and saw a wild ginger kitten dart into the bamboo thicket. Domesticating a wild cat is, of course, the height of folly, since they always make terrible pets and will probably run away. All the same, he was damn cute. But he probably belonged to somebody.

A wild cat can smell a soft heart from a hundred kilometres away. The kitten took to reappearing at about eleven every morning. Quite soon, he was discovered in the kitchen, finishing off the breakfast left by Piglet and the Duchess. He then moved uphill to Annabel's kitchen, but she had three ex-wild cats already and they were not welcoming. I decided to call him Henri Cat, after the great king of the Béarn, and of France.

'A young man with a keen eye, black hair cut very close, thick eyebrows, and a nose curved like an eagle's, with a sneering smile and a growing moustache and beard' was how Alexandre Dumas imagined the youth who would soon be King Henri IV. His description matches the face of an anonymous but contemporary drawing of Henri at the age of eighteen. He was only a few months older when his mother died and he became King of Navarre. The year was 1572.

Henry was raised by feminists, or the nearest creatures to feminists that Renaissance France recognized. His grandmother was a free-thinking princess, Margaret of Angoulême, who attracted intellectuals of all disciplines to her brilliant court. Her husband, Henry II d'Albret, who had ruled the little kingdom of Navarre wisely and well, had no male heir. Their daughter, Jeanne d'Albret, married a local duke, Antoine de Bourbon.

Henri was born in Pau and legend states that his grandfather moistened the baby's lips with Jurançon wine and a clove of garlic, an aromatic Béarnais baptism. Legend also states that Henry's cradle was a tortoiseshell. Visitors to the chateau in Pau, where he was born, are duly shown the carapace of a giant tortoise, suspended on silk ropes from crossed spears, but the castle was lavishly restored in the late nineteenth century by the Empress Eugénie and the shell was discovered in a house in the town at that time.

Henri's father then went back to the battlefield, leaving his mother, a passionate advocate of the new Protestant religion, to do as she liked with her kingdom, which she converted with fire, sword and English mercenaries. She naturally raised her son in the Protestant faith.

Jeanne d'Albret and her son were invited to Paris by another ruthless female ruler, Catherine de Médicis, the Italian-born queen-mother of France, who proposed that Henri should marry her daughter, Marguerite, in order to help reunite a country that was being torn apart by religious intolerance.

The Catholic view is that Jeanne then died of pleurisy, and the unfortunate massacre of the Protestants in Paris on the evening of St Bartholomew's Day, shortly after the wedding, just happened. The Protestant view was that Catherine had Jeanne poisoned, and staged the wedding on purpose to draw a large number of Protestant leaders into Paris so that the Catholic elite could murder them. Jeanne's unhappy ghost is said to haunt the forest of Iraty.

Henri won his place in history by the brilliance with which he tiptoed to the throne through this political minefield. He was a scruffy, garlic-breathed teenage princeling from an obscure and far-off province, and his accent was so strong the courtiers in Paris could hardly understand him.

The Pope refused to bless his marriage to Marguerite, known as *la reine Margot*, so the wedding of the two teenagers took place on a special dais built outside the cathedral of Notre-Dame. They were both in love with other people at that time, and frequently afterwards.

Somehow – Alexandre Dumas attributes it to the cleverness of his wife – Henri survived the St Bartholomew's Day massacre. According to legend, when it was put to him later that Paris would never accept a Protestant as King, he said, 'Paris is worth a mass,' and converted to Catholicism. After his marriage he spent much of his time in Paris in prison or under house arrest. He finally escaped the toxic atmosphere of the court in 1576, re-converted to Protestantism and became the very able commander of the Huguenot resistance. The King, Catherine's psychotic oldest son, died a hideous death, bleeding from every pore, either from poisoning or TB. His younger brothers did not last much longer, and Henri of Navarre became Henri IV of France in 1589. He was a popular ruler, not least for his famous promise that when he was king every peasant would have a chicken in the pot every Sunday.

Henri never went back to the Béarn, which he entrusted to the rule of his sister, Catherine. He did, however, pass the Edict of Nantes, which allowed both Catholic and Protestant religions to exist side-by-side in France for almost ninety years. Ironically, he was assassinated by a Catholic in 1610. To this day, most towns in the Béarn have both a Catholic church and a Protestant temple, and Henri remains a well-loved figure.

Ten years after Henri became king, he and Marguerite had gone their separate ways and he married the Tuscan princess, Marie di Médici. Marguerite was a beautiful and clever woman, who wrote poetry and a useful and amazingly frank volume of memoirs. Their marriage she regarded as the blight of her life, but it was an effective political alliance, and it seems a pity that it was never more, since they had a lot in common, not least a good appetite for *la vie galante*. One of the many legends about 'la reine Margot' is that she kept the hearts of her dead lovers in gold boxes, so it was perhaps as well for Henri that he was not among them.

Our First Guests

The beds were made, the croissants bought, the plans for New Year's Eve laid. I drove to Dax to pick up our first visitors, Glynn and Carrie Boyd Harte, both painters, and Henrietta Green, food writer and founder of the farmers' market movement. They arrived together on the TGV, exclaiming over the interminable boredom of the Landes. Half an hour later, and the serendipity of an outing in good company kicked in as soon as we stopped in Saliès-de-Béarn for the cashpoint at France's most picturesque branch of the Crédit Agricole.

Since everyone fell in love with Saliès immediately, and started to feel frisky after the journey, it seemed like a good opportunity to show Glynn the interior of the Hôtel du Parc. For reasons which nobody appreciates, this lovely building is in the hands of casino operators, who have filled its airy salons with fruit machines. Sedate as life in Saliès is, only a handful of old ladies are so desperate for a good time that they find the fruit machines irresistible. The place can be a ghost Las Vegas, the *croupières* in the gambling rooms sit chatting and inspecting their manicures all night and the machines twinkle into empty space.

The hotel was built in the glory days of Saliès. A builder from Oloron Sainte-Marie, J.-B. Cazenave, commissioned by a local developer, completed most of the work in a year. In good Béarnais tradition, the developer then ran out of money and a hotelier from Arcachon, on the Atlantic coast just south of Bordeaux, took over the enterprise. The hotel was finished and opened for business in round about 1893, under the direction of the owner's son, Gabriel Graner, whose initials, GG, are carved into the facades. It's an imposing building, overlooking the thermal baths, and surrounded by a melancholically unkempt park.

After the Belle Époque, the White Russian princesses and the 'sirs' from England migrated to the Riviera, Saliès fell from fashion and the hotel's fortunes continued to be chequered. An Alsatian family owned it for forty years, then sold it to a British hotel chain operating out of Jersey, who sold it to the commune in 1977, who restored it and made it into a holiday village for members of the public sector workers' union, then decided that what the town really needed was a casino.

The chief beauty of the hotel is its main hall, a huge atrium, whose walls are painted old-rose pink with squirly art nouveau flowers. It's dominated by a sweeping double staircase of polished wood, which leads up to a series of Italianate galleries. The design is strangely similar to that of the bigger Basque churches.

Off the galleries would be the bedrooms, if the present management had got around to restoring them. The atrium is so huge, twenty-seven metres high and fifty-four metres long, that it has cost a bomb to restore and money ran out before the job was finished. It usually looks the picture of Edwardian elegance all the same. On that day the potted palms had been pushed aside and the art work was hard to see because the place was packed for the weekly tea dance.

A small band played a medley of Béarnais tunes and half the company was stepping out on the floor, girls in satin jeans, matrons in chiffon, a few older men perspiring in suits. Since some traditional Béarnais choreography is a close cousin of Texan line dancing, the body of the hall was filled by a crowd of smiling and self-absorbed individuals enjoying the pleasure of their own nifty footwork.

Glynn was enraptured, so there was nothing for it but to find a seat, order a round of the pink aperitif called *pacheran* and watch the spectacle. Even the discovery that *pacheran* tastes even more like cough-mixture than Campari could not spoil the magic of the hour. Just as well the daube in the oven, intended for our dinner, would only improve with longer cooking.

Recipes

Beef Daube

Daubes, hearty casseroles, are typical winter dishes all over the south of France and in previous centuries would have been cooked slowly for hours over the embers in the fireplace. In the Béarn, they used a special pot-bellied earthenware casserole with a well-fitting lid, called a *toupin*.

The Béarnais daube is one of the simplest, and traditionally has pork rind among the ingredients. The rind makes the juice exceptionally rich, and can either be used in one piece at the bottom of the casserole or cut into pieces with the meat. Most people now would prefer their casseroled beef in reasonably hearty chunks, but in past times the daube was made with small slices of meat about 5 mm (¼ in) thick.

One old trick which is worth trying, however, is to make the daube the day before you need it, without cutting off the fat attached to the meat. Chill the daube overnight, and before reheating it you will be able to render the dish fat-free easily by lifting off the dripping that has risen to the top and congealed.

A Béarnais daube is slightly spicy, flavoured with a mixture called *quatre épices*. It's a blend of common spices which is used all over Gascony, especially in pâtés and casseroles. Coming from a region where nothing succeeds like excess, it naturally combines more than four spices, and most cooks make up their own mixture to suit their own taste, choosing from cloves, black or white pepper, cinnamon, ginger and nutmeg or mace. The spices are, of course, a Moorish legacy, imported by the invaders from North Africa who overran Aquitaine and got as far north as Poitiers in the eighth century.

Serves 8

1.5 kg (3½ lb) beef – shin, stewing beef, topside or silverside
6 shallots or 3 medium onions
500 g (18 oz) belly pork, salted or fresh, with the rind – if you are blessed with a real butcher, you can ask him to slice off the rind in one piece for you
1 bay leaf
several sprigs of thyme
6 cloves of garlic
1 tsp powdered quatre épices, or whole spices tied in a piece of muslin
1 tbsp chopped parsley or small bunch of parsley stalks
a pinch of salt
1 bottle of red wine

Preheat the oven to 130°C/275°F/Gas 1.

Cut the beef into pieces of your preferred size. Peel and slice the shallots or onions. Cut the pork into small chunks; if you have been able to buy the pork with its rind, put the rind in the bottom of the casserole, fat-side down because the skin side will stick. Put the bay leaf and a sprig of thyme on top of it. Crush the garlic.

Put a layer of shallots or onions in the casserole, then a layer of meat. Sprinkle with the *quatre épices*, or add the whole spices tied in muslin, and the salt, garlic and herbs. Add a second layer of shallots or onions, a second layer of meat, then more herbs, and repeat until all these ingredients, including all the thyme and the salt, are in the casserole. Finally, heat the wine in a small saucepan, let it boil for about 5 minutes to reduce it, then pour over the meat and flavourings.

Put the lid on the casserole, with a piece of foil or a damp cloth if it does not fit tightly, and cook in the centre of the oven for 5 hours. If you want to serve the daube immediately, simply take it out of the oven and pick out the bay leaf, thyme stalks and any whole spices – carefully, because the meat will be meltingly tender. Then serve with mashed or baked potato, or polenta.

If you're making the dish the day before you need it, you can then leave it to cool in the oven with the heat turned off, and transfer it to the refrigerator. The next day, pick off the surface fat and reheat for an hour at the same oven setting.

Hot St Clement's Cake with Jurançon

This is not a classic recipe, but my own take, with Béarnais flavours, on the light dessert cake found all around the Mediterranean, and wherever the Moors traded almonds. Jurançon wine, from the vineyards near Pau, comes in sweet and dry versions. The dry is a favourite aperitif, while the sweet Jurançon, chilled, is the proper accompaniment to *foie gras*. It is a delicate, fresh dessert wine, incapable of cloying, neither as complex as Sauternes nor as perfumed as Beaumes de Venise, though you could use either as a substitute in this recipe.

For the cake

175 g (6 oz) unsalted butter
175 g (6 oz) caster sugar
1 medium orange
3 large eggs, separated
90 g (3 oz) self-raising flour
85 ml (3½ fl oz) Jurançon wine
90 g (3 oz) ground almonds

For the sauce

1 medium orange
1 lemon
30 g (1 oz) granulated sugar
a pinch of *espelette* or chilli powder
3 tbsp Jurançon wine

Allow the butter to soften to room temperature. Preheat the oven to 160°C/325°F/Gas 3. Grease a 20 cm (8 in) cake tin. The sort with a loose base are almost idiot-proof.

Tempting as it will be to make the cake in a mixer, it would not be as light as it will be if you start it off with a wooden spoon and elbow-grease. By this method, cream together the butter and caster sugar until pale and fluffy. Grate the orange zest and fold into the mixture, then gradually beat in the egg yolks, followed by 2 tbsp of flour and the Jurançon wine. Next, take a metal spoon and lightly fold in half the almonds, then half the remaining flour, then the rest of the almonds, and finally the last of the flour.

Whisk the egg whites until firm and peaky, then, with the metal spoon, fold them into the mixture. Spoon it into the cake tin and bake in the centre of the oven for about 50 minutes, or until you can stick a skewer in the centre and pull it out unsmeared.

While the cake cooks, make the sauce which will turn it into a wickedly sticky dessert. Pare off the peel from the orange and lemon and slice into fine strips. Put the peel, the sugar, the *espelette* or chilli powder and 100 ml (4 fl oz) of water in a small saucepan and stir over a low heat until the sugar has dissolved. Simmer for 10 minutes, then leave to work up more flavour.

Squeeze the juice of the orange and the lemon. When the cake is ready, turn it out of its tin and place on a wire rack to allow the bottom to cool a little without getting soggy. Take

the strips of peel out of the sauce, add the fruit juice and the
Jurançon wine, turn on the heat and simmer until reduced
by half. Carefully transfer the still-warm cake on its serving
plate, make some tiny holes all over it with the skewer, and
drizzle the sauce over the cake until it is all absorbed. Make
a pile of the candied peel in the centre, and allow to cool
before serving. An orange sorbet, ice cream or crème fraiche
is a good accompaniment.

January

Alexandre Dumas, Béarnais at heart

Happy New Beret

Glynn needed to buy a beret. This was to go with his corduroy suit, which he had made by a tailor in Hebden Bridge in Yorkshire, and wore with co-respondent shoes, into whose origins I have never enquired, and a tweed overcoat outdoors. Whereas the proper topping for this rig in England would be a flat cap, Glynn asserted his Francophilia with a beret, and could be seen bustling round his home turf of Fitzrovia, the former Bloomsbury territory in central London, gazing keenly about from under the overhang of his favourite accessory.

A good beret is a vulnerable piece of headgear. Many a moth had got a good start in life from one of Glynn's berets during the summer break, stuffing itself into a pupa on the high-quality wool and leaving large holes to be discovered with howls of anguish round about the beginning of October. Glynn's last beret was stolen on a TGV somewhere, the price you pay for only buying the best.

He had come to the right place, because the French beret certainly originated round here, and was adopted by the Basques as a symbol of their nationalism about a hundred and fifty years ago. Therefore, I suggested, the best place to look for a beret shop would be in Bayonne, the capital of the Basque Country in France.

Bayonne was in a festive frenzy, which is its preferred

state. Architecturally, it is a dignified and prosperous city
built on the rising ground around two majestic rivers, the
Adour and its tributary, the Nive. The river embankments
and behind are terraced with handsome half-timbered
Basque townhouses, their exposed beams painted blue,
green or the signature colour of Euskadi, ox-blood red. The
shady cobbled streets rise steeply to the walls of the double-
spired cathedral.

You don't expect a city of such obvious eminence to
grab any excuse for a party, and if there is no real excuse,
to have a party anyway, but this is Bayonne's philosophy. If
you find the narrow streets below the cathedral frequented
by less than three marching bands on any given Saturday,
something must have gone wrong. I've stood in the old
town, on the cobbled *patte-d'oie* crossroads outside the exquisite pale-blue shopfront of the posh linen emporium, and
watched a different marching band jollying towards me
down each one of the five roads which meet there, my ears
bombarded simultaneously with jazz, Souza, salsa, *banda*
songs and African drums.

We arrived at lunch time, a common fault of sluggardly
foreigners in this deeply traditional region, where everything stops dead at 12.30 and you will be stared at as a
potential hooligan if you are still walking the streets at
12.35. After heated argument, bordering on a tantrum
from Glynn, we crushed ourselves around the last remaining
table in an unprepossessing caff where the day's special was
off and a tantrum in earnest threatened.

Three musicians then shoehorned themselves into a space
by the bar, and played some Basque songs. One had a small
drum, another a *txistu* and the third was a young man with
an astonishingly strong but light tenor voice who sent long
ribbons of song unfurling in the smoky air over the bowed
heads of the diners.

Glynn's tantrum turned instantly to rapture. It was agreed that Bayonne was the most gorgeous town south of Paris, that the half-timbered town houses were simply glorious, that the cafe was a perfect dream, that there was no steak and chips in the world more delicious than the cafe standard of *onglet-frites*. Henrietta – so handy to be travelling with an expert gastronome – wondered why we in England had never learned the trick of slicing what we call skirt steak across the grain this way, thus turning a cheap, tough cut into something tender and extremely good value.

In due time, we proceeded down one of the cobbled alleys and, leaving Chloe to try makeup in the Sephora store, found what could only be called a draper's shop. With its plain dark wood doors, long glass windows and generally dusty air it promised more authentic stock than the glamorous emporium at the crossroads. Behind the counter, a traditionally fey male assistant was fussing about unpacking a delivery of Basque table linen.

Basque linen, like everything Basque, is plain, striking and robust. Originally, it was woven by the farmers' wives, and used to protect their cattle from insect stings and identify them when the different herds mingled as they grazed the mountain pastures. The traditional design is of seven stripes, one for each province, on unbleached cotton or linen ground.

Your only challenge is to choose the pattern you prefer on the off-white background – red stripes? blue stripes? blue-and-red stripes? green stripes? yellow-and-green stripes? or – the new design for minimalists – white stripes? Or go mad for the very modish designer range of stripes in singing pinks and oranges?

Glynn fell into rapture again. He took delight in full colour geometry and was very fond of stripes, which featured frequently in his early work on deckchairs, beach huts, matelot sweaters, gondola poles in Venice. I truly believe he would never have painted my portrait if I hadn't owned a black-and-white-striped jacket. After stripes, he loved checks. Basque linen comes in a bold, butch window-pane check which is right up his street.

'What sizes?' asked the assistant, his tape measure round his neck like a doctor's stethoscope. A beret, he explained, must be chosen for two measurements: the circumference of the leather band which fits around the head, and the depth of the flop. The little stalk at the crown has no practical pur-pose, except to ward off bad luck.

The flop is essential. As a bra is measured by band and cup, so a beret is measured by band and flop. In past times, every Frenchman with an outdoor job wore a beret to keep his head warm and dry. For this, the headgear has to over-hang the wearer's face. So a beret worn as my father wore the specimen he collected in Normandy in the war, pulled down snugly over the skull, is of limited use.

Properly worn the beret should flop over the nose, like a limp flat cap. As it rains a lot in the Basque Country and the ethnic Basque nose is long, a good flop is essential. So is a beret made of densely felted high-quality wool that hasn't been stripped of the natural lanolin that makes it water-proof. Glynn went for the eleven-centimetre flop and the assistant got out his mini-step ladder to bring down a box of the right size.

The Basque word for a beret is *txapela*. The *tx* is pro-nounced like a slightly explosive *ch* in English, and if you say the word aloud you'll hear an echo of the Latin word for head, *capella*. The earliest record of it in France is in a docu-ment dated 1461 from the Landes, and the early pictures of men in berets suggest that they evolved from a simple square of woollen cloth worn for warmth and protection.

In 1534, when the Jesuit order was founded in Paris, they adopted a version of the beret for their novices, and called it a *biretta*. Why would the Jesuits do that? Well, the founder of the great Catholic teaching order, St Ignatius Loyola, not to mention his missionary associate, St Francis Xavier, were both Basques – Loyola from Guipuzcoa, Xavier from Navarre.

The beret became a political symbol much later, in the middle of the nineteenth century, when the Basques took sides in the civil wars in Spain. The red beret was adopted by those who were Carlists, supporters of the claim of Prince Carlos to the throne of Spain, and of the Catholic Church and the rights of the rural working class. The Carlist leaders were always drawn looking noble under a fine expanse of flop, and the Carlist newspaper was called *La Boina*, 'The Beret' in Spanish.

The red berets still come out all over Gascony, the Béarn and the Basque Country for *fêtes* and *ferias*, for village suppers, pelota matches, school sports days, the running of the bulls in Pamplona, the Carnival in Pau, the Fête du Sel in Saliès. They are worn by the *banda* musicians, the fans and anyone in the crowd who wants to get with the spirit of the event. With the red beret goes a red scarf around the neck, a white shirt and trousers and a red cummerbund.

The black beret, meanwhile, became so identified with peasant rights that it evolved into an international revolutionary accessory, popularized in the Sixties by the South American freedom fighter Che Guevara, and worn soon afterwards by the young Tony Benn. I was not sure if Glynn had fully appreciated the beret's radical implications. He was immensely pleased with his eventual choice, and we hit the motorway for home in high spirits.

Adieu to the Franc

New Year's Eve was upon us, and so was the euro. Never had the French had such an opportunity to indulge their passion for perfectionism. At the corporate level, readiness for the new currency was proclaimed everywhere. 'WE'RE READY!' yelled the banners at Leclerc, 'WE'RE READY!' shouted the posters at the gas stations. Every business, little or big, handed out their own printed conversion tables. Total-Fina-Elf had spent millions on a corporate euro-makeover, with a circular converter in the shape of a cross-eyed cartoon bird in Day-Glo colours.

I decided to use the official converter pressed upon me by the postmaster. Henrietta immediately spotted a new must-have accessory and demanded we stop at the post office to get her one – but they'd all gone. The laminated, flickering card was in the style usually found at Lourdes portraying the apparition of the Virgin Mary with an on–off flashing halo. When you tilted it, the French flag became the blue EU flag with its yellow stars, and 6.56 francs became 1 euro. The ominous countdown was on the back. 1 January, cheques, cards and bank transactions exclusively in euros. 17 February, the franc will cease to be legal tender. 30 June, the last date at which francs can be changed to euros at the post office.

From hoardings everywhere, government advertisements screamed: '*Le euro – c'est nôtre monnaie!*' The official bodies of France were stuffing the euro down the citizens' throats like the local farmers force-feeding their ducks with maize to fatten them for *foie gras*. The ducks were accepting their sad destiny much more willingly than the Béarnais.

Away from official propaganda, people didn't feel ready at all. You heard the same conversation everywhere. It started when someone shook their head and advanced the ominous proposition: '*On n'est pas prêt.*' Somebody else would shrug, shake their head in turn and agree gravely, '*On n'est pas prêt.*'

'*Non,*' emphasized the first speaker, now shaking their head vigorously. '*Non,*' repeated the second speaker. Then they both shrugged again and paused to contemplate the approaching catastrophe before one of them heaved a fatalistic sigh and said, '*Eh voilà.*'

Everybody agreed that they themselves were as ready as could be, but expressed grave anxiety about other social groups. 'Yes, we're ready,' said the wife of the proprietor of the Maison de la Presse. With a lugubrious smile, she indicated an evil-looking plastic gadget with a digital screen, sitting beside her till like a malevolent alien. 'We've got our converter. That's all we're going for. It's ten thousand francs for a new till, after all. We're ready, but what about our customers? Old people will be frightened that people are cheating them.'

'Won't you be sad to see the last of the franc?' I asked her.

'We haven't got the choice, have we?' she replied, smiling bitterly.

The vet took the same line. 'We're ready,' he said, waving a charged hypodermic around the chaotic surgery to indicate the high level of preparation that had taken place, 'but what about our patients? Some of these old farmers are still working in old francs. They'll never master another new currency.' Then he clamped the hypodermic between his teeth while he respectfully parted the Duchess's fur to find a good spot for the vaccination. Like everyone else around here, he was impressed with her pedigree, and wondered why I was complaining when I pointed out that she was hopelessly overbred and at times, like the time she tried to walk on duckweed, just too stupid to live.

In the media, the tone was cynical. All France shares a

high level of anxiety about being diddled, and the new opportunities for fraud became the focus of national hysteria. The TV news programmes dutifully visited the secret vaults near Paris where a mountain range of new notes were stacked in readiness, but once the official bulletin was over, a Saturday night prime-time dating show was dropped in favour of an investigation of scams and swindles blamed on the euro, conducted by a telly-totty in a power suit.

Le Figaro, like the rest of the press, went large on the discovery that the coppery cents, the .01, .02 and .05 euro coins, corroded easily and were possibly toxic. It also ran a massive feature headlined, 'Welcome to the labyrinth of euro-centimes', pointing out that under cover of rounding-out the prices, a mass swindle was about to take place. The FF12 cup of coffee was gong to be €2, a FF1.12 increase. The identity card photos, of which every French person needs several every year, would go up from FF25 to €4, another swindle. The biggest hike of all was going to be the price of a Paris parking meter, one of the many slot machines designed for the old FF10 coin, which would now be modified to accept the €2 coin, a 31 per cent price rise.

The *Sud-Ouest* took the emotional line, and ran a huge editorial on the last days of the franc, mourning the coin that had symbolized the nation for 642 years and whose very name resonated with freedom, since it was first struck to ransom the French king, Jean the Good, who had been captured by the marauding English at the battle of Poitiers.

There had already been an eight-page euro supplement, with an FAQ section. '*Q: Will you have to take special precautions when reading prices in euros? A: You'll probably have to be more careful of the two decimals after the comma. Euro cents will be more valuable than the old centimes — 90 euro cents, for example, will be 5.9 francs. After 1 January, you won't be able to take centimes so lightly.*'

For all the head-shaking and shrugging, in the market in Saliès, the Leclerc in Orthez, the pharmacy in Sauveterre and the *dépôt de pain* in Ossages, all the sanctimonious invocation of frightened old people, simple-minded old farmers, vulnerable old grandmothers and brainless young hooligans, the Béarnais were really quite proud of their unreadiness.

They behaved like lovers forced to put a brutal end to their affair. There was a general sense of futile regret, of an illicit passion being sadly and dutifully stifled, of people tearing themselves out of a lingering farewell embrace. The banks were threatening a strike. The Auberge de la Fontaine in the nearby village of Laàs, the only hostelry in the region whose proprietor has a real sense of humour, ran an advertising campaign for a special farewell dinner, with the slogan, 'Let's enjoy ourselves with our francs one last time!'

Infected with the national nostalgia, at Maison Bergez, we took out our francs and looked at them as if we'd never seen them before, so gorgeously heavy, so brilliantly silvery, the last currency in the world to really look and feel like money. I had an irrational sense that once this familiar little art work was gone, real money, money that weighs heavy in the pocket and jingles merrily in the purse, would be on the road to extinction and the world would go to hell with electronic cash transfers.

To us, as foreigners and Francophiles, the franc embodied all the sophistication, the exoticism and the beauty of France. The coin was a portable, everyday, national manifesto, the entire glory of France expressed in that little disc of metal. How noble to have the value side embossed with the national mission statement, *Liberté Egalité Fraternité*, and the other side stamped with the graceful figure of Marianne, the symbol of revolutionary freedom. How much more appropriate than an outdated profile of a monarch, encircled by the claim that she defended a religion of shabby origins and little respect.

No wonder the French were approaching 1 January with fear, and sadness, and regret. No wonder that they had persuaded Brussels to allow them six weeks' trial separation, and give them until 17 February to phase out their coinage. They just couldn't bear to say goodbye. And besides, the very large proportion of people with francs earned on the black – i.e. without declaring them to the taxman – needed to launder them in a hurry. Throughout Gascony, this had created a mini-property boom, as people dragged their francs out from under the mattress and bought cars, tractors, or studios in the ski resorts.

We stopped in Sauveterre to buy a dessert for our New Year's Eve supper, and found that the *pâtissier*, a willowy young man called M. Charrier, had designed a euro cake with the dough traditionally used for the seasonal *gâteau des rois*, the Three Kings Cake. This yeasty confection, glossy with a sugar glaze and decorated with candied fruits, is baked with a '*fève*', literally a bean, a tiny porcelain figure bringing good luck for the new year to whoever finds it in their portion. They also get the right to wear the gilt cardboard crown that comes with the cake.

The *gâteau des euros* completely charmed my guests, and we decided to buy it for the first breakfast of 2002. There was a muted outbreak of delight among the other customers in the shop. Glynn heard a patter of discreet applause. The new currency wouldn't work unless all the Union joined it, they explained. It was very worrying for the rest of Europe that the British government had reserved its position. But if we were buying the gâteau, perhaps the British people really did like the euro after all. So everything was going to work out just fine.

Bonjour à l'Euro

Since New Year's Eve meant a large party, various elements of which might or might not show, with or without extra guests, it was a good excuse to cook a dish that is as elastic as it is delicious, Henri IV's Poule au Pot. Henrietta, a great lover of *foie gras*, would have probably preferred the traditional French *réveillon* dish of hot *foie gras* with grapes, but my confidence was not up to handling this expensive, delicate and non-PC luxury. We finished the meal with one of M. Charrier's heavenly chocolate cakes, the Beret Basque, composed of two circles of soft, dark chocolate sponge with something fabulously rich and chocolaty between them. The upper circle is larger, causing it to flop over the filling as the beret flops over a man's head.

Our ribs thus lined, we set off in freezing fog and total darkness, to return to the Hôtel du Parc in Saliès to enjoy the promised spectacle, featuring *showgirls* from Paris. In fact, the spectacle consisted of two show girls and one show boy, each encrusted in panstick, sequins and several pairs of false eyelashes.

In vain they flaunted their permatanned ribs under the noses of those who had stayed for the Parc's FF850 (£85) seven-course dinner and were now slumped biliously in gold Lloyd loom chairs under the potted palms in the atrium, while the fruit machines winked in the distance. Carrie, Annabel and Chloe made for the temporary roulette table, which had been set up near the bar for the convenience of those who wanted to gamble without missing any excitement. Zoe, Annabel's daughter and Gerald's stepdaughter, hit the dance floor with her escort.

For a province with such a magnificent musical heritage, with folk songs so haunting they make cynical urbanites cry, the Béarn has a strange taste in DJs. A definite taste, because they're all the same. The essential repertoire combines cheesy French pop with the less demanding disco classics including Gloria Gaynor's 'I Will Survive' and 'YMCA' by the Village People. For 2002, 'Mambo No. 5' had been added to the box of hits without which no party was complete. At midnight, the disco let up for long enough to allow the showgirls and boy to twirl through the room, scattering sequins and singing *'Bonne année! Bonne année! Bonne année!'* to the tune of 'The Stars and Stripes Forever'.

At breakfast next morning, Chloe found the *fève* in the *gâteau des euros*, a tiny porcelain figure of a soldier in uniform of the Napoleonic era. We left her to start the New Year as she intended to go on, writing her next essay. Our destination was St-Jean Pied-de-Port, another handsome Basque town and a rallying point for the pilgrims making for Compostela. From the seventeenth-century citadel you can see the road to Spain leading straight into the rounded green foothills, with the vineyards of Irrouleguy to the west.

We found an ATM just outside the walls of the old town, and withdrew our first euros. After us, a young French father stepped up to the machine, his son, about eight years old, beside him. They looked at the notes without enthusiasm before the man stuffed them into his pocket.

Between Boyd Harte and Basque culture, a major love affair had begun. His original plan to draw some of the fantastic mock-gothic villas in Biarritz was almost overcome by the siren calls of half-timbered shopfronts from the back streets of St-Jean-de-Luz.

We spent a day of delights on a whistle-stop tour of the Côte Basque, Glynn setting about his assignment with the intensity of a cruising shark. He sketched incessantly in his Moleskine notebook while sending Carrie, Henrietta and me off on diversions to buy himself concentration time. The most successful distraction was Maison Adam, the macaroon shop on the main square, where a fountain of liquid chocolate was rippling on the counter.

In the cathedral, where Louis XIV was married, a cavernous edifice where the walls are lined with wooden galleries in the traditional style, Henrietta cajoled a churchwarden into switching on the lights on the reredos. Out of the shadows blazed a screen of exquisite paintings, as brilliant with gold as any Russian iconostasis. They were normally illuminated only during services, not for tourists.

The sea is tame at St-Jean-de-Luz, because the port is at the bottom of a bay so wide with a mouth so narrow that it is virtually a lagoon. The result is a wide, flat, golden-sand beach, perfect for small children, with chuckling little waves. At the much smaller port of Socoa, near the lagoon's mouth, we had one of the most sublime lunches of our lives at Chez Pantxoa, an elegant restaurant where the walls are lined with Basque-school paintings and the tables set with Basque linen and ceramics.

This is a seafood lover's paradise, and to complement some exquisite scallops we tried a pétillant white wine, *txakoli*, that has become a symbol of the local cuisine. *Txakoli* was once something that the small farmers on the coast used to make only for their own consumption, until a full-size vineyard was planted near the little port of Guéthary (Getari, in Basque) and professional wine-makers began to refine its production. The result is a deliciously fresh, light and subtle wine with a pretty hint of green in its tiny bubbles.

At sunset, we finally reached Biarritz, and strolled out to the Rocher de la Vierge on the walkway over the crashing Atlantic breakers before setting off for home. Glynn fell asleep on the journey. He had been diagnosed with 'indolent leukaemia', the first of several life-threatening conditions whose exotic names delighted him. Chloe was discovered in tears. The essay had gone badly, and she had left herself only a few days to crack it. I felt terrible for driving off to enjoy myself when she needed my support. I say support, because she always rejects actual help. We would only have one day alone together to talk it over.

Some of her friends never left themselves more than thirty-six hours for a major essay. Others of her friends spent weeks on each piece of coursework, and read every sentence to their parents over the phone. Chloe aspired to the third way, conscientious but independent. However, when she was tackling a subject that daunted her, she could spend days almost frozen with fear, unable to write a word. I suspect that it is no help to have a writer for a mother in this condition. I can never bear seeing her in distress and suddenly felt doubly guilty for enjoying myself with my friends when she was struggling with her work alone in a strange place.

Athos, Portau and Aramitz – All For One, One For All

By the middle of the month, Chloe had left, and finished her essay on time with the familiar support of the university library and her housemates. Glynn was back in London, painting frantically for his show in February, and the house was quiet again.

The weather was still bitterly cold, to the joy of the skiers and that section of the Béarnais population which makes a living in winter from the little resorts in the Pyrenees. I don't like skiing in the same way that I don't like driving – the result is marvellous but the process is stressful. I am also a crap skier, being tall, heavy and gutless, with a poor sense of balance. Furthermore, my idea of hell is a bar full of boozed-up idiots in bad sweaters reliving their antics on the black runs at maximum volume.

A mountainside in winter, however, is some kind of paradise. I love the stillness, the champagne air, the soft brilliance of sun on snow, the white-on-white landscape, the crunch of snow crystals underfoot. As it isn't possible to enjoy a snowscape properly without skiing, I will endure the sport as far as I can – which nowadays isn't much farther than cross-country, or *ski de fond*. This is lucky, because the little Pyrenean resorts, with miles of mountain trails and no facilities at all for international euro-trash, are perfect for people like me.

Before I could get to the snow, however, I found myself driving through a chapter of French literary history. After bowling east alongside the Gave d'Oloron, I had turned south, following hopeful road signs to Saragosse, or Zaragoza, in northern Spain. The road to the ski-stations ran up the valley of Bartous through the village of Aramits. This is now a handful of stone-walled barns and houses that crowd the gutter of the route to the mountains, apparently begging to be knocked down by one of the juggernauts, loaded with ewes'-milk cheeses, that come thundering down in the direction of Pau.

Aramits gave most of its name to its most famous citizen, Henri d'Aramitz, a young squire of the old military nobility of the Béarn, who was called to Paris in 1640, at the age of seventeen. The captain of the musketeers, the elite body-guard of King Louis XIII, had heard that he was handy with a sword.

One of his friends, another young Béarnais with a great reputation for fighting, named Armand de Sillegue, Seigneur of Athos and of Auteville, was called up at the same time. So was Isaac de Portau, from Pau. Portau's family title dated back to 1590, when Henri IV rewarded one of his forebears for good service as comptroller of his household. Athos and Auteville are both villages in the lush valley to the west of Sauveterre. The Three Musketeers, Athos, Porthos and Aramis, were based on real people. In Orriule, Athos, the handsome one, is our local hero.

D'Artagnan's real name was Charles de Batz-Castelmore. He came from Lupiac, a village some way north of Pau, in the Gers. His pretty little chateau, with its conical towers, is still a private home. He too joined the musketeers in 1640 and rose to the rank of *captaine-lieutenant*. He then became governor of the substantial northern town of Lille, before he took a bullet in the siege of Maastricht and died in 1673.

The life stories of the real musketeers may be read in the old archives of Gascony, and in the romance called *Memoirs of D'Artagnan*, written only a few years after his death by a contemporary novelist called Gatien de Courtilz de Sandras. This work was, in turn, discovered in the early nineteenth century by a writer of dreary historical fiction named Auguste Maquet. Maquet was never famous himself, but he found notoriety working as a researcher in the hit-factory of the bestselling writer Alexandre Dumas. 'I have collaborators,' said Dumas, 'the way Napoleon had generals.'

In his novels, Dumas romanticized the Béarn and its people on such a glorious scale that he shaped the attitudes of the whole world. Although he certainly visited the region, he never lived here. His ancestors were not born here – his mother's family were inn-keepers from north of Paris, and his paternal grandparents were a black slave from Haiti and a young aristocrat exiled there after a scandal. In spirit, however, this gutsy, witty, down-to-earth and hugely energetic genius is as much a Béarnais as any of his characters. A photograph of him around the time that *The Three Musketeers* was published shows an ebullient, hilarious hedonist whose fleshy face gazes out keenly below a grizzled afro.

Dumas's father joined the army, and became a general during the Revolution; his troops called him 'the black Hercules'. Once he returned to Europe, however, the miserable climate of northern France finished him off when his son was only four years old. Little Alexander left school at fourteen to become an office boy.

He then took part in a marathon billiards match and won six hundred glasses of absinthe. These he sold for ninety francs to finance his move to Paris, where he became a clerk to one of his father's aristocratic associates.

The young Dumas wrote up ledgers for an eleven-hour day, finishing at 10 p.m., when he sat down with his books to make up his education. He fell in love with a seamstress and they had a son – how he found the time for affairs when he worked all day and read all night would always be a mystery, even to his friends. The son would grow up to be a writer as well, known as Alexandre Dumas *fils*, and best known for *The Lady of the Camellias*.

Dumas *père* didn't have an easy start. He wrote plays which nobody wanted to produce, and self-published a short-story collection which sold only four copies. Then his late-night orgies of autodidacticism led him to Shakespeare, who he called 'the greatest creator after God', as well as the dusty works of history and bad period novels from which he grabbed characters and plots by the armful.

His genius was for animating the past as everyone wants it to be, a brilliant cascade of sword fights, love affairs, heroism, passion and treachery with a good few laughs along the way. His genius was also for finding in these dusty old tales the themes that pushed buttons with his audience. They were, like him, members of the newly literate masses who were hungry for stories that dramatized their own lives, rather than the old intelligentsia who 'enjoyed' endless revivals of Racine.

Historical fiction was already the *genre du jour*, but Dumas had a diamond instinct for giving people a good time. Coming after the nit-picking authenticity of Sir Walter Scott, the moralizing of Prosper Merimée and Victor Hugo, and the colonial primitivism of James Fenimore Cooper, his writing was a hurricane of fresh air.

Once his plays had made him rich, a media revolution swept him away from the theatre and into a new form, the serial. In Paris, as in London, newspapers began to use serialized novels as weapons of mass destruction in their circulation wars. In the mid-1830s, two popular Parisian newspapers decided to accept advertising and were immediately locked in a deadly battle for new readers.

A writer as prolific, crowd-pleasing and gifted with narrative as Dumas was a natural for the new *roman feuilleton* and his new serials were soon auctioned for massive sums. The first of these was *The Three Musketeers*. It came out in 1844, overlapping with *The Count of Monte Cristo*, which in turn ran almost concurrently with *La Reine Margot*. This, the story of the feisty princess forced into a political marriage with the future Henri IV, was cobbled together in three months for a newspaper called *La Presse*, after its editor had sacked Balzac because his gloomy work had started a haemorrhage of readers.

Dumas was writing the way his father had fought, on a Herculean scale. He wrote around ten thousand words a week, working for fourteen hours at a stretch without revising or even punctuating, dropping finished pages on the floor for his secretaries to pick up, correct and rush round to the printers.

Then a new law was passed which imposed a hefty tax on newspaper profits, and Dumas's income fell dramatically. Within a few years the theatre he owned had to be sold, as did his house, a folie-de-grandeur called the Château de

Monte Cristo, which was bought by an American dentist. In 1851, Dumas was made bankrupt.

Who cares about going bust, when a man has *panache*? Dumas immediately wrote his way out of debt, producing another forty-three novels, eleven plays, travel books, history books and his six-volume autobiography over the next ten years, all while travelling, lecturing, supervising foreign productions of his plays and planning to open a restaurant. Finally, in 1870, he suffered a stroke in September, lingered on in the care of his son for a couple of months, and died on 5 December.

Dumas was eulogized by Victor Hugo, the literary lion-king of the day, and his works sold a further three million copies over the next twenty-three years alone. Once the cinema was invented, they inspired over two hundred films. Such popularity cannot be entirely forgiven. At the time I first drove through Aramitz on my way into the mountains, Dumas's remains lay in an obscure cemetery north of the capital, not in the Panthéon in Paris, where most great French writers are interred.

Recipes

Poule au Pot Henri IV (or, in Béarnais, our Henry, *nouste Henric*)

Occasionally, you find an iconic version of this recipe, featuring nothing but the liver and giblets of the chicken, chopped and mixed with breadcrumbs, then wrapped in cabbage leaves or sausage casing and poached. This was the *poule verte*, the poor man's chicken, which, so the legend goes, was all that the peasants could afford until good King Henry brought peace and prosperity to the land. A quick glance at the subsequent history of France suggests that the poor peasants were probably stuck with *poules vertes* until well after the Revolution, but hey – why spoil a good story?

The full version, with a real chicken, is a classic Sunday lunch dish in the Béarn. Pierre Koffmann remembers it as the traditional dish for the harvest supper, finished off with a blanket of poached *brioche* dough, and served between the charcuterie and the roast. It is one of those accommodating recipes that can stretch to feed dozens and wait a reasonable time for latecomers without spoiling, and is in every way a dish to share, because the preparation can be a bit fiddly, especially for cooks of the River Café, buy-it-and-grill-it school. Its great flaw is that the poached chicken looks a bit pale to a modern eye accustomed to ready-meals glazed with caramel. The Béarnais solve this simply by serving the meat with a good, piquant tomato sauce.

Serves at least 8, if not 14

a seriously decent chicken
a Savoy cabbage
some fine cooking string or heavy thread
and you need a really large pot to hold the chicken and the
   vegetables

For the stuffing

400 g (14 oz) chicken livers, chopped
fat or oil for frying
400 g (14 oz) fat Bayonne ham (or any other raw ham)
400 g (14 oz) fresh breadcrumbs
2 eggs
a pinch of cinnamon
4 cloves of garlic, peeled and crushed
100 g (3½ oz) shallots, chopped
a handful each of chopped tarragon, parsley and chives
100 ml (4 fl oz) dry white wine
1½ tbsp Armagnac
salt and pepper

For the broth

2 white onions
4 carrots
4 cloves
bouquet garni
12 peppercorns
2 celery stalks
2 leeks
and, if you can get them, some chopped veal bones
6 whole, peeled cloves of garlic

For the garnish, per person

1 baby onion
2 baby carrots
1 baby leek
1 baby turnip

First make the stuffing. Fry the chicken livers gently in a little fat or oil, drain and mash them in a bowl big enough to hold all the ingredients. Chop the ham finely, as in the blender, and add to the livers. Add the rest of the ingredients and mix thoroughly.

With half the stuffing mixture, stuff the cavity and breast of the chicken and sew up, or skewer, the opening. If you haven't bought a trussed chicken, tie the legs together at this point to keep it whole while it cooks.

Put a saucepan of water on to boil. Break off a large, outer leaf of the cabbage for each person, and plunge the leaves all together into the boiling water for 2 minutes. Then drain them, refresh under cold water, drain again and pat dry. Spread each leaf on the chopping board and cut out the thick part of the central rib. Put a spoonful of the remaining stuffing on each leaf and roll it up into a parcel. Tie with the string and set aside.

Peel and halve the onions and carrots. Stick each half-onion with a clove – this stops them getting lost in the saucepan when you want to fish them out. Tie the *bouquet garni* and the peppercorns in a small piece of muslin for the same reason. Scrape the celery, and wash, trim and halve the leeks. Cut the remaining heart of the cabbage into portions, trimming away most of the stalk but leaving just enough so the sliced leaves remain attached.

Put the chicken into the pot, followed by all the vegetables except the cabbage, and cover with cold water. Bring to the boil and simmer for 10 minutes, then skim the surface carefully to remove any scum. Then add the veal bones, if you managed to find them, and the seasonings, and continue to simmer, uncovered, for about 2 hours, which will give you plenty of time to prepare the baby vegetables.

At the end of this time, take the chicken out of what will

now be a delicious broth, and lay it on a carving board or plate. Strain the broth and return it to the pan, keeping the ugly boiled vegetables as a soup base for another day. Put the cabbage parcels into the broth and simmer for about 10 minutes, then add the baby vegetables, for 5 more minutes, and finally the cabbage slices, which should be barely cooked and still green. Meanwhile, cut the chicken into serving pieces and arrange it on a serving plate. Moisten with a little broth and keep warm in a low oven.

Pour off, into a tureen if you have one, enough broth to serve first as a clear chicken soup. Then assemble the serving plate with the chicken, the cabbage parcels and the vegetables, drizzling a little tomato sauce over the white meat if you like, or scattering some chopped herbs over it. Put the dish on the table and let everyone help themselves. Serve with some country bread or plain boiled potatoes, and the rest of the sauce on the side.

Béarnais Tomato Sauce

A word about the classic Béarnaise sauce, that aromatic confection of tarragon, vinegar and egg yolk. It's a great thing to go with steak and chips, and would, indeed, go well with a poached chicken, but there's nothing very Béarnais about it, the restaurants of the region rarely offer it and the master works of regional cuisine never mention it.

There is a Basque recipe for a sauce to go with trout that is made on the *sauce Béarnaise* principle using mint instead of tarragon, but I've never found a reference to *sauce Béarnaise* in the traditional cuisine of the region. The whole thing was cooked up in the 1830s, in the Paris suburb of St-Germain-en-Laye, by a chef called Jules Collinet who named his creation 'Béarnaise' because his restaurant was called Le Pavillon Henri IV. He counted on the Béarnais being so far away, so unaware of events in the capital, and anyway so contemptuous of all things Parisian, that they would never know, and, if they did find out, never bother to show him up by protesting.

If there is a national sauce of the Béarn, it would be a thick, spicy purée of tomatoes, which turns up frequently with grilled meat and fish, and with vegetable gratins. Of course, you want to make this with real tomatoes, big red bulging monsters full of sweetness and flavour, which you don't find anywhere in January, but tinned chopped tomatoes, enriched with some of the sun-dried kind, are just about acceptable.

> 25 g (¾ oz) duck fat or olive oil
> 2 white onions, chopped
> 2 garlic cloves, chopped
> 700 g (1 lb 9 oz) tomatoes, peeled, skinned and chopped
> 2 tbsp chopped sun-dried tomato
> salt and black pepper
> 1 tsp sugar
> a pinch of *piment d'espelette*
> thyme sprigs and a bay leaf

Put the fat or oil in a saucepan over a low heat, add the onions and sweat until translucent. Add the garlic and sweat for another couple of minutes, then add all the rest of the ingredients, and a little water. Simmer, uncovered, for about an hour, adding more water if necessary, then remove the herbs and purée with the aid of a blender. Before serving, check the seasoning and see if a little more sugar wouldn't be a good idea.

February

'Sent Pançard – votez pour moi!'

The Big Freeze

This has been the coldest winter most people can remember. The lowest temperature recorded was 26° below freezing, in the town of Mont-de-Marsan, just north-west of here, in the Landes. Some people considered that Mont-de-Marsan is an ugly, rugby-crazed place which would only have been improved if its balls had frozen off; in Saliès-de-Béarn, however, all the fountains had frozen into icebergs and people were rolling their eyes and muttering about the cost of burst pipes and the damage to the Renaissance stonework.

The cows stood stoically in the fields, probably because the earth was just too damn cold to lie down. Their breath billowed in front of them in clouds of steam. The signs overhanging the motorway spelled out 'PRUDENCE!' in flashing lights.

I could have spent all morning watching the morning mist clear from the mountains, identifying the sharpest peaks and trying to make out the five separate ranges which Annabel assured me were there. In the afternoon, when the air was clear and as warm as it was going to get, the snow sparkled above the highest crags. Below, the mid-ranges did a constant dance of the seven veils, as the layers of air shifted.

A green shoulder would be revealed, prismatically clear, looking falsely close like a pebble in the bottom of a rock pool. Just as you were wondering if you really could count the blades of grass, the air turned opaque in that area, but cleared higher up, and a sharp, grey stone peak you'd never seen before came into focus. As I drove into Sauveterre for my *Times* every afternoon, I was in serious danger of leaving the road because I couldn't stop watching the mountains.

In French class we were learning how to describe the way you look. Punk hairstyle – *coiffé à la punk*. This dress makes me look thinner – *cette robe me minçit*, or *elle me flatte*. Nobody asks how to say 'Does my bum look big in this?' Such relief.

Renée instructs us in a more colloquial use of the word for thin. Nobody in the Béarn would dream of using a vulgar expression like 'Oh, shit!' she says. Only people in New Wave films in the Sixties actually exclaimed, '*Merde!*' And people in Paris, of whom one can believe anything. The polite usage is not '*merde!*' but '*mince!*' We try it. 'Oh – thin! I've forgotten my keys!' It sounds particularly odd when Chris, the Australian, says it.

We move on to ages. *Je suis une femme mûre*, I am a middle-aged woman, says Renée, laying her elegant hand on her girlish bosom. Literally, I'm a ripe woman. There are general gasps when Renée reveals that she is actually sixty-three. She looks at least twenty years younger. It's cheering to figure out that by this scale of reckoning, I am merely a green girl.

Screams of laughter issue from the next door classroom, where Dominique is trying to control the beginners' class. '*Non, mais alors!*' protests Renée, flinging wide the door with play-acted indignation. You get the feeling that after a lifetime of imposing the rigid discipline of a French school-room, it's quite relaxing for her to be shepherding these devil-may-care foreigners through the glories of the language.

The comedian among the beginners is Fiona, a dark-haired New Zealand girl with round glasses and sparkling eyes. In her present situation, all she can do is have a laugh. With her husband, Gordon, and their two small children, she's living in an unheated former stables in the grounds of a little chateau at the hamlet of Berenx, and watching their life savings freeze to death.

Gordon, her Australian husband, arrived in the Béarn eighteen months ago, with a ship-load of baby tree ferns. The idea was that in the mild, humid climate of the Béarn they would grow twice as fast as in their native New Zealand, and be ready to sell in the UK within a year. In New Zealand, the tree ferns can grow to sixty feet high. In the UK, and in Europe, tree ferns anywhere between three and nine feet high are the most fashionable thing you can install in an urban patio.

Gordon had a friend who had figured out that tree ferns grown on in France would turn a quick profit, and persuaded Gordon and Fiona to buy into his business. Since New Zealand wasn't offering Gordon a great deal in the way of a future, he and Fiona decided to sell up their house, sink half their cash into green fronds and come over to France.

Nobody expected the big chill, which had turned the green fronds brown and quite possibly killed the lot. Fiona invited me over to inspect the damage. Thousands of baby tree ferns, in eight-centimetre black pots, were bedded in the undergrowth in a small patch of woodland near the stables. At the start of the winter, she had covered the crowns with a thick layer of dead leaves, which turned out to be no protection at all against the freezing weather.

High in the treetops above are the wooden tree houses built by the chateau's original owner for hunting *palombes*, the wild doves who used to fly over in vast flocks on their way south for the winter. Now the autumns bring only a few thousand *palombes* and their migration route is closer to the coast. When storms thrash the trees, the hunters' hides

rattle towards total dilapidation and random planks fall off
to the ground below.

Their partner in the fern enterprise was building a green-
house to protect the stock. All the outbuildings of the chateau
are still in place but crumbling. Among them is an original
nineteenth-century glasshouse, built on to the south side of
the stable block, but between the scrolled ironwork half the
panes were smashed and nobody has thought to fix it up.

In the stable building, which unfortunately faces north
and has no windows at all on the sunny south side, the
temperature in the sitting room is just 5°; it was as cold as
a fridge. There is very little furniture. Most of Fiona's household stuff is still packed up and stored in the cellar, waiting
for the day they put the rest of their money into a home of
their own. The two children, Cam, who's nine and Margot,
six, are huddled in duvets on a divan in front of the TV.

Mardi Gras – Not to Mention *Mercredi,* *Jeudi, Vendredi* and *Samedi*

'There's a carnival in Pau,' I said. 'They're having pig racing
on Friday. Why don't we go?' Sandy didn't believe me.
Annabel said it was too cold. Fiona had just been to Pau to
take the children to the circus. Nobody else was interested,
so I set off alone.

It was already two days since the Tuesday on which the
festivities had started with the ceremonial arrival of the
bears from the mountains. Pretend bears, obviously since
catching a wild one would have been both dangerous and
politically incorrect, not to mention damn tricky. The men
in bear costumes were accompanied by others disguised as
wild men from the mountains, and they roamed the streets

indulging in a little licensed vandalism, jumping on restaurant tables and pretending to terrorize the populace.

In the mountains, the bears would be waking from hibernation around this time. There are still estimated to be a few dozen brown bears in the Pyrenees but they are not a common sight; in my year, I met only one person who had seen evidence of them, bear prints in the snow beside a mountain trail.

By Friday, the festivities had moved on to the legend of Sent Pançard, the carnival king who gets a brief day of misrule before being captured, put on trial and ceremonially burned. In case anyone should be in doubt as to the permitted scale of Saturnalia, the programme, in French and Béarnais, contained the mission statement:

> Carnival means:
> dancing and singing and bopping till you drop
> being kind, and funny, and tolerant;
> dressing like a woman if you're a man;
> dressing like a man if you're a woman;
> wearing a mask and disguising your voice;
> denouncing injustice and authority;
> winding up all the self-satisfied vinegar-pissers;
> cutting loose, rebelling, letting your fantasies run wild;
> and being proud to be Béarnais, whether you were born
> here or elsewhere.

The programme also bore witness to an impressive list of sponsors, including the tourist board, the regional development agency, the newspaper *La République*, the radio station France Bleu Béarn, the association of *charcutiers*, the Béarnais language and cultural institute, Intermarché, the vineyards, many farmers and small businesses, and a bakery.

Nevertheless, it seemed at first as if the citizens of Pau were well able to resist the invitation to enjoy forbidden delights. They were tearing out of their offices in large numbers and making for the car parks, eager to get home out of the freezing drizzle. Or perhaps they were still recovering from the all-night fancy-dress disco at the students' union the night before. Only a small knot of people, mostly with tiny children, had gathered in the small Place Gramont where the procession was due to start. Across the road, a couple of police cars were parked, their drivers standing about waiting for the action.

Quite soon, the carnival king joined us. At some point in Gascon history, perhaps when the Protestants were in charge, it was decided that the good-living population was having far too much fun with the traditional feast before the deprivations of Lent. Or perhaps the moral tale of Sent Pançard, the carnival king, has more ancient roots, and was acted out right back in pre-Roman days, when the ancient Gauls were famous pig-keepers. The character is certainly a close cousin of Gargantua, the greedy giant of Celtic origin whose exploits were satirically recorded by Rabelais in the sixteenth century.

Whatever his ancestry, the enactment of the rise and fall of Sent Pançard is the centrepiece of the carnival festivities, and in Pau the whole masquerade had been elevated into a political satire, as befits a university town and a seat of government. He had spent the week electioneering.

With a huge false belly, bright red cheeks, a tottering gold-foil crown and the essential string of sausages around his neck, an actor playing Sent Pançard worked his striped socks off pressing the flesh, kissing babies, meeting the mayor and introducing himself personally to every single member of the crowd. 'Sent Pançard,' he said ingratiatingly, 'vote for me!' The manifesto for his regime was simple: eat, drink and party on.

The carnival had been going on all week, and this was

to be the final night of sacrilegious feasting, when Sent Pançard invited his fellow ruler, San Porquin, the pig king, to a night of gluttony and excess. In due course, when about a hundred people were in the square, San Porquin appeared through a gateway to a hidden courtyard. The pig king was another actor, this time in a black monk's habit, with a string of garlic around his neck, riding on a dark brown Pyrenean donkey.

After him, a golden statue of a pig on a red-curtained palanquin emerged through the gateway, carried shoulder-high by twelve men in red and gold satin robes and black berets. As the procession formed up, various figures representing Sent Pançard's government appeared, including a fake bishop and a Ku Klux Klan figure in red satin. In front of them came a troupe of dancers in white shirts and trousers set off with scarlet sashes and green berets, accompanied by a lone fiddler.

Finally the police got back into their cars, turned on their flashing lights and moved to block the traffic on the processional route. With the dancers hopscotching gravely in the vanguard, and a good crowd of people now in place to line the route, the procession set off uphill towards Pau's largest urban space, the Place Verdun, where a huge marquee had been erected.

The pigs were not compelled to walk the whole route. They were waiting in a small cattle truck at the corner of the square, watched over by five marshals, in red jackets and red berets, armed with sticks. As the procession slowly drew level, the marshals ceremonially opened the tailgate of the van. Inside were nine pedigree porkers, blissfully asleep on their bed of clean straw. The crowd laughed and somebody told me an old Gascon saying: seven hours of sleep for a man, eight for a woman and nine for a pig.

The marshals respectfully prodded the animals awake.

They were not enthusiastic, so the youngest man was sent
into the van to heave them bodily onto their trotters, then
push them out onto the ramp to take their place of honour
at the head of the cavalcade. The pigs were all light-skinned
examples of the local breed, the Cochon Noir de Gascogne,
ranging in colour from dark ash to fresh pink with grey
spots.

Now bumbling forward at the pace of a dozy pig, the procession left the road and proceeded between crash barriers
towards the marquee. Halfway down this path was parked a
smart vintage van, reminiscent of a Harrods brougham, but
painted in red and cream, with the words *Jambon de Bayonne*
on the side.

The van was a mobile deli, whose sides could be opened
to reveal a counter, on which a massive ham was displayed
on a stand, ready to be carved. Behind this, in the body of
the vehicle, more hams dangled from the roof and a fresh-
faced young man in a red jersey was sharpening his carving
knife. His hands were covered in immaculate white muslin
gloves.

As the pigs approached the van, he began to carve the
ham into slices so thin you could have read a newspaper
through them, piling them reverently onto a serving plate
on the counter. When the pigs were level with the ham, the
procession halted for a minute, to allow the carver to bow to
them. The crowd cheered, the pigs looked thoroughly bored
and seemed determined to get back to bed as fast as possible.

The parade continued until it reached the doors of the
tent, where huge platters of fine *charcuterie* and crates of
Jurançon and Madiran wine were waiting for the festival
crowd. Beyond the aperitif area, tables were laid up ready
for the promised *repas gastronomique* prepared by the restaurant Chez Ruffet: *pâté en croûte*, jellied pig's ears, shoulder of
pork with spring vegetables, prunes with Grand Marnier ice

cream, for €24. Not having a ticket, I went home and made an omelette, but felt an entirely new sense of respect as I ripped open a packet of ready-chopped lardons.

Lent Will Be A Little Late This Year

Next morning, my description of the night of the pig king was colourful enough to inspire Annabel, and in the evening we set off together for Pau. The main event was to be the trial of Sent Pançard for the hideous crime of feasting in Lent, and we arrived in time to see him being dragged through the streets in a cage of bamboo, like an American prisoner of war in Vietnam. His fate was to endure a travesty of justice in front of the Law Courts, to be found guilty of causing all the social problems the citizens found most annoying, and then to be burned to death, accompanied by a firework display and dancing.

This time the whole town was in carnival mood. People were dressed as cows, sunflowers, clowns and political figures – Osama bin Laden and Jacques Chirac were popular. Sent Pançard's cortège was escorted by huge papier mâché effigies of the mythical giants of the Pyrenees, they who are supposed to live in caves and to have set up the standing stones and built the colossal walls and houses of boulders which can be found in the mountains.

One giant had only one eye, in the centre of his forehead. Another was stuffed with straw and covered in animal skins. A third was an old man with a three-metre beard and silver hair. The legends of the Pyrenees feature so many giants that there was probably one for every mountain. They are supposed to have given the Basque people all the wonderful discoveries that set *Homo sapiens* on the road to world domination, including fire, agriculture, metallurgy and the saw.

There was also a lady giant with a blue face and red hair, probably Mari, the Great Goddess, who was worshipped in one form or another all through Europe before the Indo-European people spread from the east with their modern patriarchal religions. Mari was supposed to travel along the chain of the Pyrenees in a ball of fire, blazing from peak to peak, accompanied by her dragon lover, hurling thunderbolts at anyone who annoyed her.

Marching along in the cold was tiring, so we sat down at a cafe for refreshment, only to be set upon by a band of students dressed as bee-keeping monks. One of them carried a pot of honey and the rest brandished wooden spoons. They were spreading the carnival spirit by going from bar to bar dipping the spoons in the honey and giving every customer a sticky dab on the back of the hand.

When we ventured into the marquee we found another Béarnais tradition in action. It is an unwritten rule of national festivities that a *fête* is not a *fête* unless at least three bands are playing at the same time. So at one end of the tent, under the red-and-yellow Béarnais flag with its two cows walking in the same direction, and a banner proclaiming '*Le Béarn, j'y crois!*' were four musicians, satin-clad and masked, one with a tuba, one with a clarinet, and two with sheepskin bagpipes.

Not very far away was a traditional brass combo playing jazz, while at the far end by the bar a huddle of singers, formed up defensively in a circle with their arms around each other's shoulders, were belting out some folk songs a cappella. There were a good five hundred people in the tent, including one man in such immaculate housewife drag that he looked like an extra from an old Monty Python sketch. Dozens of shrieking children, dressed as fruit, flowers, princesses and superheroes, played tag around the edges of the crowd.

After a couple of hours of cacophony and aperitifs, during which the three musical groups played almost non-stop, a rock band took the stage and began the evening's disco with Béarnais line dancing. It really didn't look too difficult, the people on the floor were of all ages and states of trendiness, and we were not encumbered by any husbands, partners or children who might be embarrassed, so after a while we walked into the lines of dancers and joined in.

Quite soon, we found that potential dance-partners had attached themselves. Annabel was approached by a stocky man with a weather-beaten complexion who helped her jump at the right moments by grabbing her round the waist and tossing her into the air. I found myself dancing with a lanky student who was dressed as an ear of genetically engineered maize, which meant he was wearing a Tina Turner wig, a green cape and yellow balloons pinned all over his shirt and trousers.

On hearing of our adventures, Fiona decided that she could not pass on an opportunity for the children to dress up. Happily, we soon discovered that half the towns and villages in the region were planning their own carnivals, each with their own spelling for the king's name: in Bayonne he was San Pansart; in the mountain village of Tardets, he was Zan Panzar; in Orthez he was San Pançard. In fact, the whole of February was going to be nothing but one big fiesta. Such a sensible thing to do with February, which has to be the most miserable month in the calendar.

The next weekend we piled the kids into the back of my car and went to Bayonne, where the execution of San Pansart was to take place on the ramparts of the old castle. The children did not go willingly. Cam sulked and stuck his nose in Harry Potter, volume IV. Margo whined. I tried to sell it to them by talking about the fireworks, the opportunity to eat doughnuts in the street and the burning alive of the fat man, but without success. It was like going back fifteen years, to the middle stretch of parenthood, which is all about bribery and manipulation.

The wind whistled viciously through the alleys of the old town, where every street was again occupied by a marching band, each followed by a cavalcade of people in costume. Cam and Margot were underwhelmed by the opportunity to dance along behind a large samba band and throw confetti at each other, although Margot quickly came round when she noticed girls of her own age in fairy costumes. We took her into the local branch of Sephora, the world's first make-up supermarket, and covered her face in multicoloured glitter from the sample ranges before anyone noticed.

Cam eventually stopped griping when he spotted other boys dressed as Harry Potter, in black capes, brandishing wands and with the telltale scar drawn on their foreheads in their mother's eyebrow pencil. His scowl melted and he munched through a bag of fritters from a street vendor with a thoughtful expression.

The bands eventually converged by the bridge over the Nive which leads to the old castle, and fell in behind the bloated papier-mâché figure of San Pansart, his sausage necklace resting on his ballooning belly. The Basque nationalists had made the most of the opportunity to protest about the torture of ETA members by the Spanish police, and draped a huge banner across the bridge, demanding, 'Are we still in the Middle Ages?' It seemed so.

Being a great party town and not a million miles from Spain, Bayonne was doing carnival with bags of style, as a warm-up for the great *feria* in July, when the bars don't close for a week. In the cafes around the castle square, *un happy-hour* had begun, and trays of free tapas were already on the counters to sustain the exhausted revellers.

The castle ramparts were a perfect stage for the mock trial

of San Pansart, which began with a denouncement by the master of ceremonies. 'You've stuffed your gob with food! You've pigged out until your skin's fit to burst! You're disgusting!'

The bonfire was lit immediately and the effigy of San Pansart lurched face-first into the flames surrounded by great plumes of sparks from the fireworks. The *bandas* were called upon to play him out with a blast of brass while the crowd bellowed the carnival song, 'Adiou, Praoube San Pansart'. Cam found the spectacle thoroughly satisfying and, finding that I had not lied to him about the fat man being burned to death, viewed me briefly with something which could have been respect.

The last carnival of the season was held in Orthez, by when we were fully equipped. Cam had sorted himself out a Harry Potter costume and Margot had dug out her fairy tutu and wings. Announcing the event, the Centre Socio-Cultural, its major sponsors, sternly emphasized that the regrettable new fashion for throwing eggs and flour was expressly forbidden.

Orthez, for all its medieval patrimony and its proud title of the city of Gaston Fébus, is a real old cow town, where subtlety is not appreciated. The least attractive citizen seems to progress rapidly from being a cheeky kid to a boisterous teenager, then on to become a mouth-breathing hulk in a plaid shirt or a housewife with heifer hips draped in Day-Glo viscose.

In Orthez you also find the trailer trash, meaning the travellers, or the last of the migrant workers who once travelled from village to village helping with the various harvests, but who now live in caravans beside the Gave, getting by on the dole and being generally marginalized by more prosperous citizens.

San Pançard, as Orthez conceived him, was an effigy

towed by a tractor through the streets, accompanied by one *banda* and a group of drummers. A long parade of children in fancy dress followed, and gangs of adolescents charged about trying to stuff confetti down each other's necks and cover their enemies in shaving foam.

In the trial, San Pançard was accused of being responsible for inaccurate weather forecasts and rubbish on the television. It was a freezing day and Fiona and I, having at last refined our carnivalling skills, sent the kids off to watch the bonfire while we retreated to a cafe for hot chocolate and brandy.

How's the Writing Going?

My English collapsed. With nobody in the house to talk to me in my own language, French started to take over. Halfway through a sentence, I would find myself scrabbling in my memory for the words I needed. Even simple bits of vocabulary seemed to have erased themselves. One morning, I couldn't think of the word 'adapt'. Another time, when I wanted to say 'lorry', all that came forward was the French word, *'camion'*.

English idioms vanished as well, melting away before the brilliance of French. *'Vous voulez louer le matériel pour le ski du fond?'* asked the man in the ski shop, meaning did I want to rent the complete kit including everything you needed for cross-country skiing. *'Le matériel!'* How nifty was that? One gorgeous little word with all that subtext of necessity and importance! I fell in love with *'le matériel'* and saw and heard its adorable letters everywhere, in street conversations, on newspaper ads, all over Maisadour, the agricultural supermarket. The cumbersome way to say the same thing in English just evaporated.

Soon my mind started flailing for the simplest English expressions. The whole machinery of the language, which normally turned over so smoothly and constantly, processing my thoughts and making them into words with effortless facility, had suddenly turned rusty and was clanking to a standstill.

My respect for bilingual writers rocketed. Now I appreciated the immense achievement of authors such as Kazuo Ishiguro, Isabel Allende, Salman Rushdie or Anita Desai, who could create supple and evocative prose while all the time, in their heads, two entirely different systems of thought were struggling for supremacy. Now I understood why children who were not native speakers underachieved in school. A brain working in two languages has to work twice as hard.

The effort of moving between two tongues all the time was utterly exhausting. A sustained conversation in French took as much physical effort as a ten-kilometre run. On a day when I had gone out for coffee or for dinner with French friends, I would be completely wiped out by 10 p.m.

Sandy, who speaks fluent bar French, reported the same problem. Like me, he suffered from living between the two languages and having mastery of neither. In French, we had the added problem that came with a good ear. While we still had to struggle for meaning, we sounded too good for the people who talked to us to realize that we weren't getting the whole message.

Since we both looked intelligent, behaved with confidence and sounded much better than we were in French, people would rattle on in conversation, chucking in slang and dialect and God knows what else, assuming that we were following when really we'd lost the plot after the first sentence.

Asking people to slow down didn't seem to work. You'd

get one sentence at baby speed, and then the conversation would accelerate and leave you to eat its dust. It was probably no help to us that we were living in a region where in daily life people get their ears round three living languages, French, Basque and Spanish, as well as the regional dialect, which is spoken in various strengths and with slight changes in meaning from one village or one valley to another. This means that to native Béarnais listeners most people have a funny accent, but that doesn't mean that they don't understand what's being said.

Sandy's strategy for surviving a long conversation was to nod gravely and say, '*Ah, oui.*' This, like the English 'Oh, really,' or the American, 'Oh, sure,' can be inflected in a dozen different ways to express anything from warm agreement – '*Ah, oui!*' to complete amazement, '*Ah, oui?*' or even, with a falling cadence, omniscient wisdom, '*Ah, oui.*'

If you think you're using '*Ah, oui,*' so much that you're going to be rumbled, you can progress to '*Mais, c'est ça!*', which does the same job but with a little more elegance and enthusiasm. Also useful are the expressions which you can tuck into the beginning of a statement to buy yourself thinking time, the little bits of verbal polystyrene that not only slow your sentence down while you're groping for your tenses, but also make you sound more polished and less schoolgirly.

There's '*De tout façon . . .*', which is much like the Yorkshire 'Any road up', and makes an acceptable preamble to almost anything you want to say. '*En effet*', which is close to 'actually', is handy, but a bit prissy. In intellectual debate, the equivalent is the classic one-word delayer, '*effectivement . . .*' which the worthies discussing weighty issues on the radio used lavishly, drawing out the syllables over a full four seconds.

The radio eventually came to the rescue of my English. In

the interests of keeping up with affairs back home, I had installed the ex-pats' best friend, *'le parabole du Sky'*, which was tucked into the wisteria under the eaves at Maison Bergez, its antenna pointing south to the Pyrenees and the vital satellite.

Since I had hundreds of channels of TV and radio at my disposal, all that was necessary was to pass up the mind-fracturing fun of watching the reports on Afghanistan on Al-Jazeera or aerobics on the foreshore from Sydney, Australia, and tune into BBC Radio 4 while I made my morning coffee. An hour or so with the shipping forecast and *Farming Today* was all I needed to refresh my English and keep it on track for the morning.

In the afternoon, however, a few words with the proprietor of the Maison de la Presse or a short chat with a friend on the street would be enough to send me back into linguistic no-man's-land. Fortunately, all I worked on in February was the revisions to *Mister Fabulous and Friends*, the novel I had completed seven months earlier. Already, I worried that I was losing the ability to write spot-on dialogue for English characters, but since most of what was needed was structural work, moving scenes to different places in the narrative to make it flow more strongly, this was not yet a problem.

Fire in the Mountains

On my way down from the ski-station one Sunday, I drove through a valley full of smoke. The farmers had been burning off the undergrowth, a process called *'écobuage'* in French, and known as 'swealing' in the north of England. Its purpose, as Renée explained it, was to 'clean the mountain', meaning to burn off brambles and thorny scrub, and leave the higher fields ready to grow lots of sweet young grass for the sheep who would be pastured there later in the spring.

That Sunday, Mari, goddess of the thunderbolts, was obviously watching over me, because I passed through an inferno without being harmed. The weather had turned stormy and high winds were howling over the mountains. The higher ski stations, where the ski lifts and cable cars were in serious danger, closed completely, and the departmental government had issued a statement banning *écobuage* until the wind died down. Up in the mountain valleys, the most remote farmers had either not heard of the prohibition or decided to defy it. 'Nobody told us,' they said afterwards, 'we didn't hear anything about anything.'

Once they had set a few bushes alight, the violent winds, blasting down the valleys at 100 kilometres an hour, had fanned the flames so quickly that the farmers lost control. By the end of the day the fire had raged over thousands of hectares, burning everything from the valley above Aramitz through which I drove to the lower slopes of La Rhune in the West, and threatening to wipe out areas of dense forest.

Every firefighter from Hendaye, on the coast, to Pau was called out and fought all night beside the local people to stop the blaze spreading. Eventually, in the small hours of the morning, torrential rain came down and put out the flames. Six people had died in the fires, all of them elderly shepherds who had not been able to out-run the billowing smoke.

The *Monsieur*

The carnival in Pau was the first lesson I had in the reverence which the Béarnais have for their blood stock. Gathering in public to honour their animals was a natural and important element of every festival, and the finest specimens were always selected. No wonder that nothing I was or owned won me more respect than Podge, my white Chinchilla Persian cat. So, Mr Bond, you have an animal of *pure race*?

Pure-bred cows, sheep or pigs, with bows on their forelocks, flowers round their necks or pompoms on their fleeces, were ceremonially paraded by their stockmen at a high proportion of the festivals which were staged throughout the summer. The connection between the living animal and the eating of its meat was fully acknowledged; at the Fête du Sel in Saliès, I found one sausage maker enthusiastically grilling his products on a barbecue right next to the pen where a Black Gascon sow was lying on a bed of straw with her litter of suckling pigs.

These simple ceremonies have a spiritual quality and certainly trace their origins to ancient rituals celebrating the fertility of the animals and giving thanks for their lives. They are at the heart of the respect which the French have for their food and its origins.

The legend of Sent Pançard is an unsubtle piece of propaganda against binge eating, teaching the restraint which is an important principle in an agricultural cycle in which famine would inevitably follow feast. For centuries, the pig was the foundation of a Gascon family's nutrition and a single animal, well reared, well fed and skilfully slaughtered, would provide meat for quite a large family for a full year.

It wasn't long before the rest of the world noticed the

special status of the pig in the agricultural and domestic economy of the region. The conquering Romans marvelled at the local tribesmen's skill in rearing pigs, and in the *Decameron*, Bocaccio wrote of Cornucopia, an imaginary part of the Basque Country so abundant that in the vineyards the vines were tied up with sausages.

The Gascon pig was an honoured member of the family. Living close to his owners, he would know their voices and come when called. Nobody thought it was strange to hear people talking to their pigs. He was always addressed respectfully, as *'lo Monsur'*, (Monsieur), or even *'lo Noble'* or *'lo Ministre'*. Paula Wolfert observes, 'There is a mystical feeling about these beasts on farms of the South-West, similar to the way bread is regarded in some parts of France.'

In another legend, the pig itself boasts that none of its body goes to waste. The *charcuterie* which the British admire so much in traditional French cuisine was originally devised as a varied and delicious way of preserving as much pork as possible through the depth of winter, when the chickens were no longer laying, and the fields and orchards were bare. In the days before freezers, a Béarnais housewife would set to work to preserve a year's supply of pork, making ham, *confit*, *rillettes*, pâtés, terrines, sausages and puddings.

The lean meat was either preserved *en confit*, slow-cooked in fat then sealed in a large pottery jar, or cured to make ham. The trotters, the tail and the ears were treated the same way. Small portions of ham or confit were then used in the signature dishes of the South-West: cassoulet, the bean stew, and *garbure*, the hearty soup that often comprises most of the evening meal. A thick slice of ham is also traditional with *piperade*, the Basque dish of eggs with peppers and tomato.

The liver and some of the back fat were minced and mixed with garlic, herbs and spices, sealed in glass jars or in tins, and slow-cooked to make pâtés. The fattest cuts of meat were rendered, drained, shredded, seasoned and potted up as *rillettes*. The intestines were carefully washed out, and stuffed with a minced mixture of fat, offal and meat scraps, spiced and mixed with stale bread, to make sausages.

Even the blood was saved. Glynn was hugely amused by a recipe for a dish made with nothing but the fat and blood of a duck. When the pig was slaughtered, his blood was mixed with breadcrumbs, any leftover fat and gristle, seasoned generously with *quatre épices* and poached. One recipe produced a succulent black pudding, for immediate consumption. Another method required the pudding to be dried to make the dark Béarnais sausage which actually tastes a lot better than it looks but has never found an export market.

If not to be eaten fresh, the sausages were dried or preserved *en confit*. All this bounty was then stored on high shelves or suspended from the beams in the living room, out of the reach of rats and mice. In a peasant community, the hams hanging from the beams were a symbol of the wealth of the household.

There is another story about Henri IV, who, when installed on the throne among all the magnificence of the royal court in Paris, was visited by his old wet-nurse from Pau. When she saw that there were no hams hanging from the ceiling, she exclaimed, 'Henri! My love, you must be starving – I'll send you a ham as soon as I get home!'

The gastronomic crown of this tradition is Bayonne ham, to which the French foodie establishment has accorded AOC status, meaning that the title can only be applied to an item produced according to a strictly defined method. Like the hams from Parma in Italy or Serrano in Spain, a Bayonne ham is salted then air-dried, so the slices are dark red and translucent.

The meat must come from a pig raised in the Béarn, the

Basque Country or the Armagnac region, and cured using
salt from Saliès-de-Béarn and from Bayonne. First the fine
white salt from Saliès is rubbed into the pork legs over a
three-day period, giving the ham its dense flavour and
colour. The cured hams are then stored in boxes of coarse,
greyish Bayonne salt for a year, before being rubbed with
pepper and hung up to dry. Refined diners usually like their
Bayonne ham wafer-thin, but the traditional slice preferred
by the Béarnais is a whole lot heartier.

Recipes

❦

I found a recipe for traditional carnival fritters, called Rats'
Tails, an enriched step up from everyday doughnuts, which
are often flavoured with orange-flower water. This wasn't
difficult to buy. The small blue bottles of perfumed flavouring were in every shop and on the stalls in the markets
selling nuts, olives and spices.

Orange-flower water is one of the Moorish legacies in
south-west France. In Morocco, and all over North Africa,
market traders still sit beside small hills of fresh orange
flowers and rosebuds, heaped up simply on a cloth on the
ground. The blooms are bought by the spice merchants,
who distil their own essences from them. The label of
the French-produced orange-flower water confessed to both
natural and artificial flower essences, but it was still a delicate flavouring that instantly evoked hot summer days in
the dead of winter.

In Béarnais cooking, orange-flower water is often used
in desserts and pastries where an English recipe would
call for vanilla. Not content with a single note of aroma,
many Béarnaise cooks make up their own mixture of sweet
flavourings, using orange-flower water, citrus peel, rum,
Armagnac, anise and almond extract in various proportions.

Rats' Tails

4 eggs
100 g (3½ oz) caster sugar, plus extra for dredging
500 g (1 lb 2 oz) plain flour
20 g (¾ oz) or a small packet of yeast
50 ml (1½ fl oz) oil
100 ml (4 fl oz) double cream
1 tbsp orange-flower water
oil for deep-frying

Break the eggs into a spacious bowl. Beat them lightly, then beat in the sugar, flour and yeast, little by little. Add the oil, cream and orange-flower water and continue beating until thoroughly smooth.

Put the frying oil over a gentle heat. Take a generous teaspoon of the dough and roll it between the palms of your hands to make a long, thin rat's tail. Continue until all the dough is shaped, by which time the oil should be hot enough to fry the fritters in batches until they are golden and puffed. Drain, dredge with sugar, and hand out to hungry children in paper cones.

If making Rats' Tails for adults, add a few dashes of rum to the batter.

Crème Caramel au Fleur d'Oranger

Once in the cupboard, the orange-flower water became a compulsion. I used it to sprinkle on a winter fruit salad of oranges with toasted almonds, or on slices of grilled pineapple to be served with ice cream. It gave a wonderful lift to milky nursery puddings, and a new zing to a simple *crème caramel*.

My *crème caramel* recipe comes from my tattered, butter-splattered, first-ever recipe book, Len Deighton's *Action Cookbook*. The *crème caramel* recipe is on page 118, and I've used it so often that the book now falls open there. Deighton, as well as a thriller writer extraordinaire, was a damn fine cookery writer and, after Elizabeth David, one of the best-known authors who popularized French cooking in Britain in the Sixties. He learned to cook as a student waiting tables to pay his way through art school.

850 ml (1½ pints) milk
6 eggs
225 g (8 oz) sugar, vanilla sugar if you keep it
1 tsp orange-flower water
butter for greasing
1 orange, peeled and sliced prettily

You will need

A mould – with its dark caramel top and creamy custard-coloured sides, *crème caramel* looks great in any shape of mould. I use a glass ring mould or a fluted kugelhopf tin.

A water jacket – which means a shallow dish or tin filled with water. This diffuses the oven heat and stops the *crème caramel* cooking too quickly and getting hard and ugly, with those bad little bubbles. If you can rest the mould on something like a couple of wooden skewers, to keep it off the bottom of the container, the result is even better.

This is a very simple dish, so you will get the most luscious results with the very best ingredients – fresh organic eggs and fresh organic whole milk. If you choose industrially produced eggs and half-fat milk, you get something lighter, paler and lower in fat and calories. It's an easy dessert to make in the morning of, or the day before, a dinner party and leave peacefully in the fridge until you need it.

Preheat the oven to 160°C/325°F/Gas 3. Scald the milk, which means bring it almost to boiling point. In a bowl of at least 1.4 litres (2.5 pint) size, beat the eggs and 90 g (3 oz) of sugar thoroughly. Slowly pour the milk into this mixture, beating all the time. Add the orange-flower water.

Put the rest of the sugar in a heavy-bottomed small saucepan and melt it. It should go dark brown, but not black. Grease the sides of your mould with a smear of butter; don't grease the bottom, the cooked caramel will unmould of its own accord. If you don't keep butter, use a film of oil, but don't resort to any kind of spread for greasing the mould, it will taste revolting.

Pour the caramelized sugar into the bottom of the mould, tilting it to coat evenly. Then pour in the custard, put the mould in the water jacket, put it all in the oven and cook for about 45 minutes. It's better to err on the side of caution with the heat; after about half an hour, check that the *crème* is actually cooking. The surface should have risen a very little. If not, turn up the heat – cautiously – and check again in five minutes.

When the *crème caramel* is cooked, take it out of the oven and let it cool before putting it in the fridge to chill. To serve, run a knife around the edge of the custard, put the serving plate over the mould, take a deep breath, say a prayer, hold the plate steady and turn the whole thing over. The *crème caramel* should flop gently down into a puddle of its own sauce. If it doesn't, give it a gentle shake. Fill the mould and the saucepan with cold water to dissolve the remaining caramel.

Decorate the plate with the orange slices and serve.

March

Golden-glazed confit pot

The snow melted. There were four different species of violets blooming in the garden: very tiny dark purple ones, bigger purple ones, blue-and-white speckled ones and pink ones. They were so abundant that it was impossible to walk across the grass without treading on them. 'You don't have lawn here,' said an English woman with a wistful voice and a little house in the next village. 'It's more like meadow, really.'

The weather was milder, but still stormy. I began digging the vegetable garden. The original patch had been almost overgrown with grass, and nothing but some strawberry plants had survived. Being under the mimosa tree, whose gloomy overhang was taking over the ground about the rate of two metres a year, it was doomed anyway.

I'd asked for a book on growing vegetables for Christmas, and Chloe had given me Monty Don's *Fork to Fork*. In his previous incarnation, Monty Don had a wonderful jewellery shop in Knightsbridge, on Beauchamp Place. I still had at least two pairs of his ear-rings, including some fabulous diamanté chandeliers, which I did not anticipate wearing that year.

His book is full of inspiring pictures of a vegetable garden as a jewellery designer would plan it, intricate, precise, neat square beds of velvet-black earth, hoed to total submission between little willow fences. The garden of Maison Bergez is more a piece of wilderness. Almost a mountain wilderness, since it slopes steeply. There are plenty of hazel bushes, with long straight branches, from which I could have made little fences easily, as long as I had no plans to do anything else with my life for a few weeks. But the ground is uneven and no portion of it is anything like flat. It divides into the tamer area close to the house, where the grass is finer and there are a few flowering shrubs, and the wild area beyond a geriatric lavender hedge, which gets the full sun.

I spent a wet morning drawing an ambitious plan for a semicircular plot in the sunniest position, divided into four triangles like a demi-Camembert, with a new lavender bush at the inner corners and wigwams of hazel twigs for beans and sweet peas on the uphill sections.

Sweet peas are my favourite flower. On my eighteenth birthday, the first time a man ever gave me flowers, it was a posy of multicoloured sweet peas. There's something utterly romantic about the intense scent and the brilliant colour carried by blooms as fragile as butterfly wings. Back in London I could only manage to squeeze a few sweet peas into a pot on the patio. Now I wanted to grow them in towers of flowers, the way I remembered from the gardens of my childhood.

The downhill sections were to be devoted to tomatoes, courgettes, herbs and artichokes. I had been fantasizing about growing artichokes for years, imagining the huge grey-green fountains of foliage topped with great purple globes. In Ossages, in the terraced vegetable garden behind her house, Marie grew enough artichokes to feed an army. I once complimented her on them, and explained that in London an artichoke could cost as much as fifteen francs. She looked at me with a mixture of pity and horror, and the next time we went for dinner she treated us to a huge platter of artichoke hearts, fried in butter and piled three deep.

In December and January I had gone out with gloves, hoe

and secateurs to exterminate the brambles which had invaded the beds around the house. Adding these to the dead leaves, the fallen branches, and all the sad detritus of neglect, I had made a bonfire over half the projected vegetable patch. The potters, out walking their three yappy white dogs, came in to inspect the works and offer advice. No way could I have a bonfire without permission from the *mairie*, they said. Rubbish, said Annabel. But the mayor was said to be very correct. So I compromised, and let the fire burn slowly on a still day. The ash was added to the heaped leaves on my very first compost heap, down on the far side of the garden. A compost heap! What joy.

The fire had done what I hoped it would do, and burned off the grass and weeds over a large area. With the beds marked out with string, I left this easy bit until last, and began digging into virgin turf. It was such hard work that I could only manage about an hour a day, which was handy since I was so impatient to start planting that I would never have got any writing done if I'd been able to dig all day.

A routine established itself. I wrote from 9.30 a.m. to 1.30 p.m., by which time it was 12.30 in London, the hour at which publishers go out to lunch and newspaper editors need their copy for the next day's edition. I lunched *à l'anglaise*, on bread and cheese, then went out to dig until 3 p.m., by which time the shops in Sauveterre would be open and I could make the trip in for my newspapers and the post. I would then be back at my desk at 4 p.m., which was 3 p.m. in London. Talking to my editor becoming increasingly important.

A red squirrel appeared in the walnut tree as soon as the icy weather gave way to milder days. Soon he was waking me up at dawn every morning by dancing all over the roof. He was extremely shy, and never came out if he thought that the cats or I were in the garden, unlike Squirrel Nutter, the grey squirrel who stops by my London yard, who runs down the tree trunks yammering insults at Piglet and the Duchess.

Fat Rabbit, however, was not shy in the least. He deluded himself that if he froze, and allowed only his jaws and whiskers to move, I wouldn't be able to see him. He spent long periods posed like a rabbit-shaped tea-cosy, thinking that he was invisible. This worked perfectly on Piglet, who stalked importantly around the garden looking for game and never noticed that there was an overfed rodent right in front of him. Fat Rabbit had a favourite patch over by the new compost heap, and sat there, as still as a cardboard cut-out, watching me at work. Since his eyes were on the sides of his head, he could turn a full profile and still keep me in view.

A Proposition

By now, dropping into la Maysou to pass on my *Times* had become almost a daily habit and Gerald had laid in a bottle of gin especially to tempt me over at aperitif time. Annabel cleared her throat nervously and announced that the Club International Salisien would like me to give a talk about writing to their members. On the face of it, this should have been easy. I have a standard lecture on storytelling and popular fiction which adapts to almost any occasion, even as an after-dinner entertainment for a convention of dentists.

Translating this, however, would take me about a week and I was not at all certain that my French was up to expounding my theories of narrative structure. Annabel proposed that we consult Annie-Claire Despaux, a professional translator who found the club useful for keeping up her English.

We met in Annabel's family room on a Sunday afternoon. Annie-Claire had carried the Frenchwoman's devotion to the silk scarf to the extent of knotting one casually around her polo-neck sweater. She was a fine-boned, vivacious woman whose eyes shone with intelligence.

The name of Despaux has been prominent in Saliès-de-Béarn for centuries. Jean d'Espaux, a master surgeon, appears in the city records in 1765. By 1793, the year the revolutionaries executed the king in the Paris and urged citizens to hunt down aristocrats like dogs, the Salisiens were protesting that there was no unrest in the town, ex-nobles and peasants got along fine, and pointing to D'espaux the elder, described as a merchant, who was colonel of the national guard, and his son Jean Despaux (sic) who had served with the guards since the age of fourteen, as exemplary citizens. Note the naive meticulousness with which the Salisien authorities identified the father as a land-owner, but called the younger by the complete name which confirmed the family's revolutionary politics.

A Pierre-Zéphirin Despaux-Faget was first Deputy then Mayor of Saliès between 1854 and 1870. The family town house, built in 1793, still stands on the Place Jeanne d'Albret, one of the tall, half-timbered, steep-roofed buildings which makes the centre of the town look like a fairy-tale illustration by Arthur Rackham. Annie-Claire doesn't live there, but in a modern home in the spacious out-skirts of the town, where she works on English-to-French book translations for a publisher in Paris.

Her late husband was a pillar of les Amis de Vieux Saliès and made the name of Despaux even more prominent by founding a nursery on family land adjoining the RN117, and a garden centre in the village of Baigts-de-Béarn, on the same road. Despaux is a very good garden centre, the best place in the region to find the classy border species as opposed to trays of lurid bedding plants, but no longer a family business.

I had turned my speaking notes, a few scribbles on a postcard, into a coherent text, and printed it out. In the section where I usually talked about fairy tales, mythology and the collective subconscious, I added the strangely similar stories of the discovery of the hot springs in the region, all legends of the universal wisdom-of-nature genre.

In Saliès, Gaston Fébus discovered the salt spring when out hunting. The viscount wounded a boar, and the animal instinctively ran to the hot spring to bathe its wounds in the curative waters. Being a magical animal, the boar could speak, and its dying words to the hunters were, 'If I had not died here, none of you would live,' or, in Béarnais, '*Si you nou y eri mourt arres no y bibere.*' Frankly, this is one of those resonant bits of folklore that doesn't make sense. Not to me, anyway. If the waters are so curative, why didn't the boar get better? And the hunters were going to live anyway, weren't they? All the same, that's the legend, and the boar's words are carved on the fountain on the main square, so there can be no argument about them.

Other local legends are more coherent. There's a mountain spa which was reputedly found by an old war horse whose owner couldn't bear to kill it, and abandoned it in a remote valley. One slurp of the magical spring and the venerable charger came cantering down the valley to meet his master, as sprightly as a young stallion. In Dax, the story goes that a Roman centurion who had been called to the front threw his arthritic old dog into the river to drown it, rather than abandon it to suffer while he was away fighting. The waters worked their magic, and the centurion found his dog jumping up to greet him when he returned from the battle.

The club's secretary, who was Dutch, had already translated the biography on the back of my last book. I sounded so much more impressive in French. My style of writing (*une brillante satirique sociale*) and the highlights of my career to date (*elle a écrit 7 nouvelles dont la dernière, 'Épreuve d'Amour', est une comédie romantique. La production de Tom Cruise l'a retenue pour un film avec le star Nicole Kidman*) lost the weary familiarity which an author gets after writing the guff on book jackets for fifteen years, and took on a fresh, new glamour.

Describing the actual subject of the lecture, however, had been a problem. 'Storytelling' is one thing, *'comment raconter des histoires'* isn't the same thing. *'Narration'* didn't quite do it, either. The words for 'plot' and 'narrative' didn't have the same meaning, either. In fact, there seemed to be no way in French to express the idea of constructing a narrative as part of literary technique. No wonder the French New Wave authors were so mad for the deconstructed novel.

Imagery turned out to translate more accurately, so it was much easier to talk about the process metaphorically: *'C'est une sorte de danse, de chorégraphie, ou, par le jeu de l'imaginaire, l'auteur et le lecteur, en harmonie, se plaisent a créer, ou plutôt recréer, des images dont ils son porteurs.'* This sounded like the splendid stuff I heard French intellectuals discussing on the radio. Indeed, Annie-Claire herself was an adept user of *'effectivement'*.

Translating only two paragraphs took over three hours, so we decided that the best way to manage *'la conférence'* was for me to speak in English and for Annie-Claire, on her sit-up-and-beg typewriter, to provide a digest of the lecture in French. I would then input this on my computer and print out lots of copies to distribute to the audience.

Having reached decisions with which everyone was happy, Annabel made a fresh pot of tea, and Annie-Claire told me about the failed attempt by the local preservation society to get Saliès and its environs protected as a UNESCO world-heritage site.

There are so many stories of similar failures, and so many tourist enterprises which fizzle out, that I suspect the Béarnais have never been convinced that they needed the help of outsiders to make their economy work. They're extremely jolly with travellers at a person-to-person level, but they've never liked the idea of hundreds of visitors traipsing through their valleys. Perhaps the sleepy air of the South-West makes it all seem like too much trouble. Or maybe they simply share the live-and-let-live philosophy of their Basque neighbours. The story of the decline of Sauveterre is a sad example.

Once, Sauveterre-de-Béarn was a prime destination on the pilgrim route to Compostela. For pilgrims from the north of France, trekking down to St-Jean-Pied-de-Port and planning to cross the Pyrenees through the pass of Roncesvalles and head for Pamplona, the most direct route lay through Sauveterre, which had a splendid stone bridge across the deep waters of the Gave d'Oloron.

In the days when the Landes was a pestilent swamp, even pilgrims from England, who used to sail over to Bordeaux before they started walking, favoured this route. In the Middle Ages, two million pilgrims were making the trip every year. Three of the principal routes, the *chemins de* Tours, Vezelay and Puy, converged just north of the town.

Pilgrims were huge business. Not only did they pay top prices for their guides, board, lodging and walking gear, but they were also happy to make big donations to the churches they stopped at along the way. Throughout the north of Gascony there are many imposing Romanesque abbeys whose stonemasons were paid with pilgrimage money.

Before its fortunes changed, Sauveterre also managed

to build itself a splendid pilgrim church, with a beautiful Romanesque doorway and the traditional blue ceiling painted with gold stars. The bridge, however, fell down some time in the eighteenth century. Instead of rebuilding it as fast as they could, the townspeople began a leisurely debate about the sort of bridge they wanted, no doubt fuelled with whatever was preferred as an aperitif in those times.

They ended up arguing for forty years, in which time the pilgrims had to make other arrangements to cross the Gave. By the time Sauveterre finally built a new bridge, the pilgrims had found another crossing and taken their custom elsewhere for good.

The Most Beautiful *Brocante* in France

I wanted to go to Ahetze. All I knew was that Ahetze is a tiny Basque village near the coast and on the third Sunday of almost every month it has a flea-market fair, one of the biggest in the region. I forget who told me about it, but something about the idea sounded excellent. Besides, I had a yen for some twirly garden chairs in nice rusty ironwork.

Willow was away and Fiona wanted to take the children up to Iraty to play in the snow. Annabel, used to trawling the auction houses of Pau for fine art, was not attracted by the prospect of a flea market. Sandy-and-Annie were doing lunch for the young Irish couple who were thinking of buying her house. In the end I went on my own with instructions to call in on Les Écossais on the way back, and give the Irish husband a motivational chat about skiing.

Lorries are forbidden on the roads in France on Sunday, and there was so little traffic on the motorway that I counted the vehicles I passed on the forty-minute trip to the junction with the busier coast road. Six other cars going in my direction, twenty-two coming the other way. If bliss can be attained on a motorway at all, I made it that morning.

Ahetze was easy to find, hardly ten minutes from the St-Jean-de-Luz Nord exit from the coastal motorway. The road, typical of the inland lanes of the Basque Coast, ran purposefully along the high ground, between fields which even in the dead of spring were like emerald velvet, patched with russet swatches of bracken or copses of beech.

Suddenly you found yourself running downhill, and there was the village in front of you, a picture-postcard vision of half-timbered Basque houses standing majestically around the church. In the flat, whitewashed bell tower, two bells swung in round-topped niches.

Even here, less than twenty kilometres into the foothills of the Pyrenees, Basque architecture is quite unlike that of the Béarn. To new eyes, the houses look more Tyrolean than anything else. They're massive, made to shelter an extended family under a low-pitched red-tile roof. Under the eaves is a space for the doves, who come and go through neat triangular holes in the outer wall.

There's usually a decoratively carved wooden balcony at first-floor level, traditionally used as a dry storage area for firewood. The window shutters and the exposed beams are painted a bold colour, most often ox-blood red, though dark green, brown and blue are also popular. The massive front door is hung under a stone lintel on which the names of the family's founding couple are carved, with the date when they set up the new home.

Often the Basque national symbol is often carved in the top corners; it evolved from pre-Christian sun-worship and looks like four teardrops swirled together into a rounded swastika. A Basque house tries to face the east and always has a name, written diagonally on the front wall, in paint or wrought iron.

The price of the emerald velvet, of course, is that the Basque Country has the highest rainfall in all Europe; it's even wetter than Éire. The Irish are going to feel right at home here. On that day, however, the sun was smiling down through big fluffy cumuli, burnishing the green grass and the white-walled village houses.

The flea market was clearly a whole-village effort. The children were out on the hedge banks directing vehicles to park in neat lines on the nearest field, from which it was a short walk down a lane lined with primroses to the first stalls. These were selling the high-end of *brocante* desirables, the vintage cafe-ware, cottage-kitchen enamels, early twentieth-century coffee bowls, dressing-table sets, 'bedroom' pictures and small mirrors.

Moving on, I came to the realm of agricultural antiques. Here were the old cattle yokes, forks, spades, rakes, trowels, bird cages, horse shoes, rat-traps, watering cans, butterfly nets, fishing rods, sieves, shoe lasts, bottle stands, plate racks, egg carriers, grape baskets, milk churns, plough shares and prune dryers. The prune dryers are shallow ovoid wicker scoops, like giant snow shoes, on which plums were spread out in the sun to turn into the famous Agen prunes.

So far, the stalls had lined the narrow village streets. As I drifted out of the agricultural tat section to the serious old iron department, where garden seats, tables, urns, statues, bedsteads, light fittings, plant stands and fountains lay about, their rust patches twinkling in the sun, I realized that every inch of available space in this village was going to be covered in goods for sale. Every lane, every alleyway, every sports ground, every large room, every car park – everywhere except the church itself and the graveyard around it.

The car park in front of the village's two shops was a

battlefield of buying and selling, where everyone with furniture had set up to take advantage of the space. The dealers' vans, circled like cowboys' covered wagons, were parked with their wheels on the grass verges and leaned at crazy angles. In front of them were the tables covered with sheets and sheltered by fluttering sunshades, crowded with a pell-mell selection of goods.

True tat rubbed handles with real pearls. You could buy anything from a very nice art nouveau marble sculpture of a child's head to a well-used photocopier, circa 1979. Ahetze was like Portobello Road in the Sixties, though the clientele were more conservatively dressed and the breeze carried a whiff of the Atlantic ocean rather than of patchouli oil.

The school sports hall housed the down-market textiles, the linen tea towels monogrammed in traditional red cross-stitch, the frayed damask guest towels, the washed-out napkins and their cotton envelopes, the scalloped fabric shelf-edgings edged with lace or embroidered naively with animals and fruit.

Up a stone staircase, and the posh linen was discovered in the pelota court, transformed into the bottom drawers of a thousand Basque brides. Here I could have spent all day among the snowy mounds of treasure, reverently unfolding and refolding the embroidered sheets and admiring the drawn-thread work, the stylized deco or nouveau mono-grams, the insets of lace, the embroidered flowers, the matching pillowcases, bolster covers, nightdresses and curtain panels.

More steps led up to the church car park and the funky textiles, the chenille curtains, the velvet cushions, the lengths of faded chintz and printed linen, the smocked farmhands' shirts, and the very old and very rustic linen sheets, woven in the nineteenth century and earlier, by hand, on small cottage looms, from thread that had been hand-spun.

Once these old linen sheets, some of them nearly as thick as blankets, were despised as coarse and fit only for peasants. Now they are one of the most prized items in the fashionable catalogue of French country antiques, the first choice of the international yuppie designer for running up loose covers or curtains with 'the divine flop factor'.

Dealing in linen is strictly a woman's business, so *the* most prized buy, the ultimate fetish item, is one of the yellow-glazed earthenware pots originally used for confits, on which both the men and women dealers are comfortable making a profit. To give you an idea of the scale of the profits they make, I was buying coarse linen sheets at around €15, while they sell in London at up to £150. Fine linen sheets without embroidery were up to €20, sold in London for up to £100, and the confit pots, depending on size, were up to €50 at reasonable *brocantes* and up to £120 on the King's Road or in Portobello. I have even found a confit pot – admittedly a very fine specimen – on sale for £300 in Notting Hill Gate.

Every confit pot is a different shape and the golden glaze is a different shade; the older the pot the darker the glaze. Some, which were used for haricot dishes, are dappled with the marks of the beans. They are wide-mouthed and made with a pair of looped handles on the shoulders, through which they could be suspended from a ceiling beam. Confit pots are so fashionable, and such easy items to sell, that some dealers simply barged through the door of small country sales as soon as they opened, bought every confit pot in the room, and drove off for breakfast twenty minutes later without wasting a thought on the more obscure collectables. This market means that the confit pots are becoming rare.

Possibly the pot dealers missed a trick or two. The single biggest mark-up I discovered was on a humble moulded-glass salt and pepper cellar, which nobody at Athetze would have bothered with and at a Béarnais *vide grenier*, the equivalent of a boot sale, would have gone for €1 or less. At one of London's temples of French country style, these were offered with a ribbon-tied hand-lettered label reading £29.50.

I sat down with a coffee in the weak spring sun, outside the village's one buzzing restaurant. The array of gorgeous, evocative and underpriced goodies felt overwhelming. I needed a budget and buying policy. For today, it would be €100 and nothing for which I didn't have a specific use. For the future, I would run to embroidered linen only if it had my own initials on it. And, if the price was right, old linen sheets and confit pots, because . . . well, it would be daft not to and they *were* lovely.

The squirly ironwork chairs of my dreams were sitting right across the alley from me, at €7 each. €21. The table to go with them, big enough for four, or for one writer and her laptop, was down in the car park, painted mud brown but it would be the work of a lunch-hour to fix that. A bit of a rip-off at €40, but it was in good nick. €61.

On the way back from leaving a deposit on the table, I passed a sweet-faced, white-haired woman fussing over a pile of sheets, while a man of the same age, presumably her husband, sat on the tailgate of their van, enjoying a pipe. She was evidently too much of an amateur to have a pitch in either of the main linen areas. Perhaps . . . yes! A few minutes' browsing revealed three gorgeous sheets of fine, pure linen, with simple ladder-stitch borders, priced at €15 each. They would have been the last remaining under-sheets of a trousseau; the more decorated top sheets had already been sold.

Haggling is expected, of course, though it goes against

the grain with an English person when something so lovely is priced at a fraction of what it would be in London. 'Would you take €40 for the three?' I asked her.

Her husband, who had abandoned his pipe and bustled over to watch his wife make money, got quite excited. 'Three fifteens are forty-five,' he calculated, 'but she's offering forty for all three . . . that's a good deal, you ought to take it.'

'Is this your husband?' I asked her jokingly. 'Whose side is he on?'

A pained look flashed into her eyes. The husband looked utterly foxed. Clearly the Gascon sense of humour stopped at the Basque border. I apologized as fulsomely as I could. She apologized back. Her husband concentrated on relighting his pipe. The money changed hands and I scuttled away before another opportunity for embarrassment opened up. €101. I wasn't going to beat myself up for one euro.

Listening to the babble of conversation around me, I realized that Ahetze was a trilingual event. French, obviously. Basque, obviously. And Spanish. The Spanish dealers were unmistakable. With their dark hair, flashing eyes, cowboy boots, leather jackets and tight jeans, they out-Lovejoyed Lovejoy. The Spanish were buying strictly for their home market, anything in black metalwork or dark wood, no twee faded French cottage knickknacks for them.

As I wandered back to the car with my arms full of sheets, trying to pick out phrases I recognized from this agreeable babel, I heard something completely familiar and utterly unexpected: an East End voice, speaking English. It came from a tall young man with a number-two haircut, who was talking to an even taller young man with a small white dog in his arms and a Paul Smith scarf. *A Paul Smith scarf? An East End accent?*

'Good heavens,' I said, the words hopping out of my

mouth before I could stop them. 'I haven't heard a London voice for weeks.'

'Nor have we,' said the speaker, and he laughed a good, nasal, East End heh-heh-heh.

They had been in France two weeks. They lived in Castagnède, a pretty village on the far side of Sauveterre, famous for its restaurant, la Belle Auberge. The speaker couldn't remember his phone number. The one with the dog could. We agreed to do tea the following Tuesday.

At Iraty, Fiona's dog, a wire-haired terrier called Scruff, was whirled up in a tornado and dropped from a great height — fortunately into a snow-drift.

Lunch with Marie and Robert

Marie, of course, had invited me to lunch immediately I arrived in Orriule, but on a day when Annabel was away and I had already invited Gerald over for pot luck. Like most of my neighbours, she and Robert have enough to do with keeping up with their family, but at last we found a date that worked for both of us. 'Come and eat some *confit*!' she chortled down the phone.

If you want to do justice to lunch with Marie and Robert, it's a good idea to fast for a couple of days first. Robert and their son, Christian, are capable of sitting at the table and watching her bring a procession of home-prepared delicacies out of the kitchen, then graciously selecting a few morsels and passing the loaded plates onwards, but my admiration for the cook won't let me do that.

Indirectly — and not very indirectly at that — it is thanks to Robert and Marie that I am here at all. Some years ago, Willow and Tony, having decided to settle in the region, began house-hunting. Willow's method of doing this is simple. She goes to every estate agent in the chosen area and asks to see their cheapest property.

In this case, it was a small farm cottage with no mains services, surrounded by maize fields, near Ossages. Robert and Christian Lafargue were the nearest builders, and got the job of converting the cottage into an elegant home, complete with a galleried double-height reception room and a wide balcony overlooking the valley.

Ossages was then almost a ghost village. The last *auberge* was shut and the *dépôt de pain*, less than a shop but still a place you could buy bread, closed at the same time Willow and Tony moved into a caravan in what was supposed to be their garden. Some of the finest houses in the village were either standing empty or seriously dilapidated. Robert and Marie's children were still in the area. Their two daughters were married to local businessmen and Christian was living at home, running the building firm with his father and still, in theory, looking for a wife. However, their grandchildren, like the rest of the young people in the village, had moved away, first to study and then to build careers in Bordeaux or Bilbao.

Slowly, Robert and Marie looked over these foreigners who had bought into their community, who wanted walls built lumpy, beams left exposed, window sills shaped free-hand and a bathroom with a power shower to every bedroom, who ate dinner instead of lunch, had friends instead of relatives and were content to rattle around in a vintage Mercedes instead of trading in a brand-new Peugeot every couple of years.

It must have been a steep learning curve on both sides. Willow and Tony, used to houses with foundations, didn't appreciate that their cottage, like many old buildings in the Chalosse, had been chucked up on a sandy slope with no foundations at all. Only the stone mass of the chimney

breast stopped the whole structure sliding down the valley.
Willow wanted to move the fireplace. Christian mentioned
underpinning. Willow said they couldn't afford it. I was
talking to her on the phone when the walls did their house-
of-cards trick and I can still remember the scream.

Week by week, mutual trust developed. It was over a year
before Robert mentioned that his great-grandfather had
built the house. When the first part of the job was done,
Marie invited the clients to lunch. It was noted with enthusiasm by all the female Lafargue relatives that Tony bore a
striking resemblance to Julio Iglesias.

In time, some friends of Willow and Tony came to visit
and decided to buy a substantial *maison de maître* in a nearby
village. Instructions were faxed to the Lafargue office, and
translated by Tony, who speaks fluent English, French and
Spanish. After three years of this, the friends reappeared and
moved in with Willow and Tony for the final six months of
snagging and general agony. The wife then picked a fight
with her old friend and never spoke to her again. Time
passed, and the foreign community developed the notion
that the wife was an English aristocrat.

Marie and Robert sided firmly with Willow and Tony.
'*Un peu bourgeoise*,' Marie says of the wife, making clear
that this is a courteous understatement of her real views.
The house at Berenx was going to need ongoing work, but
Lafargue et Fils had enough work for the next two years and
blood was thicker than water – because by now, Willow and
Tony were part of the family.

Robert is a man of immense respect, which he has earned
in a lifetime of fair dealing and wise advice. When people
pass him on the street, they say, '*Bonjour, Maître Lafargue*.'
He encouraged my friends to buy their present home, a
handsome village house facing the church. It needed saving

from the decades of neglect; the ageing owner would soon need residential care and her family needed the money.

Under the wing of their adoptive parents, my friends were inducted into village life. The mayor smiled upon them. They sold their first house to another English family. Now there are six houses in and around the village belonging to non-French owners. Ossages is almost fashionable. The village has a shop and cafe. Somebody has just opened a *brocante* but the prices are ambitious. All these matters were discussed over the *confit*. By half-past two, everyone had finished their coffee and went back to work.

A Literary Evening at the Hôtel du Golf

The Hôtel du Golf was built mostly of concrete in the 1970s, and beside the glory that is the rest of Saliès it looks rather plain. Nevertheless, the Club International Salisien had determined that it was the ideal venue for my *conférence*.

Andrew and Geoff, my new friends from Castagnède, came. Sandy-and-Annie came, and bought champagne because the Irish were indeed going ahead and buying their house. Willow and Tony, newly returned from exterminating the cockroaches in their Spanish villas, came. Annabel, *la vice-présidente*, came with Gerald and her handsome thirtysomething godson. Fiona and Gordon came with Cam and Margot, and Cam crawled over the floor in front of the front row like a commando. Dominique came, and had the new experience of trying to follow a conversation in a foreign language for an hour. Roger was in England and sent his regrets. The Mayor of Orriule was also invited, but couldn't come; she was a birdlike young woman who dropped in on me one morning at Maison Bergez, apologizing for not calling before and inviting me to the Mother's Day fete.

Annie-Claire, more than ever like a bright-eyed robin, introduced me to the young owner of the excellent local bookshop. I'd seen the French edition of *Heartswap* in his window the previous year, but he had no recollection of stocking it.

The rest of the audience were club members and seemed, on average, to be British and confused. My party piece contains one splendid joke, at which they laughed uproari-ously, and it did seem that they were taking in the good stuff about narrative, mythology, the collective unconscious, Joseph Campbell and the legend of the hot springs.

But then it was time for questions. The first was in English, from the lady with the wistful voice. 'All these bestsellers are written to a formula,' she said. 'What is it?'

About half an hour earlier, I'd explained that there was no formula and it was this irritating misconception that had led me to get interested in plot structure in the first place. 'Er – as I said at the beginning,' I said, trying not to sound insulting, 'there is no formula. There is only classical narra-tive structure, which is capable of infinite interpretation.' She looked disappointed.

The next question was in French, from the Club Presi-dent herself, Gracienne, who had turned up in stilettos and a black power suit with a peplum. 'Why aren't there any pictures in your books?' she demanded.

Annie-Claire waded in to try to help. We went for some-thing on the lines of words being the medium in which I preferred to express myself. Gracienne looked disappointed.

Annabel's godson asked: 'Why was your first novel a bestseller?' Well, what could I say? Because it was brilli-antly written, exquisitely constructed and, most crucially, it was exactly the right book at the right time. 'Well, why don't you do it again?' Because I grew up, along with my readership. Because it's not in my nature to churn out a blockbuster every two years. Because I'm an artist and we have to move on. He looked disappointed.

Afterwards, we attempted to enjoy a dinner of excruciating slowness, thereby blighting the romance of the hotel's only guests, two lone salespeople, a man and a woman, who sat sadly at their separate tables. Gerald, I noticed, talked animatedly in French to Gracienne until way past midnight without a hint of tiredness.

Recipe

Confit de Canard

This, the great signature dish of all Gascony, is hideously abused in Britain. I was once silly enough to order a salad with duck *confit* in the restaurant at a West End fashion emporium. A minute inspection of the limp leaves that arrived some twenty minutes later revealed no meat of any kind. I suppose the chef decided to try it on because most of his clientele 'eat' a salad by flicking the leaves about for a while, then mashing a few of them with a fork before pouting resentfully and shoving the plate aside. The tiny minority who actually swallow then rush off to the lavatory to make themselves sick. Easy to put invisible *confit* on the menu with that kind of customer.

If you are ever actually served duck *confit* in Britain, it's usually slimy, pallid, greasy and revolting. To be strictly fair, you can have the same experience in a downmarket *auberge* anywhere in Gascony, too. In Britain, trying to make your own *confit* at home is almost as unrewarding – I've read recipes by otherwise reputable cookery writers who suggest that the cook in a hurry can just mock up a decent duck leg *en confit* by tossing it into the deep fryer. Trust me, you can't.

You can't make duck, or anything else, *en confit* in a hurry. It's a dish that was originally cooked over embers in the corner of an open fire, while the cook and her family got on with their lives nearby. The essence of its deliciousness is that the meat is briefly cured in salt, then its fat is rendered very slowly, then the meat is cooked in the fat so slowly that it practically melts. Pierre Koffmann remembers that his grandmother didn't consider that the first part of the cooking had been completed successfully until she could pierce the meat with a piece of straw.

This slow cooking, followed by slow cooling and a process of preservation in fat, gives the meat a velvety texture and a deep, mellow flavour. Without giving each phase of the process its due time, the chemical changes that create the texture and flavour will not take place. A piece of duck *confit* should also be golden and gorgeously crispy on the outside – it's a close cousin to the classic air-dried duck dishes from China, another great duck-eating nation.

Prepared properly, *confit* should not be greasy, and should offer the maximum of crispiness for the minimum of calories, because the cooking is finished by again heating the pieces of preserved duck slowly in the oven until all the fat has run off. Most modern hobs and ovens can cook *confit* perfectly well on their lowest settings.

You will need

    a duck – the French raise a particular strain of heavy-built Muscovy duck which carries generous deposits of fat. If you're in Britain, your best bet will probably be a Trelough duck, from English Natural Foods, who will also be able to supply you with . . .

    duck fat – even if you've picked a duck with plenty of fat under the skin, you probably won't have enough for the cooking process. See if you can scrounge some more from the butcher, or buy a tin of ready-rendered duck or goose fat, sold quite reasonably in French supermarkets or butchers, and at an exorbitant price in some British delis.

a bay leaf
sea salt flakes
black pepper
a saucepan
a casserole
whatever you're going to preserve the duck in – glass
    preserving jars or an earthenware pot
greaseproof paper
time
patience

If you've bought your duck from a proper butcher, you can ask him to cut it into pieces for you, leaving you with two breast portions, or *magrets*, two legs, two wings (minus the tips) and the carcass with its skin and fat. Leave the skin on the pieces to be preserved.

Like the peasant's pig, every bit of the duck was considered eatable, and so a traditional *confit* operation would preserve the heart, the gizzard, the feet and the head, as well as the skin of the neck stuffed with sausage meat.

Crush the bay leaf to powder and mix with lots of salt and some finely ground pepper. Sprinkle some of this mixture into the bottom of a casserole, put in the pieces of duck and sprinkle on more salt mixture. Turn the pieces once or twice to make sure they're salted all over, cover the casserole and leave overnight for the salt to draw out moisture and lightly cure the meat.

Render the fat from the rest of the skin and the carcass. Cut the skin into small pieces and pull out any fat from the body cavity. Either put the skin and fat in an ovenproof dish into a very low oven, or simmer them in water in a saucepan on a very low heat. After about 90 minutes, all the available fat will have run out. Strain this carefully into a container. You will be left with the *graisserons*, a luxurious advance on pork scratchings. Add any scraps of meat left over, sprinkle with salt and brown in the oven before cooling and keeping for aperitif time.

Take the duck pieces out of the casserole and rinse off the salt mixture under running water. Pat them dry with a cloth. Wash out the casserole, dry it, and pour in the duck fat. Set the casserole over a low heat until the fat is warm and liquid, then add the duck pieces. There should be enough fat to cover them completely. If there isn't, cook them in instalments using the same fat. Simmer the pieces in the fat for about 3 hours.

Turn off the heat and leave the duck pieces to cool in the fat overnight. In the morning, wash out your containers with boiling water, dry them and put a little salt in the bottom of each to sweeten any juice that runs from the meat. Pick out the pieces and pack them loosely into the jars.

Reheat the fat remaining and strain off and keep the clear layer which will rise to the top, leaving the meat juice and the cloudy fat behind. (These will not keep long, but you can use them to enrich gravy and for general cooking.) Pour the clear fat around the pieces of duck in the jars until they are completely covered. Tap the full jars gently on the work-top to get rid of air bubbles. Leave to cool, making sure that none of the pieces touches the side of the jar (one reason to prefer a glass container).

If you intend to eat the *confit* within a month, you can now lay a circle of greaseproof paper on top of the fat and put your containers in the fridge. If you want to go the whole nine yards and let your confit mature for up to a year, add the circle of greaseproof paper, seal the jar tightly and sterilize in boiling water for 30 minutes, before cooling and storing.

Traditionally, jars of confit were often sealed with a layer of lard, which is denser and more air-proof than duck fat, covered with a piece of cloth which was tied down tightly and kept in the cool room adjacent to the kitchen, called a *chambre obscure* because no ray of sun was ever allowed to warm it. If your home is centrally heated, the only sensible place to keep your confit may be the fridge.

When you want to use some pieces of confit, leave the jar in a warm room until the fat is semi-solid and you can withdraw the pieces easily. If you have to speed things up, warm the jar in a saucepan of simmering water. Don't even think about the microwave.

Let the fat drip off the meat, helped by very careful scraping if you're in a hurry. Put the pieces on a roasting rack and reheat them in a slow oven for about 40 minutes to an hour. If the skin is not crisp after this, either turn up the heat in the oven or pop them under the grill. If the skin still isn't crisp, it's likely that you bought the wrong sort of duck. In this case, the cheat's way forward would be to sizzle the portions briefly in a pan, in a mixture of duck fat and olive or nut oil.

While you are reheating the duck, you can also brown some cubes of parboiled potatoes in a little duck fat, with some garlic, sliced shallot and thyme or rosemary. Quite often, *confit* is served with nothing more. However, the Gascons, like the English, see an affinity between duck and green peas, and sometimes serve confit nestled into a dish of peas cooked with baby onions, herbs and cubes of Bayonne ham. A piece of *confit* is also essential to finish a *cassoulet* or a *garbure*.

April

Edmond Rostand, author of
Cyrano de Bergerac

The termites hatched out in the middle of the Queen Mother's funeral. I had two guests with me, two old friends, both called Penny. 'Tuppence!' cried Roger joyfully, when I asked him to dinner to meet them.

The Pennies are two of my oldest friends, and have custody of those precious domestic bits I'd have been mad to trust to my tenant. Penny B lives around the corner from me in London, works for the BBC and is looking after my Victorian terracotta urn with its topiary box ball. Penny C lives in Somerset and teaches children with learning difficulties; she and her husband have custody of the Brayfield collection of art deco ceramics.

My landlady's sofa, by that time, had been tastefully draped in antique linen sheets. We had finished dinner and were sitting by a glowing fire watching the television on which, thanks to *la parabole du Sky*, we had enjoyed highlights of the proceedings in Westminster Abbey from the first tolling of the bell to the last skirl of the pipes. It was when I got up to make the coffee that I saw dozens of black insects crawling up the back of the sofa.

Termites look like small flying ants. They crawl about with a horrible determination while their wings unfold and dry out, then they fly off and pursue their termitey way of life outdoors, until they lay eggs. When the eggs hatch, the termites can reduce a house to rubble in a couple of years by burrowing under the walls and eating their way up through the woodwork.

Softwood – pine, as in floorboards – is what termites like best, but they won't turn their noses up at hardwood, like oak beams. By the time they are ready to swarm they will have reamed hundreds of channels inside a solid plank, hollowing it out to the extent that the householder will be able to push in the surface with an ordinary kitchen fork.

Year one, the skirting boards. Year two, the level of a light switch. Year three, almost at the ground-floor ceiling. Year four, into the ceiling but, if you're lucky, they won't take out a whole oak beam. Year five, if the house is still standing, they're approaching the roof. By year six, the house can be nothing but a heap of stones.

Termites create a peculiar dry smell which a person with sensitized nose can detect as soon as he or she walks through the door. Sandy and Annabel had both been warning me for months that I was in for a nasty surprise in the spring. After watching the termites for thirty seconds, I could see the little beasts were hatching out of the kitchen door frame.

Fortunately there was a good supply of insecticide in the house. The Pennies were intrepid and a short episode of shrieking and spraying took care of the first infestation.

When we came down in the morning, another few hundred had hatched from the door frame between the sitting room and the hall, and were crawling all over the floor and up the walls. For the rest of the hatching season, I took to getting up early and having a good spray before my guests appeared.

With the termites came a moral dilemma. Gascony is probably the termite capital of France. Its humid climate is just what they like. Officially, termites are considered so deadly that their presence must be notified to the *mairie*. It's illegal to rent out an infested house, and if a house is sold, as Sandy-and-Annie had just discovered at a cost of €5,000, the seller has to provide a certificate proving that any possible termites have been exterminated.

I took advice. Possibly, my landlady had been told about the termites by the previous tenant, but was in total denial, terrified of the expense of treating them. Annabel, who had a vision of billions of termites crawling intently up the hill to La Maysou, licking their tiny chops at the sight of her gorgeous Béarnais roof, voted for going straight to the *mairie*. I preserved a few specimens in a jamjar as evidence and decided to wait until the landlady visited in May, feeling sympathy for a woman on a fixed income faced with a crippling house-repair bill, and not wishing to find myself suddenly homeless either.

Everywhere I went that week, perfect strangers, hearing my English accent, put their hands on my arm in sympathy and said, 'Ah, you've lost your Queen Mother.' Some of the shops even put a picture of her in their windows. *Paris Match*, on the other hand, took a few pages out from its normal coverage of starlets and psychopaths to give the Frenchwoman's view of the courtship of that scheming hussy Elizabeth Bowes-Lyon by the great plonker, the future King George VI, *dit* Bertie.

'At the time, the young aristocrat had only one aim, to cosy up to the royal family. She made friends with one of the princesses of the blood and, cunningly playing on the relationship, penetrated the circle around the Prince of Wales. Later he would sum her up as "a frigid little bitch", something to bear in mind when recalling her bottomless loathing for him and Wallis Simpson . . . Bertie fell madly in love with her, but Elizabeth snubbed him. Lumber herself with this timid great oaf, neurotic, ulcerated, mad, addicted to whisky and, on top of it all, with a stammer? She who was the idol of London, courted by princes, for whose forget-me-not-blue eyes a famous Scottish seducer had just broken his engagement? She had higher hopes.'

Later on, the writer noted that this 'Mrs Windsor' went on to be praised by de Gaulle and to do lots of heroic war work, but that just proved what a calculating two-faced minx she was. *Ah, oui.*

The First Chapter Is Always The Worst

Mister Fabulous and Friends is still on my desk. It was time to get some fresh minds on the subject. In London, when I needed feedback, I just handed the problem text to whoever walked through the door and asked for reactions. There seemed no reason not to do the same in Orriule. I printed off five copies of the most recent redraft and handed them out to the Pennies, Willow, Andrew, and Sandy-and-Annie.

Ex-pats are massive readers. They find books far more comforting than people who are surrounded by their own language and culture. They may have TV, but the hour's time difference makes it much less compelling to an offshore audience, and people quickly lose their feel for the grain of life back home, so that soap operas and reality TV are just incomprehensible to them. I suspect, also, that people who choose to leave their native country to live in rural France are also choosing to reject *EastEnders* and everything it stands for.

My instant workshop responded gallantly to a writer in need of a reaction. Willow said she was confused. Andrew never found the time to read it, which is the most eloquent way that anyone can tell you that you've failed to grab their attention. Sandy-and-Annie looked terrified and said nothing. Penny B was far too polite to tell her holiday hostess anything she might not want to hear.

Penny C, however, was characteristically analytical, and gave me a good idea what I needed to fix. In literature as in life, I'd picked the wrong man. She just plain didn't like him.

Mister Fabulous is an ensemble piece about five men of fortysomething, and I'd started by introducing the nicest of them. Big mistake. Nice guys, in literature as in life, finish last. You can have a nice guy in a book but he can't carry the plot. Same goes for a nice girl. I am not the first to try making narrative water run uphill in this way. After all, when Margaret Mitchell wrote *Gone With The Wind*, she actually intended her heroine to be Melanie Wilkes.

Mister Fab was really about men and their friendships, something women find eternally mysterious since we can't understand how people can have a friendship when they avoid talking about anything that matters and only communicate in grunts. However, to get my readers into this book, it was unwise to pick on the gentlest of them. Much better to have all five together and looking damn butch. Since they were all still bonded by the band they'd formed in their student days, the opening scene was obviously the band on stage.

I decided to rewrite my first chapter and, with one bound, I was free to start my screenplay.

The House that *Cyrano* Built

We went on a day trip to Cambo-les-Bains. Cambo is a beautiful little town in the Basque Country, a collection of pretty houses scattered along the edge of the River Nive. Here in the foothills, the river that is a broad mini-

Mississippi by the time it gets to Bayonne is a torrent which roars through a forested gorge.

Cambo is famous for three things. There is a huge spa complex, built above a hot spring. The main room is visited by art lovers for its bas-reliefs by Gabriel Rispal, and a lovely art deco fountain designed by the architect Henri Sajous, where gold mosaic sparkles through the waters. There are so many huge palms in the grounds that the whole estate looks as if it is in Beverly Hills. Recuperation is a big industry in France, and Gerald was sent to the convalescent centre at Cambo for three months to recover from his bypass operation.

Cambo also has an excellent restaurant, called Chez Tante Ursule. It's a perfect place to try the classic Basque specialities and mountain cooking in particular. It does suffer from its decor, being a huge, gloomy room with a tiled floor, a massive fireplace and lots of stuffed animals glaring down from the walls. Irritatingly, this means it's cosy in winter but oppressive in summer, which is the only time that Cambo's third attraction is open.

This is Arnaga, the house that *Cyrano de Bergerac* built, a gigantic Basque-style villa created by the poet and playwright Edmond Rostand when he retreated to Cambo to recover from the overwhelming success of his play. We decided that April, when the house opens after the winter, but the gardens have not yet been ruined by excessive planting of municipal begonias, was the perfect time to visit.

Although they both won their place in history by immortalizing Gascon musketeers, and Rostand grew up feasting on Dumas's historical romances, the two legendary writers could not have been less alike. Rostand was born into a privileged and prominent Provençal family. 'Always remember that your life had a rosy morning,' wrote his father, a banker in Marseille.

Born in that city on April Fool's Day 1868, Rostand was a slim, fine-featured young man with soft skin, a delicate aquiline nose and black, heavy-lidded eyes. He was always exquisitely dressed and, being himself painfully sensitive, was known all his life for his kindness and empathy with other people. His only real vice was clothes — he loved to dress well and even after he'd settled in the rural obscurity of Cambo he wore a different outfit every day.

The summer before he went to Paris to study law, Edmond fell in love with an ethereal, well-connected young poet, Rosemonde Gerard. They met in Luchon, a hugely fashionable spa town in the central Pyrenees, and lived in Paris after their marriage.

Edmond Rostand wrote poetry and plays ceaselessly, no doubt to the detriment of his legal studies. He had some minor success, writing lyrics for the composer Chabrier, and his literary skills were also called upon by one of his friends, a shy young man hopelessly in love with a girl who barely knew he existed. Edmond coached his friend to woo her, and wrote his love letters for him, with such success that they soon married.

Just before he and Rosemonde married in 1890, he paid for the publication of five hundred copies of his first book of poetry. He sold only thirty of them. 'This young man will never do anything worthwhile,' prophesied one of Rosemond's advisers.

Edmond began to submit comedies to the Comédie-Française. He crashed into depression every time he was rejected, but eventually succeeded, and made the acquaintance of the legendary actress Sarah Bernhardt. She in turn introduced him to Constant Coquelin, a veteran actor whose extraordinary voice was praised by Henry James as 'the most wondrous of its kind that the stage has ever known.'

Rostand called himself a 'smuggler of idealism' and was

absolutely clear that his duty as an artist was to appeal to the widest possible public while pursuing the highest intellectual ambitions. He wrote a serious work for Bernhardt, which flopped, but by then, although battling through another suicidal depression, he was already working on *Cyrano de Bergerac*.

Cyrano, like most of the leading characters in the play, was a real person. Born in Paris in 1619, he took his name from the town in which he was brought up, Bergerac, which is up in the Dordogne valley, near Bordeaux. He became a musketeer, fought alongside Dartagnan at the siege of Arras, but died at the age of thirty-six in Paris when a plank of wood from a building site dropped on his head.

The real Cyrano was also a writer of some note, celebrated for his daring political satires and for a number of comedy sci-fi epics. Rostand researched his life meticulously, read all his works, then put away his notes. He gave himself complete freedom to create the Cyrano of the stage, the poet who is judged by the woman he loved more on his long nose than his fine mind, and whose heart is big enough to help a better-looking man to court her.

The entire story is a metaphor for the tragedy of Rostand's own condition, and the paradox of every writer's existence, forced into loneliness by their work and condemned to live through less sensitive souls. It was also an elegant condemnation of the cynicism and materialism of the times.

The first night of *Cyrano de Bergerac* was in Paris, in the depth of winter, 28 December 1897. Constant Coquelin, Bernhardt's friend, played the title role. Edmond, who was only twenty-nine years old, was so convinced that the play would be a flop that he hugged him in tears, saying, 'Forgive me for dragging you into this disastrous adventure.'

What followed was one of the great historic events in the French theatre. *Cyrano* was an instant hit. The audience went wild. Edmond was dragged on stage to take a bow halfway through the play. Women threw their gloves and their fans on the stage, men threw their opera hats. At the end, Coquelin took forty curtain calls, after which the curtain was simply left up. The audience stayed, applauding and singing the 'Marseillaise' until they were exhausted, then lingered in the streets outside until the small hours of the morning, laughing, crying and hugging each other.

The critics too raved about *Cyrano*, calling it not merely a masterpiece but a work which restored the honour of the French theatre and gave the whole country the comfort of knowing they had a new genius in their midst. The show sold out for two years and the new genius was immediately awarded the Légion d'honneur.

He followed up quickly, with another historical verse play, called *L'Aiglon*. Written for Sarah Bernhardt, it was also hailed as a triumph. For Edmond Rostand, however, success was even more stressful than failure. He became withdrawn and paranoid, then collapsed with pneumonia. His hair fell out and his doctors told him he wouldn't survive another winter in Paris. One of them recommended Cambo, and so the playwright, chronically ill at the age of thirty-two, arrived with Rosemonde and their two sons and rented a house.

Apart from their love of the musketeer era, the other passion Dumas and Rostand shared was for building. Edmond soon fell in love with the gentle beauty of the Basque countryside and appreciated the genuine warmth of the people. When his health recovered, he bought a white Arab mare and went for long rides, often getting lost when his mind wandered in a poetic reverie. Eventually he found a place he wanted to call home, a small plateau of land above the Nive valley, and began to design his dream house. A smaller river, the Arraga, bordered one side of the estate and he adapted the name, which in Basque means 'water on the stones', for his mansion-to-be.

Rostand must have endeared himself immensely to his neighbours by choosing to build a house in the Basque style, instead of the classical chateau which his background would have suggested. Arnaga, which we approached from the front, walking down the long formal garden between the walls of topiary beech that enclose the ornamental lake, seemed to be colossal, even beside the massive Basque farmhouses. It's also asymmetrical, making it a Belle Époque take on the traditional form. Edmond designed much of the house himself, and amused his family after dinner with his plans, sketches and cardboard models of the building.

For the interior, Rostand commissioned the leading artists of his time to create a palace. In the great hall are murals by Gaston La Touche illustrating poems by Victor Hugo and, in the small games room, a charming frieze, illustrating French folk songs, by George Delaw. Opulent nudes by Hélène Dufau loll around in the library, and delicate fairy-tale paintings by Jean Veber decorate Rosemond's boudoir.

As we found the house, a desk had been installed in the little Empire study, which is panelled in lemonwood. It's an elegant room, but Rostand seldom worked there. While the rest of the family had spacious bedrooms overlooking the lawns with views out to the mountains, the writer found himself most comfortable in two little rooms over the porch. His bathroom was a hydrotherapy spa in itself, designed to allow him to profit from the healing powers of the local waters even when he was too weak to go outside.

An incurable workaholic, Edmond continued to write at Arnaga even on days when he could not leave his bedroom. *Cyrano* and *L'Aiglon* were constantly revived in France and toured the rest of the world. His poems were acclaimed but his only new play, based on the antics of farmyard animals, was a disappointment.

A stream of smart visitors, from Paris, from Biarritz and from the still-fashionable spa towns round Cambo, kept him entertained, but Arnaga, for all its strange mixture of intimacy and grandeur, was not a happy house over the next seven years. The Rostands' marriage, once such a joyful and nurturing relationship, broke up and both Edmond and Rosemonde found new lovers. Edmond's younger son Jean, who remained loyal to him, became a celebrated biologist and philosopher. Maurice, the elder, who sided with his mother, was a successful writer and a flamboyant homosexual.

On 10 November 1918 Rostand left Arnaga to go to Paris, planning to complete a great poem celebrating the end of World War I then oversee the New Year production of *L'Aiglon*, by now a theatrical tradition. He burst into tears when he left. The omens for his trip were sinister; earlier in the day, his lover, Mary Marquet, had been telling his fortune with cards and turned up the ace of spades. A little later, one of his white pigeons flew into the room and fell dead in front of the fireplace.

In Paris, he immediately caught the flu, the deadly strain that was to kill more people than the war itself. Pneumonia set in again, and Edmond Rostand died in less than a month. Arnaga was inherited by Rosemonde, who let Jean live there only four years before selling it. She claimed she needed the money, but, given the royalties rolling in from *Cyrano*, the decision looks more like pure spite. The great house passed through the hands of several owners, including a Parisian couturier and a Brazilian arms dealer, before the town of Cambo-les-Bains bought it in 1961, and turned it into the museum it is today.

Election Time

Everything around me seemed caught up in a frenzy of growth. In my garden, the grass was knee high and so full of flowers that I couldn't bear to mow it all. The trees were suddenly lush with foliage and the fields blazing with dandelions. M. Lavie's tractor was out until ten at night, getting the earliest maize planted. Within hours of the seeds touching the earth, rows of bright-green cotyledons appeared, changing immediately to the first trembling leaves of the region's major crop.

Beside this sudden upsurge of new life, the first round of the Presidential elections seemed a dry, distant and irrelevant event. Some of the candidates issued coloured brochures, which stood around in the supermarkets looking for takers. 'France doesn't know where she's going any more,' proclaimed one. 'She has lost her destiny. The world financial markets do what they want with her. More and more, the law of the jungle is taking over our society.'

So – what did the candidate propose in the way of policies? 'Define a coherent law and order policy! Revalue work! Keep France as a great political force!'

In the media, the arguments were passionately anodyne. A radio talk show would introduce a 'debate' but the speakers, whatever their affiliation, waffled so energetically that they were totally unable to argue with each other, or even define any issue on which to argue except the ever-popular 'security', which in Britain would be called 'law and order', and on which everyone was in agreement anyway.

Small wonder that the candidates seemed to have no purchase on the minds of my neighbours. The major law-and-order issues in the Béarn were fatal road accidents and con men preying on pensioners. Either of these events would

make a headline in *La République*. Were a crack-house raided
in Orthez, it would probably merit a special supplement on
the imminent collapse of civilization.

In our French class, Renée took time off from the *partitifs*
to lay out the landscape of her country's politics. This
election was for the President, she explained. It was the
first round, in which any candidate who could scrape up
five hundred signatures of support could stand. There were
going to be sixteen candidates, and this first vote would get
them down to two.

As for political parties, well, there was the Left, represented by M. Jospin, the Prime Minister, and his Socialist
Party. She introduced him with great satisfaction. There was
the Right, represented by M. Chirac, the President, and his
Rassemblement pour La République, which she managed
to name in a resolutely fair tone but with a telling lack of
enthusiasm.

Then there were minority parties, like the Greens and
the Communists. And then there was the far Right, led by
M. Le Pen. But that – and here Renée actually shuddered –
that was fascism, and that would never be accepted by the
French people, who would never forget the Nazis and the
atrocities of World War II.

Outside our classroom, everyone was deeply bored by this
routine exercise in democracy, and expected Jospin and
Chirac to emerge as the front runners. On the eve of election
day, photo posters of the candidates suddenly appeared on
the notice board outside the *mairie*, with the key points of
each manifesto printed below. On the day itself the countryside was utterly calm and still, with only the constant drone
of the tractors breaking the silence, until the dead of night,
when the first news of the disaster was broadcast. Suddenly,
taking advantage of the darkness, a handful of Le Pen

supporters took to the lanes and drove around for a couple of hours, jubilantly sounding their car horns.

The next morning I got a flurry of emails from England headed *Achtung Baby* and *Sieg Heil*, which I didn't find too funny. The Béarn had awoken to find itself part of a country that was halfway to fascism, and the region went into shock. For the first time, people asked me what I thought, and how people in England had responded to the result. 'We're worried,' I said. 'We have our own fascists and they are bound to be encouraged by this.' It seemed an acceptable answer, allowing for some shared headshaking and expressions of gloom.

Jospin had polled only 16.1 per cent of the votes, and so the final race for the Presidency was between Chirac, with 19.8 per cent and Le Pen with 16.9 per cent. On the television, sobbing students, clutching handfuls of their pre-Raphaelite hair in despair, were interviewed outside the Socialist Party HQ. Le Pen was filmed at a rally of his supporters, unwisely leaping around a thrust stage decorated with mock flambeaux, which made him look like an elderly demon capering arthritically in the mouth of hell.

Overnight, Le Pen posters appeared on a hoarding around a municipal building site in Saliès. The mayor immediately directed a workman to scrape them off, a task he performed with great ceremony before the approving eyes of the whole town. A single graffito for the Front Nationale appeared on the bridge carrying the slip road to the motorway, and was officially painted out the same day.

Jospin had carried only eight departments, seven of them in the South-West, so Gascony as a whole could hold its head up. The maps which quickly appeared in the local papers showed that the Landes and the Gers were solid Jospin country. Our department, 64, had voted Chirac but that, it was generally agreed, was only the fault of the Basques, who were notorious diehard conservatives.

By the weekend, over two thousand students were on the streets in Pau, demonstrating against 'hatred and racism' with hastily hand-drawn placards and red-and-yellow Béarnais flags. Naturally, a complement of Béarnais singers and musicians were among them, with an African drumming club to underline the mood of the meeting. Those who had voted for the minority candidates openly blamed themselves for the disaster.

They soon had their own slogan: 'first, second, or third generation – we are all the children of immigrants'. 'That's the end of the *bof* generation,' said a more mature onlooker, meaning that none of the demonstrators would ever let themselves sink into apathy again. However, they went home in an orderly fashion, unlike the mob in Paris who had to be dispersed by riot police with tear gas. The cops shouted, '*Ça suffit!*' before they fired, an exclamation normally heard from kindergarten teachers at the end of their tether.

A Night on the Town

It was Gordon's birthday, so a party of us convened at a local restaurant. It has an atmospheric little garden, a playroom with a TV for children, a reasonable menu and an owner, Laurent, who makes up for all the rest of the miserable sods running restaurants in Gascony by his gentle, witty character. He's gentle with the gypsies and the migrant workers as well. As every other bar, cafe and eatery in the region had banned them, they were in there every night, which means that the only other customers were foreigners, tourists and people from out of town.

'Why does everyone hate the gypsies?' asked Fiona.

'People think they cause trouble,' said her French friend, Françoise.

Elegant, cosmopolitan and an exemplary mother, Françoise was nevertheless as marginalized in her village. 'I'm going crazy,' she said bluntly. 'I can't wait to leave.' Her crime was to be temporarily without a husband. He is a world-famous maker of violin bows, and he had been head-hunted by an American orchestra. He was in a state capital in the Midwest, setting up a bow-making school, and Françoise was waiting out the school year before the whole family went out to join him.

Perhaps Françoise's neighbours didn't believe this story. Or perhaps it never occurred to them that Françoise, on her own with two children under five, could stand a little company from time to time.

Françoise therefore had no friends and neither did her children, except for Fiona, Cam and Margot. They met through the village school. Fiona was struggling to master French, but Françoise was almost bilingual, and could explain the expectations of the French school system.

Whatever her age, a single woman hereabouts, like Françoise, Annie-Claire or Gracienne, and one or two others who I'd met, was expected to be content to devote all her time to her family, no matter how far away they might be living. Women did not have friends, they had sisters-in-law and cousins. Women were not expected to have lunch or dinner together, they cooked for their families, and entertained women friends for elegant little teas only. Women were not expected to have interests, except those passed down to them by their husbands. Even a discreet affair wasn't likely; single Frenchmen over the age of thirty were as rare as hen's teeth and husbands preferred the safety of other men's wives. The only men who took up with these dangerous creatures were the foreigners. Thus Roger had not been lonely for long.

I soon appreciated the enormous leap of understanding which Robert and Marie had made in realizing the importance of the procession of friends who arrived at Willow and Tony's house. The idea of friendship, let alone of an urban family, was completely alien in this community, where life was conducted at home, behind closed shutters, the way it had always been, and no deviation was accepted.

The other guests were two young English ex-pats, second generation now since they arrived here as children and went to the local schools. They too were both bilingual but they spent most of their time with the English-speaking community, which was just big enough to keep them in work.

The evening did not start well. There were a bunch of men by the bar who were so pissed that they were acting like Charlie Chaplin playing drunk in a silent movie. Even Laurent was eventually provoked to the point of asking one of them to leave. In the garden, the drunk turned and started to argue. Laurent, who had just taken our order, patiently stood his ground. Eventually Gordon and his English friend, a huge young man of around 6ft 5in, went to see if he needed help.

The drunk then reeled out of the gate. Laurent came over to our table, not to thank his two supporters, but to tell them that their intervention really wasn't necessary and they should have let him sort the affair out by himself.

An hour or so later, when our food finally arrived, the men at the bar were getting noisier and more animated. One of them had rolled a gigantic spliff and sat smoking it, defiantly waving it in the air between each puff. The rest were arguing among themselves.

The argument began to move, up the bar, down the bar,

up the bar again. People began to wave fists. Suddenly, a big man at the far end of the bar pulled out a pair of pruning shears and slashed at the air.

The rest backed away, and the fight – it was definitely a fight now – spilled into the playroom. Fiona and Françoise, as one woman, screamed and leaped up to grab their children.

The fight surged back up the bar, and now the man facing the hulk with the shears had a knife in his hand. When they saw it, all the rest of the women in the restaurant screamed, and their menfolk, seeing a fine excuse to run out on their bills, began to get up and leave. Within sixty seconds we were out on the street, with the young Englishman carrying Margot and Gordon still in the bar, standing beside the patron like a good Aussie mate.

After a while, the drunks spilled out into the street and staggered away, two of them to the camper van which seemed to be permanently parked outside the restaurant.

We collected up enough money to cover the bill. When Gordon finally joined us, we stuffed it into his hands to give to the owner, who then appeared, carrying a gigantic bottle of Ricard. With a wan smile, he apologized for the ruined birthday, pressed the bottle into Gordon's arms and refused to take the money.

Gardening News

I had artichoke plants. Three artichoke plants. I bought them as seedlings in the market in Orthez. They were only a few centimetres high, but growing so fast you could almost see them bulking up by the minute. The wisdom of Monty Don warned me that I couldn't expect an artichoke big enough to be worth eating in the first year, but, I reasoned, the climate round here was much kinder than his in Herefordshire and I might just be lucky.

I also had infant beans, peas, courgettes and tomatoes. The sweet peas had got their tendrils around their wigwam. I thought my vegetable garden was looking good, but my guests disagreed.

'You're letting the weeds take over. You're not out there every day, are you?' Penny C said, at 2 a.m., after dinner with Roger, who had been so entertaining that our faces were stiff from laughing. In the morning, she went out and started hoeing. Within half an hour she was back, looking sheepish, having hoed the top off one of my artichokes. One down, two to go.

To make amends, Penny put her skills as a wicker sculptor to good use and built me a bamboo screen to hide the compost heap. By now, this was a teeming hillock of biodegradation, alive with insects of every possible kind. The screen was much appreciated by the birds, who sat on it in dozens, taking their time in picking out the fattest beetles and the tastiest ants before fluttering down to start feasting.

By the end of the month, the cicadas had started, churring away around the clock. Their sound, bringing memories of hot summer holidays, suddenly made Orriule seem glamorous and exotic. Soon afterwards, the first bats appeared at twilight, swooping around the garden as soon as the sun started to set behind the acacia trees.

Recipes

It was asparagus time. Was it ever asparagus time. Andrew and Geoff found that there was so much asparagus in their garden that they had to give it away, which, since it was the green colour which the French despise and the British prefer, made them extremely popular even with people who startled visibly upon meeting a gay couple.

In the markets, the stalls were suddenly heaped with bunches of white asparagus, while the green was often just sold by weight from a great heap of stems. It was surprising to see the despised green asparagus on sale at all – maybe people were only growing it because they'd always grown it, ever since the days of Eleanor of Aquitaine.

To the taste of the rest of Europe, the green asparagus which the English like has an overpowering flavour, makes your breath smell and has a nasty diuretic effect. The white asparagus, which the English consider insipid, is achieved by blanching the stems, rendering them succulent and delicate.

It's possible that class also creeps into the question because only the smallholders in the markets were selling green asparagus, while it was almost impossible to find in smart greengrocers or in the supermarkets. It was, clearly, a peasant taste. And happily available at a peasant price.

To my mind, it is better to roast green asparagus than do anything else with it if you intend to eat the spears whole as a starter. The flavour is more intense, the texture just as toothsome and the likelihood of getting the tips to the table intact is much higher with roasted asparagus than with the traditional poaching or steaming.

To roast your asparagus, line a roasting tin with foil and oil it liberally with a light olive oil. Rinse the raw asparagus, drain it and cut off the dried-out ends of the stems, evening up the length of the spears in the process. Pile the asparagus into the roasting tin, sprinkling with coarse salt and more oil as you do so, cover loosely with another piece of foil and roast in a medium oven for about 10 minutes. Serve hot or cold, probably with the aid of barbecue tongs, so useful for picking up unmanageable food.

The Belle Auberge in Castagnède served an exquisite starter made with asparagus in both colours, accompanied by herb-flecked spoonfuls of *greuil*. The name for this white, light, very slightly sour dairy product is pronounced almost like the English 'gruel'. *Greuil* is another peasant taste. It's sloppier than *fromage frais*, thicker than yoghurt and tarter than curd cheese, and much enjoyed in the Béarn and Basque Country, as is *caillé*, curdled sheep's milk which is sweetened to make a satiny junket. In this recipe, low-fat *fromage frais*, sharpened with a squeeze of lemon, would be a good substitute for *greuil*.

Salade des Deux Asperges 'Belle Auberge'

For each person

6 fat asparagus spears, 3 green and 3 white
light olive oil
1 tsp each of chopped fresh chives and chervil (chervil,
    having a lighter flavour than parsley, is a better choice
    for this delicate taste combination, but it can be hard to

find and a small amount of minced flat-leaf parsley
could be used instead)
1 tbsp *greuil* or *fromage frais*
salt and white pepper
white-wine vinegar
a handful of mixed salad leaves – mache, sorrel, baby
spinach, rocket, flat-leaf French parsley, whole chervil
sprigs and any kind of lettuce would be good, plus, for
a pretty colour contrast, some tiny red chard leaves with
scarlet spines

Roast, steam or microwave the asparagus until just tender,
toss in a little oil and leave to cool.

Fold most of the chopped herbs into the *greuil* or *fromage
frais* and season with salt and pepper.

Make a light vinaigrette with the oil, vinegar, salt and
pepper. Use half of it to toss the salad leaves, and heap them
in the centre of the plate. Arrange the asparagus spears on
top like the spokes of a wheel, tips to the centre.

Boil some water, take a teaspoon, dip it into the hot water
to warm it briefly and use it to mould the herb mixture into
3 egg-shaped mounds and put them on the plate between
the ends of the asparagus. Finally, sprinkle with the remaining chopped herbs and drizzle with the remaining dressing
before serving.

Asparagus Omelette

A lovely thing to do with white asparagus, and an excellent
scam for making it go further if you have only one bunch
and a lot of people to feed. It's also a good way to use up
asparagus stems if you have a lot left over after making a
posh starter.

For each person

2–3 eggs, according to size, as fresh as you can get
salt and white pepper
1 dsp grated Parmesan (optional)
2 fat or 4 thin asparagus stems
some chervil
light oil
unsalted butter

Break the eggs into a bowl, season with salt and pepper, and beat very lightly, hardly more than mixing the yolks and whites. If you're stuck with the sad, pale, gutless eggs that result from industrial-scale farming, add the Parmesan now to give the dish a better flavour and colour.

Slice the asparagus thinly, keeping any tips intact. Chop the chervil, but not too finely, so that some of the pretty leaves remain whole.

A proper French omelette is nothing like the neat, turd-shaped item which the British call by the same name. It's a loose, fluffy thing, a mere cloud of protein with not much shape – Marie's famous *omelette aux piments* is much more like scrambled egg. To make one, you need to be chivvying the beaten eggs around the pan all the time, just allowing them a few seconds of peace before you tip the finished omelette onto a plate.

In a heavy frying pan, heat the oil, then add 1 tsp butter. Sauté the asparagus until tender – it happens very quickly. Pick out the tips and keep them safe on a plate. Then, working as fast as you can, turn the heat up to maximum and pour in the eggs. Using a spatula, muddle the eggs about with the asparagus as they set, aiming to distribute the asparagus evenly in a creamy omelette that will have only a bit of shape.

Help the omelette out of the pan onto a serving plate and decorate with the reserved asparagus tips.

Marie's *omelette aux piments* is one of Tony's favourite dishes. She makes it with the long, thin, mild, green peppers which are a speciality of the Landes, which she simply chops across into bite-sized chunks, then sautés briefly in the pan before adding the eggs. Myself, I'd prefer to slit the peppers lengthways, scrape out the seeds and chop them finely, but that's probably why my *omelette aux piments* just doesn't taste as good.

May

Pedigree Blondes at St-Palais

The Blondes Next Door

Last week, there was nothing to hear but the buzzing of insects and the rustling of growing grass. Now there is bellowing. It's the cows. If they're not bellowing because they're calving, they're bellowing because their newborns have been taken away to be vaccinated and tagged. The hillside rings with the noise of bovine outrage all day.

In Britain, the calves would also be dehorned in their infancy, but these are the most beautiful cows in the world, the Blondes d'Aquitaine, and nobody wants to put them through that. The worst they do is to wait until the horns are grown and saw off the pointed tips, to remove the possibility that a cow will accidentally disembowel her cowman, or one of her sisters, with an idle toss of her head.

The Blondes were . . . well, blonde. All over. Any colour from the palest cream to the darkest butterscotch. Long before the breed was officially recognized, there had been cattle with creamy coats, light-brown noses and pale eyelashes in the South-West of France: the Blonde's close family look strikingly like cattle in the cave paintings at Lascaux, the prehistoric *Bos aquitanus*.

The Blondes' favourite occupation, even more than munching the sweet new grass, was lying down comfortably in the warm sunlight and looking out across the valleys with their big, long-lashed eyes. The major task for the stockmen who had to parade the pedigree bulls at the summers' fetes was stopping them from taking the weight off their hooves at the first opportunity and settling down to ruminate in the middle of a main street.

My farmer neighbours kept these gentle beasts in family groups, a bull, his cows and their calves all together. The bulls were mere four-legged toy boys, usually younger than their mates, because by the age of about eight they got grumpy, then aggressive, impossible to manage and doomed to the abattoir. They were massive and muscular, with superb definition reminiscent of the young Arnold Schwarzenegger, and despite their bulk they were nimble enough to give an exhibition of natural insemination at any time, even pausing for a shag while they were being herded through the village to a fresh field.

The Blondes are exceptionally docile because they were in part bred from the old Béarnais cattle, who were all-purpose farm animals reared principally to pull carts or ploughs and provide milk. Their meat was a great luxury, seldom consumed by their owners. They lived, not in vast herds, but in twos and threes, kept by the thousands of small farmers in the South-West. In the Landais farmhouses, they were also part of the heating system, being stabled in winter on one side of the building while the family lived on the other. The old photographs show a half-door between the living room and the barn, through which the cows were occasionally allowed to put their horned heads and breathe warmly over the family.

Even in the nineteenth century, only farmers in the north of France were rich enough to keep shire horses to work their land. In Gascony, the draught animals were cattle. They were looked after just as the members of the family which they almost were, and sent to work with a crocheted fringe over their eyes to keep off the flies, and often a linen smock over their backs and forequarters to protect them from insect stings. Théophile Gaultier, travelling down to Spain in 1840, noticed them as soon as he reached the Landes.

'Around here you meet the first vehicles drawn by oxen. The chariots looked quite Homeric and primitive; the oxen were harnessed by the head to a single yoke, decorated with a little frill of sheepskin; they had a soft, serious and resigned air, truly sculptural and worthy of an Egyptian frieze. Most of them wore trappings of white cloth, which protected them from midges and horse-flies; nothing was stranger than to see these oxen in shirts, who slowly turned towards you with their wet, shining muzzles and the big dark-blue eyes which the Greeks, those connoisseurs of beauty, found so remarkable that they described the goddess Hera as having "cow's eyes".'

The Blondes are also wonderful parents. The cows get pregnant readily and the shape of their pelvis makes it particularly easy for them to give birth. A Blonde cow will produce six to eight calves in her lifetime, which means she can still be a productive farm animal up to the ripe age of fifteen.

Another of the breed's useful characteristics is that the calves are born very small-boned and slim, so their survival rate is very high. They bulk up quickly and when it comes to be sold, the veal is proudly labelled '*élève sous la mère*'. The label often has a picture of a calf diving for its mother's udder, reassuring the purchasers that this is free-range meat, not the product of a cruel and unnatural rearing process.

The breeders created the Blonde in 1962, when it was clear that tractors had replaced ox-ploughs and the northern beef cattle, the Charolais and Limousin, were going to take over unless the Gascons took steps to stop them. They described the process as a 'reunification'. The registered Garonnais and Quercy breeds were crossed with the pale

Pyrénéen cattle, among which many separate strains were recognized including the toffee-coloured Béarnais.

Their mixed heritage shows in their crazy horns; some just look like the nursery-rhyme cow with the crumpled horn. Some of them have incurving horns carried almost over their eyes, and some of them develop the wonderful lyre-shaped horns which are characteristic of the old Béarnaise cow.

The Blondes turned out to be terrific beef cattle, muscular, lean and light-boned. Their hides also turned out to have a unique type of hair which stopped them sweating excessively in hot weather. By the Seventies, the Blonde had been exported not only to Northern Europe, America, Canada and Australia, but also to Brazil, Colombia and Mexico.

While the new Blonde was taking over the world, however, the old mountain breeds were dying out. Only three Béarnais bulls and a few dozen cows survived by 1981. Béarnais nationalism came to the rescue and by 2001 the numbers were up to fifteen bulls and 112 cows. The rare cattle were celebrities: when a couple of prize specimens went to the Paris Show, the *Sud-Ouest* put their picture on the front page. So we were honoured that two lyre-horned Asturian cows and their calves were sent to meet the public at the opening festivities of the Château at Laàs.

From Caravan to Chateau

By 1 May, it was, as the Gascons say, raining like a pissing cow. Fiona and her children watched the black clouds and the dripping trees with dismay, since the family had just moved into the smallest caravan any of us had ever seen, just about big enough for the four of them to lie down to sleep if all their possessions were stuffed under the bed.

Right.
Maison Bergez,
shaded by pollarded
catalpa trees

Below.
The squirly
ironwork chairs
of my dreams

Lunch at Maysounabe – clockwise from left: Sandy, Chloe, Willow, Benjy Lewis, who's in charge of restoring a local chateau, London fashion writer Shelley Vella, Tony, Andrew, Jan Weller, who works in a school in Bordeaux, Geoff and Annie

Andrew,
out walking
with Otto and
a guest

Esprit de
Beverly Hills:
Margaret by her
front gate

Above. Poster for Rostand's instant hit, *Cyrano de Bergerac*

Left. Hercules fell in love with Pyrène, the shepherdess

Saliès-de-Béarn, the bandstand. Watercolour by Glynn Boyd Harte

Detail from Roger Hallet's panorama of Saliès-de-Béarn,
showing La Terrasse.

Above.
Rock pools at
Biarritz

Left.
Saliès-de-Béarn:
townhouses
overhanging the
River Saleys

'More than I could possibly have imagined, I miss the mountains.'
The Pic du Midi d'Ossau above the Lac de Bious-Artigues

The Duchess: 'So, Mr Bond . . .'

Piglet hunting among the violets

They had been thrown out by their business partner, who decided that he needed the whole building as a 'party house', and that the children would just cramp his style when he arrived with his guests. Their partnership in the tree-fern nursery had thus been terminated.

The guests for whom the family had been evicted were allegedly to be major investors interested in underwriting their ex-partner's scheme to create a Disneyworld-style dinosaur theme park on the outskirts of Saliès. It was not a total fantasy – Roger, in his round of chats with the mayor, had seen the plans for it – but it seemed unlikely that international financiers would go for it.

The caravan was on what should, by then, have been their own land. The *notaire*, the lawyer handling the sale, had promised them that the process would be completed by May Day. The transaction showed no sign of emerging from the various committees who have to approve it, but the owner of the property had graciously allowed them to be squatters on the land.

The caravan was in a little village called Bellocq, uncomfortably close to the RN117, and mostly made up of rather urban nineteenth-century terraced cottages. Although it's not typically rural, Bellocq is still not completely devoid of romance, having also some vineyards, a wine-making cooperative and an imposing ruin which is the oldest *bastide*, or fortified town, in the Béarn, built around 1200.

Their property was made up of three small buildings crushed together on a back street. Between them, they had quite a few walls, a couple of roofs and a bit of a ceiling. They hadn't got water, electricity or drains. Until Gordon's British friend came round with his digger to flatten the land at the back, they had a lot of brambles and stinging nettles. The garden ends in a steep cliff, at the bottom of which the Gave de Pau runs shallow and swift. They had visions of running a scenic B&B, maybe, if they could get planning permission, even a little cafe, with tables overlooking the sparkling river.

The day they moved in, various members of the foreign community descended to wish them well. The rain held off for a few hours, and the children ran about, playing with their new neighbours and bringing us sprays of cream-coloured acacia blossom.

Sandy-and-Annie arrived with the camping toilet they'd used when they began restoring their own house. Andrew and Geoff arrived with a platter of barbecued chicken. I brought a *pastis landais*, a dessert cake which is an extra-rich variation on the *brioche*, from the famous baker near Amou. An elderly English couple who'd set up a B&B close by came empty-handed, perhaps to reassure themselves that they would have no competition.

Gordon had decided to start burning the old, infested timbers and we sat about in the smoke, wishing them well and trying not to look as horrified as we felt. Being British, we considered renovating a house a normal rite of passage. All of us had gone through a time of plaster dust and negative plumbing. We remembered the meals eaten off tables made from old doors and breeze blocks, the loos flushed with buckets and the showers begged from friends.

We were itching to sort the site out with plastic canopies, duckboards and camping gas, but Gordon and Fiona seemed too exhausted and traumatized to move. Most of the tiny tree-ferns were sprouting green now, but it would be another year at least before they were ready to sell. Gordon was confident that their partner would pay them back their investment, but there was no contract. 'They shook hands,' said Fiona gravely. 'In New Zealand, if you shake hands on something, that makes it square and legal.'

It was still raining a few days later, when Fiona, Margot

and I left the boys to be boys and went to the festival at Laàs. Laàs is a village in the valley below Orriule, on the edge of the Gave d'Oloron. It's a fine example of what a mayor with ambition can do for a rural backwater. While the surrounding hamlets snooze in contented decay, with crumbling buildings and muddy cart tracks, Laàs is tarted up to the eaves, with fresh paint and blooming window boxes. This titivation works for everyone, and Laàs is a popular place for a family stroll on Sunday afternoon.

The war memorial and the tiny bridges over the little River Laà are in perfect repair. Every house has a former function which is proclaimed by an artistically engraved slate plaque on the wall – 'The Skittle-Maker's House', or 'The Pottery'. Another plaque records the history of the tiny old church. There is also a new church, on the main square, and a hostel for the Compostela pilgrims equipped with the essential pelota court. Across the road is an ambitious but erratic restaurant devoted to Béarnais specialities, the Auberge de la Fontaine.

The square itself is called the Place Brigitte Bardot, because, as a plaque with very tiny print explains, Brigitte Bardot could perfectly well have been born there. As the whole of France knows, BB was actually born in a Paris suburb and now lives near St Tropez, but these facts have not been allowed to stand in the way of the village's pride in its attractions.

The grandest of these is the Château, a small but pretty mansion of seventeenth-century origins, built in the classic style rather than the Béarnais, with a slate roof and three rows of tall, white-shuttered windows. Its position, on a wooded cliff overlooking the Gave, is spectacular and its gardens exquisite – when, of course, it's not raining like a pissing cow.

The Château's last owners were some art collectors from

Normandy, who died childless and left the building, with some good paintings, a lot of curiosities and some magnificent Aubusson tapestries, to the departmental government. To amuse visiting children, the home field is planted with a maze of maize every year, while the grounds are the site of festivities all summer long, beginning with what was billed as 'Transhumances Musicales'.

At this time of year, the farmers in the mountain villages move their sheep and cattle up to the summer pastures, where, after the cleansing of the ground through *écobuage*, the new grass is already long and sweet. The process is called *transhumance*; it's the excuse for another festival. The Basque shepherds used to decorate their cows with wreaths of flowers and their sheep with stripes of paint and pompoms of wool in bright primary colours, originally so that they would know whose was whose after all the animals were herded up into the mountains together.

The animals are still decorated, and there is still much consumption of aperitifs and exhibition of old photographs to make everyone pleasantly damp-eyed and nostalgic. The *transhumance*, however, is nowadays accomplished by cattle truck and horsebox, which means that flocks of the long-fleeced Pyrénéen sheep could spend the winter in pastures as far north as Orriule. On days when it was too misty to watch the mountains on my way into Sauveterre I would stop and watch the sheep instead, bustling around their field in twos and threes, their long dreadlocks swinging down to the grass as they cantered around.

The sheep are a nimble mountain breed and are allowed to keep their horns, which are as long, twisted and curved as an antelope's. The first time I ever saw a sheep with a full-grown pair I was driving up on the road to Pamplona with a friend, another novelist, called Mavis, an inherently lady-like character who did not take to the bucolic charms of deep France at all. We were crawling along in thick fog, which suddenly cleared to reveal an extremely startled ram, poised on the tips of his hooves in the centre of the road, his horns quivering with alarm.

Behind the ram emerged first one, then several, then a whole herd of massive Pyrénéen cattle, all with big iron bells clanking around their neck. The road was well and truly blocked; visibility was about ten metres.

Mavis suddenly found some *African Queen* spirit, and stepped regally out of our rented Renault. She approached the mixed herd at a dignified pace, clapping her hands like a school teacher and calling out, 'Come along, now. Come along.' The ram freaked completely, leaped vertically in the air off all four hooves at once, then bounded up a crag and away into the wall of mist. The cattle followed him serenely, and we were able to drive on.

The 'Transhumance Musicales' turned out to be five days of music and dancing in a large marquee, observed from a distance by the lyre-horned cows, who stood patiently in their muddy enclosure, munching the wilting remains of their garlands.

The inside of the tent was divided into three sections: an auditorium, with a stage, curtains and seating for at least three hundred; a changing and backstage area; and the bar, which remained open throughout all performances, selling softs, half-litres of beer and generous plastic beakers of Rosé de Béarn.

We decided to see a spectacle called *La Flabuta de Pyrène*, starting at 2 p.m. In this relaxed part of the world, there is a tradition called the Béarnais quarter of an hour, which is usually around three-quarters of an hour, and is the minimum permitted period which may elapse after the official starting time of any event before things really get under way. The custom of the Béarnais quarter of an hour allows for two vital regional pastimes, chatting and consuming aperitifs.

Even in these grand surroundings, it was exactly 2.45 p.m. when the master of ceremonies took to the stage. He looked familiar; I had last seen him with a violin, leading the dancers at the carnival in Pau. Keeping time with crisp beats of his bow, he reminded me powerfully of Pete Postlethwaite in *Brassed Off.*

'Well,' he said, 'the Béarnais quarter of an hour is up so let's get started.' The audience laughed. As the spectacle was to have two hundred performers, it was likely that all the spectators, except us, would be their relatives. They were completely mixed in age and social status, from immaculate middle-class children to elderly men in workers' overalls.

The dancers and singers too were of all ages, shapes and sizes. There were some sturdy teenage girls in orange chiffon, but most of the rest wore variations on the Béarnais national costume. For the women, this meant a long skirt with a printed apron, a white blouse, a fringed shawl and a headscarf, with white espadrilles tied with red ribbons. The men appeared in white shirts with black waistcoats, dark, striped breeches and knitted leggings of natural wool pulled over black espadrilles. They all wore berets, and in one dance the most acrobatic boys held the beret in both their hands and jumped over it.

The master of ceremonies helped us out by narrating the legend of the creation of the Pyrenees. 'Hercules, coming back from the edge of the known world, stopped here and thought how nice it would be to live the life of a simple shepherd.' The audience sighed in agreement.

'He fell in love with Pyrène, a shepherdess, but the gods were angry when he said he wanted to marry her and sent a pack of wolves to tear her to pieces. In his rage and grief, Hercules picked up the biggest rocks he could find and hurled them at the gods. Where they fell to earth, the Pyrenees were born.' The audience sighed again, this time with what sounded like the sheer contentment of living within sight of such a magnificent geographical event.

The local edition of the *Sud-Ouest* reported that the spectacle was full of *joie de vivre*, and said that the two hours rolled by *sans lassitude*, which in Margot's case was not exactly true. She perked up considerably when we took the guided tour of the Château and were invited to admire the impressive bourgeois dining room, with its built-in china cupboard stuffed with Baccarat crystal and fine porcelain.

Fiona talked about how she could see Cam and Margot learning the Béarnais songs or maybe playing recorders in a school orchestra. She adored the Château, and said she was longing for the house to be habitable so she could invite her mother over to see it. But as soon as she stopped talking, Fiona's eyes filled with tears.

At the caravan in Bellocq, it took a month to get the electricity connected, largely because Gordon didn't understand the man from the electricity board when he explained that the meter needed to be in a waterproof cupboard. People dropped by with casseroles. After a couple of weeks, in which the rain never let up, Gordon got some sheets of industrial plastic and fixed up a canopy over the camping toilet, and another outside the caravan door to keep the immediate area dry. The children stayed in school until 6 p.m. to do their homework, because there was nowhere they could work in their new home.

One day when the rain stopped for a few hours I called in and found Fiona alone with a smouldering fire of termite-eaten beams. She was wandering about the garden with her eyes unfocused, clutching a small tortoiseshell buckle set with diamanté which she'd found in the mud, the picture of a gutsy girl in the process of losing it.

May Day, May Day

Until the second round of the presidential election on 5 May, the Béarn suffered agonies of anxiety. The normal favourite topic of conversation, the weather, certainly provided enough incidents for people to talk about, but all they wanted to discuss was politics. In a nearby village, Burgaronne, one man had voted for Le Pen; everyone knew who he was and nobody was speaking to him.

In Bordeaux on May Day, the Western Revolutionary Communist League and a dozen less grandly named organizations staged a demonstration that got at least forty thousand people out on the streets. In Paris, four hundred thousand people hit the boulevards to urge their fellow-citizens to vote against Le Pen.

The Club Internationale de Saliès-de-Béarn was in ferment, and no member was more tortured than Annabel. One of their French members was said to have stood up at a Socialist Party meeting and made racist remarks about Muslims. The report came from Annie-Claire, who was no longer a paid-up member, but was determined to get an apology out of the guilty one before the name of the club was besmirched, and wrote a letter to the whole committee about the alleged outrage.

As vice-president, Annabel found herself in the hot seat, pressurized by Annie-Claire to do something but having no idea of what to do and a great fear of doing anything. Her telephone rang all day, with committee members eager to chew over the issue. The club's treasurer, a Hungarian businessman whose English wife's family had owned a holiday home near Castagnède for thirty-five years, felt so hassled by this pack of warring women that he resigned.

Nobody, however, had said anything to the alleged

offender, who whizzed obliviously about the town on her bicycle with her lips fixed in the habitual half smile. She seemed to be living in a world of her own, unaware of the conversations that ceased abruptly as she approached and the speculation that erupted as soon as she was gone. In a few days later, she announced that she would give a little party, on a Moroccan theme, and warmly invited us all. A few days after that, she called the party off, saying that not enough people could come.

'You don't actually know what she said,' I pointed out to Annabel. 'It might not be true. Why don't you just ring up the Chairman of the Socialist Party and ask him what happened?' She squeaked in sheer distress.

Annabel was also afraid that if Gracienne, the club president, got embroiled in the drama, she too might resign. Annabel would then be under pressure to take the role of president. The position carried responsibilities. There are rules governing clubs and societies in France, even one whose members' main activity is sitting in a cafe having coffee and practising their languages every Tuesday.

The original purpose of these regulations is to stamp out political corruption at the grass roots, an objective which many critics would argue has been pursued with tragic naivety. Nevertheless, associations as blameless as the Guild of Painters or the yoga class in Saliès, the hunting clubs or the concert society run by Babi and Thierry must be properly constituted and must also produce, for public scrutiny, financial accounts and a record of their activities. Gracienne had a difficult task in explaining these imperatives to her multinational membership and her only reward was the distinction of being able to attend the annual national conference of international club presidents.

Being a part-time antiques dealer, Gracienne also had the expertise and contacts to put on a rare-book fair at the end of the month, and a *vide grenier* in the Salle Multiactivités in Orriule was planned for September. If she resigned, these plans would collapse, and the club's only project would be a bring and buy plant sale, called a Plant Stock Exchange, in a couple of weeks. I could appreciate Annabel's anxieties.

She succeeded in stonewalling until election day, when the Gascons went to the polls in indignant numbers. In some areas the turnout recorded was five times as high as in the first round of voting. The same spirit was abroad all over the country. Le Pen was routed, France was stuck with Chirac for another five years, everyone heaved a sigh of relief and went back to the real business of May, which is enjoying it.

Great Myths About The French, No. 1: They're Lazy

May is the month that gets the French a bad name. Most years, the rot sets in at Easter, which is followed by Ascension, then Pentecost. All of these are major religious festivals, rating at least a long weekend if not a full week of holiday, and before God gets his due respect, the state claims its own share of time off with the May Day bank holiday.

One way or another, almost the whole month disappears in celebrations. Everyone is so used to this that the banks don't bother putting up formal notices of the bank holiday opening hours, they just shut their doors and assume everyone can work out when they are going to re-open.

If they get a lot of public holidays on top of the legally enforceable thirty-five-hour working week which had just been introduced, that is not to say that the French are taking it easy. This is the mistake the departing American Ambassador had made earlier in the year, when he said goodbye with an objectionable tirade, telling the French to pull their socks up. And the Americans wonder why everybody hates them.

Those actually entitled to the thirty-five-hour week, like the post lady or the bank manager, claimed it most apologetically, because the other half of the community was self-employed and, in France as in Britain, had their boss's permission to work an eighteen-hour day. My neighbour, M. Lavie, was always out before eight every morning and, at busy times, worked far into the night with a searchlight on his tractor. The only day he took off all year was 15 August, the Feast of the Assumption of the Blessed Virgin Mary.

On working days, the French take their famous lunch hour, but it's a strict 12 to 2, or 12.30 to 2.30, and then it's back to work. One glass of wine is allowed. The doctor worked until 9 p.m., four days a week, and all day Saturday. And a lot of French people have two jobs. Around Orriule, people could be shopkeepers and poets, farmers and DJs, farmers and office workers, caterers and maintenance men.

French women, married or single, have three jobs, since they also have all the family organization to do, including servicing relationships with distant family members and giving a helping hand to relatives who are frail or sick. Not to mention the shopping and cooking. The ready-meals which take up half the average London supermarket get no sale in France. Only a stressed urban Frenchwoman would feel justified in using them and besides, they're mostly uneatable.

French people work very, very hard at keeping their families together. Almost all their spare time is spent with families, and even in Paris many people never have dinner parties except with their cousins. No teenager or older relative, for example, is expected to go to see the doctor or dentist alone. When I found myself spending a lot of time in the orthopaedic clinic in St-Palais, it was noticeable that every elderly woman with a broken wrist was accompanied by a prosperous-looking son of forty something, who had taken the afternoon off for the purpose.

The French also work hard at enjoying themselves, and a lot of the pleasures which at first glance seem to be selfish also benefit their families or communities. Thus the hunters, the anglers and even the ramblers keep the ecosystem in balance, earn some extra money and bring home some treats – like venison, trout or mushrooms.

Volunteer work was an industry in itself. In the school holidays, the mature skiers and surfers were called in to take parties of school children to the beach or the mountains. IT experts gave computing lessons and native speakers taught Spanish or English. Anyone with an HGV licence would be called upon to drive a senior citizens' coach party off on a gastronomic day-trip to Spain.

Four More Great Myths About the French

1) *The French have exquisite taste.* With all those begonia-encrusted roundabouts garnished with bad sculpture? Icky postcards of cute kittens? Painted wirework loo-roll holders wreathed with ivy? Sub-Corbusier vertical slums? Vomit-yellow Provençal-print tablecloths?

2) *The French are terribly emotional.* No, they're extremely repressed. This I fully understood only when I saw those among my neighbours whose views were irreconcilable conducting their unspoken vendettas with perfect politeness and expressionless faces. In French society, anything likely to provoke social discord – gossip, a strong opinion, a contentious subject – is immediately stifled. One of my friends, teaching at a French secondary school, was disciplined for

allowing the debating society to tackle social issues; like Eliza Doolittle at Ascot, she was advised to stick to the weather and everybody's health.

3) *French women are elegant*. Not a certain sector of the clientele in Leclerc in Orthez, believe me. French women are as capable as any other possessor of two X chromosomes of pouring their backsides into polyester slacks and going out with five centimetres of regrowth on a really bad tint job. The elegance some of them seem to have is really conformity. They prefer uniforms to fashion – the silk scarf with everything, the sailor stripes for the beach.

4) *The French love food*. What they really love is things being the way they always were. From a British viewpoint, that certainly means enjoying fresh, flavoursome, well-cooked food instead of something industrially grown, pre-cooked badly, chilled for two weeks, tarted up with E numbers and sold in a packet with a big coloured picture of how the dish is supposed to look. But the French do not love any food which is not their own, meaning not of their region, let alone not of their country. Persuading a provincial French family to swap green beans for Brussels sprouts is almost impossible.

Party Time

In a country region, all the traditional enjoyments are labour-intensive. The life of the community is hugely energetic. Suddenly in May every town and village was advertising something – a concert, a *vide grenier*, a flower show, a cycle race, a *bal des jeunes*, a *soirée dansante*. Suddenly the sober people who seemed to have been in bed and asleep by nine every night were out dancing until dawn. When the

big barn at the top of the hill was used for a disco, Gloria
Gaynor was belting out over the valleys all night.

Even the Centre Socio-Culturel in Orthez decided to end
the adult-education season with a party. Celebrations were
planned for the institution's twentieth birthday, including
a jumble sale, a Caribbean buffet and a *concert salsa*. The
three-day event kicked off with a debate, 'To be a parent
today – how do you help your child to grow up?', mediated
by a local psychologist.

Renée and Dominique anxiously asked us to bring in
our photos and our national flags for the anniversary *fête*.
I found a good picture of our Valentine's Day lunch at
the Vietnamese restaurant owned by the family of one of
our members, at which both classes had squeezed around
the long table under the pink lanterns. It seemed to hit the
right multicultural note; there was, I detected, a certain
nervousness in the Centre about how the work of teaching
foreigners French would be perceived. It was as if, all the
rest of the year, Renée and Dominique had chosen not to
draw attention to this subversive activity, and were now
worried that the wider community would disapprove.

The riches of the region included so many live bands
that there seemed to be one in every village, and all the
summer meant was a constant cultural exchange between
the valleys. Their names were inexplicable – Capibara,
3,14, The Wilde Country (American country and western),
Confit'Danse and Dingle Bay (both with Irish leanings),
Box'son, Papar'oc, Aistrika, Tabasco, Parpalhon, Blue
Ridge, Ibiliz – the only name that made sense was a very
popular combo called Cows. They pronounced it 'Coos'. No
words were more evocative of that summer than the names
of these bands, printed on the smudgy little posters that
appeared on every municipal notice board.

Veni, Vidi, Vide Grenier

After I met Andrew, a great hole in my life was filled. A hole about the shape of a gay friend who is madly witty, brilliantly astute, curious about everything, willing to stop for lunch, who used to be an antique dealer and had a large empty house to furnish.

Andrew and Geoff threw themselves into their new life with an enthusiasm that was like a hurricane of fresh air after the winter-weary apathy of some expats. At Masounabe, the long shelf of HP sauce bottles, almost the only thing they had brought out from London, stayed untouched as Geoff experimented with local produce. Everything was new, fresh and exciting to them. They even believed the long-standing rumour that an Irish bar was going to open in Saliès.

As soon as I introduced them, Annie and Geoff bonded inseparably, on the grounds that neither of them liked speaking French and both of them smoked, that Annie couldn't drive and Geoff could. When, to general amazement, McGuire's Irish Pub (proprietor, M. Tom McGuire) did indeed open and started serving Beamish ales along with the traditional *pression*, it also became clear that Annie could drink so much that Geoff felt virtuous drinking half as much, and the two of them could happily spend all evening perched on bar stools.

This left Andrew and me free to get on with having fun, as we defined it. Andrew hated driving, and I didn't mind it. Andrew was learning French as fast as he could, but I spoke it better. I didn't know much about antiques, but Andrew did. We agreed about almost everything else, so there was nothing for it but to do the *vide grenier* season big-time.

Andrew and Geoff had built up a flourishing photographic studio in the most fashionable part of the East End.

Their only problem was that they hated living in London. First they lived near King's Cross – Andrew did a hilarious impression of a prostitute who chose to provide a client with a blow job on their front steps; when they asked her to find another venue, she swore at them without removing her client from her mouth.

They moved to Marylebone, and came home from lunch one Saturday to find that they had been burgled. The thieves had got in by cutting the front door in half with a chainsaw. So Andrew and Geoff decided to rent out their smart flat, bought a left-hand-drive Range Rover, got Otto, Geoff's West Highland terrier, a pet passport and set off to drive around the Mediterranean looking for somewhere they could move their business. Not all of it, just the management, some of the big fashion catalogues and any other shoots that needed exotic locations.

Fortunately for us, they hated the food in Spain, so they drove on to France, felt more cheerful by the time they got to Pau, then fell in love with the Béarn, and with a big farmhouse high on a hillside above the village of Castagnède. Maysounabe (it means New House, a pretty common Béarnais name) was surrounded by huge oak trees. It had gorgeous pargeting under the eaves of its classic Béarnais roof, a garden with borders most lovingly stocked by the previous English owners and a huge barn which was destined to become the studio. Apart from that, it had stupendous views of the Gave valley, an Aga and a bed.

Since they were intent on a whole new life, they had left their furniture behind in London, which meant that Andrew was licensed to shop. He started out with a glass-fronted mahogany cabinet, smothered in carved flowers and garlands, for their kitchen, and said, 'If you're going to live in France, you might as well live in a whore's handbag, eh?'

One of his favourite hunting-grounds was a huge old

garage full of fine furniture and old trunks in St-Palais. The owner, a young Basque who used to be a supermarket manager, was so handsome he got known as Cute Guy, and he had a great eye for an Empire bedstead or a Louis Vuitton Gladstone bag.

On the way back from Cute Guy was Dog Man, an older and more rotund Basque dealer who had two huge barns full of treasures in the depths of the countryside, found with the help of hand-painted signs promising 'old furniture'. There we found wonderful old oak coffers carved with Basque designs, and dating from the 1600s or earlier. Which did not mean anyone had thought to brush the dust and chicken feathers off them lately.

Dog Man's village had a church with a three-bell campanile and an orchard bearing bright red apples and grazed by spotted Black Gascon pigs, a sight so picturesque it could have been straight out of a 1930s nursery-rhyme illustration. Dog Man got his name from his magnificent one-year-old pure-white Pyrénéen mountain dog, a breed originally favoured by the shepherds. 'Nice dog,' we said, sincerely. *'Il est beau ou quoi?'* Dog Man replied with pride. He's good-looking or what?

We got on the motorway and scoured the *trocantes*. The word is probably a mixture of *truc*, meaning trick or deal, and brocante. Pau and Bayonne each have several on their outskirts. Anyone who wants to sell something brings it to the *troc* owner, who puts a price on it and displays it in his showroom, taking an agreed percentage of whatever it fetches. *Trocs* sell anything from an old lawnmower to the irresistible black oak cupboard carved with scallop shells and marigolds which is now in Chloe's bedroom in London.

We discovered that, like Ahetze, many villages and towns had regular flea markets. Helpfully, all of these, from the epic to the humble, from Bordeaux to Toulouse, plus the big-city auction sales, the huge seasonal antiques fairs and special events in the decorative arts, were listed in a wonderfully enthusiastic monthly newspaper, the *Gazette des Ventes*. Since even Ahetze can suddenly decide to cancel itself at times of year when stock is low or buyers sparse, the *Gazette* was added to my essential reading. Our vocabulary began to grow exponentially: *enchères*, auction; *particulier*, a private seller; *pomme de pin*, literally a pine cone but also a bed-knob.

On Sundays, there was usually a *vide grenier*, one up from a car-boot sale. *Vide grenier* means 'empty the attic'. They took place in sports halls and *salles multiactivités*, organized by the local ACCA or the fire brigade or the village school. The advertising wasn't sophisticated – somebody with a computer printed up a few posters which were stapled to telegraph poles near the main road junctions. A few local *brocante* dealers usually took part, but most of the sellers were ordinary people trading in their children's in-line skates and Barbie dolls.

One Sunday, we drove for an hour into the dreamy Chalosse, which was now a shimmering ocean of buttercups. We decided that being there must be like dropping some heavy-duty Sixties narcotic like a Quaalude. Neither of us had ever done this, but in this undulating landscape, where everything is slow, sunny and blissful and time seems to disappear, your mind definitely feels altered.

Our destination was a *vide grenier* in the hall of a tiny village. It had a surprisingly large range of stalls; as well as the local people, there were Africans with leather bags and Bob Marley banners, a Basque cheese vendor and plenty of specialists in agricultural antiques and café ware, which meant Ricard water jugs, St-Raphael ice buckets, Cinzano ash trays.

The next Sunday it was the turn of another Chalossois village, Mouscades, which has what must be the smallest bullring in France. It would fit into the miniature arena in the Spanish village of Mijas about four times. The bullring in Mouscades, however, is intended for the cruelty-free local sport, the Course Landaise, in which there is no matador, only *écarteurs*, and the *sauteurs*, who jumps over the horns of the charging animal, like the bull-dancers painted on ancient Cretan vases. Some of the Gascons also enjoy Spanish bullfighting. The best matadors and bulls come up for the big *ferias* in Bayonne and Dax every year, and the fans go down to San Sebastian or Pamplona, but it's an urban, cosmopolitan thing, whereas the Course Landaise is a central part of the village heritage.

After Mouscades there were a couple of *vide greniers* in ugly villages along on the RN117, then a small one in a tiny Basque hamlet in a green valley near Aramits, then the first of the really big sales in Pomarez, yet another Chalossois venue, and the centre of Course Landaise culture where the sport's annual festival takes place in July.

The stalls were spread out on the sand of the arena itself, and the tarmac of the car park and the linoleum of the sports hall. Many dealers came, with many treasures, over which we lingered a long time, restoring our energies with trips to the buffet for an Armagnac *crêpe* or a slug of thick black coffee.

By now, we had discovered the unwritten rules of the *vide grenier* game, as they are observed in the Béarn.

1. No *vide grenier* shall start before decent people have finished their breakfast, or 9 a.m., whichever is the later.
2. Thereafter, the Béarnais quarter of an hour shall be strictly observed. Any buyer offering money for goods before the quarter-hour has expired is obviously one of those ill-mannered dealers from out of the region, and may be ignored.

3. Sellers may continue to unpack until 11 a.m., or later
   if they had a hard night. (Andrew took time to adjust
   to rules 1, 2 and 3, being used to British sales for which
   the sellers started to queue in the pitch dark at 5 a.m.,
   when the buyers would already be banging on the van
   windows.)

4. No item shall be considered too humble or bizarre to be
   offered for sale, nor too grand. An old anorak is as good
   as a Kenzo linen dress, and a cracked flower pot as
   desirable as a brassy-looking statuette of some oriental
   goddess which turns out to be solid gold, four centuries
   old and worth thousands.

5. If any item offered for sale has a chip, tear or other
   fault, the seller shall considerately point this out to the
   buyer before taking the money.

6. Any buyer claiming to be able to sell an item on eBay
   for thousands of euros is obviously deluded and shall be
   heard with a pitying smile.

7. The seller shall not feel compelled to assist the buyer in
   examining the stock. It is not necessary to unfold sheets
   or demonstrate the working of any machinery, merely to
   keep chatting to one's neighbour and allow the buyer
   to browse in peace. (My favourite rule, apart from 9
   below.)

8. If any item shall be dropped, making a loud crashing
   sound, the entire room may roar with laughter and call
   out: *'C'est vendu!'* ('It's sold!')

9. A bar and *sandwicherie* shall operate for the duration of
   the *vide grenier*, offering coffee, bacon sandwiches, beer,
   wine and other snacks according to local taste.

10. Notwithstanding this, all exhibitors are free to bring
    their own three-course lunches with fresh bread and
    wine. They may avail themselves of any cooking
    facilities in the building to reheat *daubes* or *cassoulets*,

     and may dine with the use of such chairs and tables as
     they may be trying to sell.

11. The lunch hour shall last from 12 to 2, at least.

12. Sellers should not be disturbed while cooking or eating.
     During the lunch hour, one dealer may be appointed
     to handle, on behalf of the others, any transactions
     suggested by delinquent buyers wishing to do business
     while sensible people are eating. In confirming prices,
     a wave of the glass or gesticulation with a piece of
     bread may be interpreted as the appointee considers
     appropriate.

13. Prices on unsold items need not be reduced towards the
     end of the day, and any seller suggesting this may be
     treated as insane.

The Town Called Love

On the way back from Pomarez, we stopped in a bustling
little town called Amou, which has retained an air of prosperity and consequence from its pilgrim days, or maybe even
earlier. It got its name from the Romans, who called it
'Amor', or love, and found nearby the only real hill in the
region, on which they built a large camp whose sentries could
have seen a barbarian horde coming a hundred miles away.

    A river runs through Amou, a gentle big stream called
the Luy de Béarn, spanned by a pretty bridge and shaded by
immense old lime trees which soar over the arena and the
site of the Sunday market. They also shade a rather grand
restaurant, le Commerce, also known by its owner's name,
Darracq. Le Commerce is impeccable; it goes in for formal-
ity and white tablecloths, simple achievements but notable
in a country that seems to believe that the uglier the plates
are, the better the food will be. The menu features grills

and roasts, with the most exportable classics of the regional cuisine. At lunch, the terrace seems a tad close to the road that also runs through Amou but on a warm evening, when the scent of hay creeps in from the meadows, the swallows are diving around the square tower of the Romanesque pilgrim church and there is no traffic, it's deeply pleasant.

While we waited for our meal, we amused ourselves designing our coats of arms. I got crossed pens quartered with chickens. Andrew and Geoff got the dog Otto and their new kitten as supporters. Sandy-and-Annie's escutcheon featured crossed roll-ups and a set of false teeth. This was because, after years of gentle and not-so-gentle urging, Sandy was to visit the dentist. Three things had brought about this change to the habit of a lifetime. Firstly, he'd got hardly any of his own teeth left. This had been the case for some years, but when you're an ex-pat it's easy to lose a grip on what's considered normal by the rest of the world. When the proprietor of the Belle Auberge cracked a joke about his gummy smile, Sandy simply decided to stop smiling and boycotted the place. Nor was he about to be told by his sons that nobody in Britain goes around with no teeth any more.

Secondly, the sale of their house had gone through, and they could no longer plead poverty. And thirdly, it was doctor's orders. Sandy is an enthusiastic steak-eater, but had been suffering from indigestion. The doctor, finding he had just a couple of incisors left, told him firmly that meat needed to be chewed before swallowing, and sent him to the dentist.

I tried and failed to lure Andrew on to Gaujac, where the gardens were coming into their own. This is where the Romans built their camp; five hundred years later, a local noble family built a strange new chateau on the same site, neither of vernacular nor classic design, but modelled on a Cistercian priory, with all the rooms leading off a cloister. The present owners open it to the public, and have established a real plantsman's garden, which now includes the French national collection of clematis.

Gaujac became notorious in the ownership of the Montespan family. Louis-Henri de Pardaillon de Gondrin, Marquis de Montespan, was a volatile character who helped to get the Gascons their bad name. His first big mistake was to marry a famously witty and lusciously beautiful young woman from the Poitou region, Françoise de Rochechouart, who had changed her Christian name to Athenaïs because it had more style. Athenaïs may have been an absolute scream but she was also ambitious, and from the day in 1660 that they left for the court of King Louis XIV at Versailles, she had her eye on the King.

Seven years later, the King had eyes only for Athenaïs. She had a moment of doubt, and begged her husband to take her back to the country, but he told her she was just being egotistical. The King then dumped his first mistress and instated Athenaïs as his consort. The Marquis then made his second big mistake. He minded.

At Versailles, the correct behaviour for the husband of a woman to whom the King had taken a fancy was to adopt a low profile and find good reasons to be out of town. This would immediately be rewarded by a string of well-paid official positions and extra titles. This was not for the Marquis. Was he not a Gascon? Did he not have his honour, not to mention his *panache*?

The Marquis kicked up an unseemly fuss. He raged, he stormed, he complained loudly and in public, and when he got drunk he beat up his wife. His uncle, a grand archbishop of the fire-and-brimstone Jansenist sect, was foolish enough to take his side, preaching censorious sermons and persecuting unfaithful wives in his bishopric.

So the King banished the Marquis to his estates, the normal punishment for an unruly aristocrat. It meant he was sent home under house arrest, and one of the houses chosen was Gaujac, undoubtedly because it was a hell of a long way from Versailles and close to the malaria-infested swamp that was then the Landes. Defiantly, he arrived with his son and daughter by Athenaïs, and with a pair of antlers lashed to the top of his carriage to symbolize the cuckold's horns. He then invited all the neighbours to a mock funeral and buried Athenaïs in effigy, ascribing her demise to 'coquetry and ambition'.

Athenaïs bore at least nine children, seven to the King, and put on a great deal of weight. She was eventually supplanted by the King's last mistress, the dreary and self-righteous Madame de Maintenon, who alienated Athenaïs' sons and drove her away from Versailles. The Marquis, however, scorned to catch malaria and eventually pulled himself together. He moved to Toulouse, and was then allowed by the King to return to Versailles. I like to think of him stomping across his lawn at Gaujac, impatiently scanning the landscape for the sight of the messenger from the court who never came to tell him his wife was coming home.

Meanwhile in the Garden . . .

22 May. My first sweet pea today. I picked it and put it in a little vase on top of my computer. It scented the whole room.

The so-called lawn looked like Prince Charles's wild-flower meadow, teeming with camomile daisies, ragged robin, dark blue bugle, sky-blue speedwell, the earliest of the purple cornflowers, and some crimson-petalled orchids. At the same time, primroses and violets were still flowering in shady corners.

Every herbivore in sight was nose-down all day, doing justice to the banquet. The cows, who lay down the minute the sun came out, were trying to graze as they reclined. Annabel's donkeys had got grotesquely fat, in their different styles. Lulu, the white mare, had a crest of fat on her neck and rolls of fat between each of her ribs, while Coco, her Pyrénéen consort, being a mountain animal in need of winter insulation, was evenly covered all over.

I picked my first strawberries, which were more exciting as a concept than a dessert. The slugs had got there first. The wild strawberries tasted much better; there were so many plants at the edges of the garden that I could go out to pick a handful for breakfast every morning.

A week or so later, after a few dry days, my own strawberries were much better. They were an elongated oval shape, deeply red, gorgeously soft and sweet, quite unlike the sour, cold things bought in supermarkets at home. They were of a local variety called 'Garrigues', and the first commercial crop of the year got the front page in the *Sud-Ouest*. When Andrew's parents and his Aunt Rose came to visit, I mashed some wild and garden strawberries into Eton Mess and decorated it with crystallized petals from the deep-red rose climbing up the front of Maison Bergez.

I also had the first cherries, a small, light-scarlet variety which suffered hardly any bird damage. This is surprising, because in most gardens the birds wait until the exact day that the cherries are ripe and then swoop down to strip the tree, which they can do in a few hours. The children, when they were off school for one of the bank holidays, were allowed to sit up all night to be ready to run out at dawn banging saucepans to scare away the winged marauders.

The lines of peas were flowering, but not growing very tall – I wondered why, then checked the seed packet and found I'd planted a dwarf variety. The broad beans and the runner beans were looking good, the tomatoes were getting

under way and the courgette plants could only be called
'*cousteau*'. This was another new word which I was enjoying.
It means beefy, butch or muscular. Thus one could translate
the famous undersea explorer, Jacques Cousteau, as Jack
Butch.

All the woods were laced with cream – the petals of the
acacia flowers. The hill on which Andrew and Geoff lived
was covered with so many of these tall, hard-wooded trees in
full flower that their scent rolled down to greet you; it was
like driving into a wall of honey halfway across the valley.

The weather was operatically temperamental. For a few
days it was like some caricature of good growing weather,
brilliant sunshine one minute, bucketing rain the next.
Then there would be storms. One morning I woke up to
see a blanket of mist in the valley below; by the time I'd
made my coffee, the mist was all around the house, so thick
I could hardly see the road.

When it was hot now, it was hot, over 30°C at least.
The rivers were raging grey-green torrents, and Sauveterre
was suddenly full of kids who'd been rafting, squelching
up from the river in their trainers, looking happy and
exhausted.

Sometimes the mountains were invisible in a heat haze,
but sometimes the whole range was so brilliantly clear I felt
sure I could see every stone on their snowy sides. When the
air was so transparent, the mountains seemed to move closer,
then drift away again as a veil of cloud came down.

One Monday, when I was just leaving Annabel's house,
we had a tornado. As I stepped out of her kitchen, black
clouds rolled up from the South-West and covered the sky.
By the time I'd walked downhill to my own gate, a huge
wind was thrashing the hedges. With it came a blizzard of
acacia flowers, and then, by the time I'd run all over the cottage locking down the shutters, a swirling gale was ripping

branches off trees. In the morning, the garden was full of torn-off branches of mistletoe. At Chris's house, the wind slammed the bathroom door with such force that it knocked a hole in the wall.

The First Cuckoo

I heard the first cuckoo, calling in the wood by the tile factory. Several pairs of blackbirds were nesting and ceaselessly combing the garden for worms. From twilight onwards they scolded the cats non-stop, until I went and got Piglet in just for the sake of some peace. Annabel pointed out the beautiful liquid call of a golden oriole, coming from the bamboo thicket by my gate. We also had a wren, hardly bigger than the yellow butterflies now dancing over the flowers. He was extremely aggressive, and at first poured such vicious abuse on Piglet that he took fright and ran indoors.

At the far end of the garden, under the huge oak tree, were some sawn-off oak logs, grouped around like the table and chairs set up for a leprechaun's tea party. As I passed by them one afternoon, I found a woodpecker frantically chipping the oak stumps to shreds in search of the beetles which had already bored them hollow. These were the notorious _capricornes_, another insect capable of condemning a house to death, and in a few days they had completely destroyed a section of oak trunk about two feet in diameter.

At dusk, the churring of cicadas was joined by calls from the big brown toad who lived by the stop-cock on the water pipe. Huge bugs began to fly about and a hornet came to visit my office every evening, flying in for an inspection about six, droning around officiously for thirty seconds, then flying on his way.

After him, a cinnamon-coloured beetle about fifty milli-metres long tried to get over the kitchen window sill; there was no need to deal with him, because his own clumsiness eventually sent him tumbling out into the flower bed. In the bathroom, exquisite grey moths, some with orange eyes on their wings, lined up on the window panes.

All this delighted the cats. The Duchess went out every morning, picked the softest spot on the bank of grass beyond the catalpas, and spent all day alternately dozing and watching the butterflies. Piglet's claws had grown as hard as steel, and he wanted to be out all night, prowling the bamboo thicket, or sitting on the kitchen window sill watching out for game, and also for Henri Cat, the ginger kitten, who was now to be found in the kitchen on most days when I came home from Sauveterre. He whisked out of the window and into the wood shed as soon as he heard me. Of course, it is folly to try to domesticate a barn cat but allowing him to live in the woodshed would, I reasoned, definitely discourage the mice.

Recipes

Blonde d'Osso Bucco à la Landaise

There are far more recipes for poultry and pork in the traditional cooking of the South-West than there are for beef and veal. This is, after all, a cuisine of the people, who could only eat the cheapest and least-esteemed cuts of meat, while the roasts, steaks and chops were enjoyed by the *milords* and the bourgeois. One of the most popular cuts of veal is the *jarret*, the equivalent of the shank of lamb, which is often pot-roasted. It's also cooked in slices, which we know in Britain by its Italian name, osso bucco.

This is my adaptation, using Jurançon wine and pine nuts, a classic Landais ingredient, with the veal shin in a sauce made with onion, celery and anchovy, rather than the traditional tomatoes. Fear not, the anchovies dissolve and enrich the sauce undetectably – absolutely no hint of fish. The veal shank is cut through the bone; the marrow is kept intact in the cooking and is considered a great delicacy. It's also bursting with vitamins. But if you have to feed people who can't deal with bone marrow, this dish is nearly as good made simply with chunks of veal shin without the bone.

Serves 4

4 good slices of osso bucco
oil and butter for sautéing
a little flour for dusting

salt and pepper
2 red onions
4 sticks of celery
3 cloves of garlic
9 salted anchovies
half a bottle of Jurançon wine (if you can't get Jurançon,
    use any other slightly sweet white wine)
500 ml (16 floz) stock, or water
the pared rind of 1 fresh, unwaxed lemon
4 tbsp chopped parsley
4 tbsp pine nuts, toasted until pale gold

Preheat the oven to 150°C/300°F/Gas 2.

Wash and dry the osso bucco slices, taking care to get rid of any bone crumbs. Set some butter and oil to melt in a heavy-bottomed casserole over a medium heat. Mix a handful of flour with a pinch or two of salt and pepper – if you put it all in a plastic bag the whole process is easy and not too messy. Dust each slice of veal with the seasoned flour, and when the casserole is sizzling but not burning, fry the slices on each side to seal them.

Chop the onions and the celery. Crush 2 cloves of garlic. Wash the anchovies, pull out any visible bones and chop them.

When the meat is sealed, remove from the pan and set aside on a plate. Put the onions and celery in the pan, reduce the heat and cook gently until the onion is transparent. Then add the garlic and anchovies, and cook for a couple more minutes. The anchovy scraps will start to melt.

Pour in the wine and turn up the heat to reduce it a little. Put the slices of meat back into the casserole. The liquid and sauce ingredients ought to come up around the sides of the slices, but not cover them, so if you need to, add some stock or water to get enough liquid in the casserole. You don't want the dish to burn.

Cover the casserole and put it in the oven for 2½ hours, checking occasionally and adding more liquid if necessary. To get an attractive golden colour on the meat, uncover the casserole for the last half-hour and glaze the slices with a little butter.

Chop the lemon zest, parsley and remaining garlic very finely together – this topping is known in Italian cuisine as *gremolada* – and mix in the pine nuts. To serve, transfer the meat slices to a flat serving dish. Taste the sauce and if you like add some more stock and seasoning. Pour the sauce around the slices of osso bucco, scatter the *gremolada* and pine nuts over the top, and serve with plain boiled rice or a simple risotto.

Acacia-Flower Fritters

This is Pierre Koffmann's recipe, which marinates the flowers in rum before turning them into fritters. This elevates the dish from a novelty snack for children to a sophisticated dessert. It's delicious – but it's worth trying once without the rum to enjoy the delicate honey flavour of the blossom.

Acacia blossom grows like wisteria blossom, in long panicles of tiny flowers. You may have to break them into manageable sprays before trying to cook them.

Serves about 6

100 ml (4 fl oz) light rum
50 g (1½ oz) caster sugar, plus extra for dusting
12 sprays of acacia blossom
100 g (3½ oz) plain flour, sifted

    3 eggs, separated
    1 tbsp oil
    a light oil, such as sunflower oil, for deep-frying

Mix together the rum and sugar and macerate the flowers for
half an hour.

   Meanwhile, prepare the batter. Put the flour into a large
bowl, make a well in the middle, and add the egg yolks and
oil. Beat gently with a wooden spoon, gradually adding a
little water to make a soft paste which will coat the back of
a spoon. In another bowl, beat the egg whites until stiff,
then fold them into the batter.

   Drain the flowers and stir the rum and sugar mixture
into the batter. Heat the frying oil until it is sizzling. Dip
the flowers in the batter, then fry them in the hot oil until
golden brown. Drain well on kitchen paper, then sprinkle
with sugar before serving.

Eton Mess *Tante Rose*

I suspect that this famous English dish derived from the
kind of mess schoolboys make when they mash their ice-
cream to a slurry. It's a crafty thing to do with less-than-
perfect strawberries or damaged meringues, and in this
variation the gritty little wild fruits add an extra dimension
to the texture while the pink peppercorns lift the flavours.

   For each person

   about 100 g (3½ oz) large fresh farmed or garden
      strawberries
   sugar to taste
   3 pink peppercorns, softened in a light sugar syrup
   about 2 heaped tbsp whipped cream
   about 30 g (1 oz) wild strawberries

1 meringue
3 dark-red rose petals, crystallized

Put the large strawberries in a large bowl, mash them roughly, add a little sugar and the peppercorns and leave to infuse. Whip your cream into soft peaks in another large bowl – don't overdo it, or the cream will get too solid. Roughly fold the cream into the strawberry mess, then add the wild strawberries, then enough sugar to make the mixture a little less sweet than you intend the finished dessert to be. Keep a few of the reddest wild fruits for decoration. In yet another bowl, break the meringues into chunks.

Just before serving, fold the broken meringues into the fruit and cream mixture. Pile it into *coupes* or glasses and decorate with the crystallized rose petals and wild strawberries. (To make crystallized rose petals, choose perfect petals from the darkest, most fragrant red rose you can find. They need to be dry. Preheat the oven to its lowest setting. Beat together with a fork the white of 1 egg and 1 tbsp caster sugar, then paint both sides of the rose petals with this mixture. Set the petals carefully on a sheet of baking paper or foil, put them on a baking sheet and leave them in the barely warm oven until they're dry and brittle – an hour should be long enough. When they're cool they're ready to use, or to keep for a few days.)

June

Sauveterre-de-Béarn:
le Pont de la Legende

The Blues, Real Bad

Even Gascony was ready for a French victory in the World Cup. A tractor dealership on the road to Oloron put all its blue tractors in a line at the front of its yard, under a banner reading *'Allez les Bleus!'* All the gas stations and supermarkets were adorned with giant posters of Zinedine Zidane. The Maison de la Presse made a window of its new stock of football magazines, and the sponsored merchandise ran from the obvious footballs and jerseys to more recherché items such as tins of sardines.

These were small investments compared to the big national players who had decided, in defiance of common sense, basic instincts, expert opinion and recent history, that France was now a great soccer-playing nation. Hadn't they won the cup the last time? Hadn't they defeated Brazil, that race of footballing giants? Well, then, obviously they were going to win again.

To us, the foreigners from a truly great footballing nation, the proper pose was of indulgent non-involvement. 'They don't know,' said Gerald in a kind voice. 'They've never even been in with a chance before, and last time they won. Some of their players aren't bad. You've got to expect them to go over the top a bit.'

'They've got no Gary Lineker,' said a more recent arrival from Britain who'd just noticed the bias against bad news that afflicts all the French media. 'They never had a Jimmy Hill. They haven't got any real experts so they haven't got anyone to tell them how it is out there.'

The madness extended to two particularly confident advertisers, who had actually pre-recorded vastly expensive commercials celebrating a French victory.

The nationwide mood of jubilant anticipation staggered when the French lost their very first match to the little-rated team from Senegal. The commentators jabbered and the newsreaders floundered. The players gave the traditional ashen-faced interviews but to us, long-term devotees of Ron Knee broadcasting, they showed no sign of appreciating the seriousness of their country's situation. Football was no longer a sport to be discussed by people who'd actually played it, but some new kind of reality TV, so the studios were filled with a bizarre parade of minor celebrities who twittered jaunty banalities at the camera.

When the Blues went down and out to Denmark, the nation plunged into despair. 'This will teach humility,' said Annie-Claire, with the satisfaction of a non-fan reprieved from weeks of soccer mania. Adidas turned on a sixpence and whacked out a new commercial with a slogan borrowed from Kipling, 'Losing makes you stronger!'

That was on 11 June. On 8 June, the Biarritz-Olympique rugby team had won the national championship. Their colours were red and white. In the Béarn and the Basque Country, the way forward was clear. The blue banners were pulled down, the blue tractors were driven to the back of the showroom and the blue flowers were uprooted from the municipal displays. In their place appeared red banners, red tractors and red flowers, not to mention red berets, red jerseys and red sweatbands. The glowering features of Zidane were replaced by the blond head of Christophe

Milheres, on posters adorned with triumphant flashes. *'Terre de rugby!' 'Allez B-O!'*

'You can't expect them to have the same concept of loyalty as we do,' ruled Gerald. TF1 screened a final analysis of the Brazilian victory, a sedate performance by the cosmetically perfect 'experts' talking in front of an audience of Disneyesque children who were dressed in brightly coloured clothes and waving Brazilian flags. It looked like a rehearsal for a vintage Michael Jackson video.

Chloe Returns

I collected the limp remains of my daughter from Dax station. She was alone. The plans to arrive with between seven and thirteen inseparable friends and head off to Pamplona in July for the running of the bulls on the festival of St Ermin had collapsed, because nobody had any money, everybody needed to work through the summer to get some and none of them had yet done the literature module on Hemingway which would have sold them Pamplona properly.

Between a month of revision and exams, and the week of partying required to celebrate the end of that nightmare, my daughter was speechless and grey in the face, ready to sleep for three days. By which time, I sincerely hoped that the rain would have stopped.

As day after day had dawned grey and chilly, and squall after squall had blown down from the mountains to soak the already-sodden ground, people were beginning to get anxious. The Gaves were raging with water. Although it is rated one of the most beautiful regions of France, up there with Brittany and Provence, the Béarn is much less lavish in marketing its charms. While the Côte Basque resorts lived for the holiday season, very few inland businesses would suffer badly if the summer turned wet. On the other hand, some tourists came, and people wanted them to have a good time, especially the children. Up at La Maysou, Gerald was getting the house and garden ready to welcome parties of Zoe's pupils, lurking indoors cursing while it rained then dashing out to weed the flower beds and paint the shutters the minute the sky cleared.

Everyone had a prediction. It would stop raining on 15 June, because it always did. It would stop raining on 20 June, because that always happened when you had a cold winter. It would stop raining on 10 June, because the shape of the clouds over the mountains told you so. 'It will stop raining on 12 June,' said Gerald with his usual sublime confidence. And it did, just in time to greet Chloe when she recovered. I had fixed a hammock between the walnut tree and an ash tree in the garden, and she lay in it contentedly, reading through a new supply of chick-lit from the English-language department of Amazon.fr and giggling when the golden butterflies settled on her toes.

We then enjoyed a week of perfect weather, with pure white puffs of cloud scudding across the brilliant blue sky. We went up to La Maysou one day and found Gerald taking a break, reclining on a lounger on the terrace watching the clouds as they drifted past and remembering what fun it was, when he had just got his wings as a Spitfire pilot, to fly in and out of little clouds on glorious days like these.

The vegetable garden powered into life. The first courgette flowers opened, big orange trumpets just begging to be picked, stuffed with a little fresh goat's cheese and herbs and eaten. The peas and broad beans were ready, and were miraculously free of blackfly. Most miraculous of all, the two undamaged artichoke plants were now huge fountains of grey-green foliage, out of which thrust sturdy stems bearing purple-tipped baby artichoke buds. The one which had been decapitated was half the size of the other two, but growing energetically.

For a few days, we enjoyed the kind of dreamy domestic lifestyle depicted in Conran-inspired photographs of life in France. I couldn't quite persuade Chloe to wake up in time to see the sun rise over the mountains, so we breakfasted late and luxuriously on a slice of leftover *pastis landais* with one of my growing collection of home-made jams. (Home-made, that is, by one of the market vendors.) One of the local dogs, a golden-haired mongrel with a madly affectionate nature, sometimes ran in for some extra petting, wearing half an iron chain instead of a collar.

The mornings slipped away peacefully. We discussed my ambition to keep chickens, by now a well-rounded fantasy featuring a little chicken house out by the compost heap and three birds, to be named Jeanne, Corisande and Sancie after the queens reckoned to be the good eggs of Béarnais history. Chloe was sceptical, but prepared to indulge me. I had drawings. I had costings. I had a hilarious book which Andrew had lent me, which advised that a chicken house should be trim and neat, not a ramshackle assemblage of fence posts and bits of rusty old corrugated iron. Clearly the author had never seen a proper Béarnais chicken house, since this was exactly the vernacular style. Andrew also was determined to keep chickens, but Geoff was against him. He said he didn't like to think about eggs coming out of a chicken's bottom.

After the chicken debate, I could get a morning's work in while Chloe enjoyed a bath. I had sent Nick Marston, the emperor of Curtis Brown's media department, an outline and the first twenty pages of my screenplay about the friend-ship between two great lovers of France, Henry James and Edith Wharton. He had sent me an email containing that kiss-of-death sentence, 'There is some good writing here.'

Nick was not totally discouraging, and asked me to finish the work, but with this book and my new novel to complete in the coming year, I would have no time until the following September. In fact, I urgently needed to crack on with the new novel, *Wild Weekend*, or the schedule would start slipping away from me.

This was to be the first summer for six years that I had not had a book published. It felt more than a little strange. I had a curious sense that I was fading away and becoming invisible, particularly when I sensed that I was with one of those big-talking expatriates who was making up a false identity. My French acquaintances, although they politely asked for copies of my books to read, still seemed overawed by the idea that a real writer was in their midst. I felt happiest with Marie, who seemed to accept my explanation that writing was just a job, and so I produced books just like she produced *confits*.

The only publication coming out with my name on it was a short story in *Magic*, an anthology published in aid of the charity One Parent Families. For some years, I had been one of the charity's trustees. Sarah Brown, wife of the Chancellor of the Exchequer, had edited the book and gave a launch party for it at 11 Downing Street. I flew back for this, leaving Chloe in the custody of Andrew and Geoff.

Unfortunately, there is more to being an author than writing the books. I've never been confident of my abilities in that part of the job which is about working the room at literary parties. I have two problems with this: I feel like a hypocrite even when I'm flattering people I genuinely admire, and I can never get it out of my head that a party is supposed to be fun.

I watched nervously as other writers jostled to be photographed next to J. K. Rowling and queued up, elbowing aside their competitors, for the privilege of laughing at one of John O'Farrell's jokes. A year ago, I realized, the fact that I just can't behave like this would have sent me home totally depressed. Now it seemed amusing. I found a kindred spirit in Emma Donoghue, whose story of two rival boatmen in Louisiana was one of my favourites. We formed ourselves into the too-sensitive-to-live tendency and lurked at the side of the room, where we found an equally shy fugitive from the House of Lords, Baroness (Ruth) Rendell.

He's a Vegetarian

Michèle Roberts had written a story which summed up Geoff's predicament perfectly. It was called 'Please Excuse My Husband – He's a Vegetarian', and concerns a couple who take their holidays in France. The husband, sick of watching his meat-eating wife tuck into one delicious meal after another while he is contemptuously dismissed with an omelette, says, 'They're so intolerant, the French, of anything different.'

'Oh, darling,' his wife replies, 'it's just not in their culture, that's all.' By the end of the story, the wife has acquired some of the timeless skills of the rural French carnivore, and the husband has come to a sticky end.

Andrew thought this tale was highly amusing, and Geoff did not. He was not finding life easy as a vegetarian and was struggling to master the French language. Often, he gave up on the menu when we went out to eat. Instead, he gave the waitress a flirtatious smile and hopefully mumbled, '*Vegetarian?*' This strategy produced two choices, a cheese omelette or a mushroom omelette. Sometimes the chef, feeling embarrassed that he was sending out such a poor dish, would toss in a few *lardons* and ruin the whole thing. The salad makers were inclined to do the same, adding chicken livers, gizzards *en confit*, strips of duck breast, slices of ham and chunks of Béarnais black pudding to innocent bowls of lettuce.

Geoff had been a chef himself, cooking first for the patrons of the English National Opera and then for his own clients at the studio, but trawling through the regional cookbooks revealed very few vegetarian recipes. Most of France is still eating on the values of their peasant days, when meat was the only real status symbol, and the more meat you could eat, the richer you obviously were. Thus vegetables meant poverty, and serving a guest a vegetable dish was virtually an insult. A couple of women, lunching on their own, might get away with a little *gratin*, but otherwise the only role for vegetables was to garnish the meat.

To make things worse, vegetables were what the animals ate. The maize, which was now 120 centimetres high and getting visibly taller every day, was intended for export and to fatten the ducks and the beef cattle. The less delicate vegetables which the British like to eat, marrows, parsnips or swedes, for example, are also considered fit only for animals by the French.

The local taste was rigidly conformist. Leeks were eaten in the winter, along with chicory. Green beans were eaten in the summer. Slices of squash or pumpkin might be contemplated in the autumn. Haricot beans were grown to be dried and eaten in the winter. A salad might be made of one of three recognized lettuce types, *laitue*, batavia or escarole. And that was pretty much it, a tragedy in a land where every seed that fell to earth grew as heartily as Jack's beanstalk.

A Trip to the Cinema

Films are one of my greatest pleasures in life. It was, in fact, the discovery that foreign films were shown in repertory in the local cinemas that was a clinching factor in my decision to leave London for a year. Saliès, St-Palais and Orthez all had little local cinemas which showed a wide range of films, the imports often being screened in '*version originale*' with subtitles and their original soundtracks. Pau and Bayonne had real art-houses, as well as small multiplexes.

However, getting someone to come to the movies with me had been a challenge. Annabel ventured out to see *Amélie* with me, but our diaries never had a window big enough for a trip to Pau for something more ambitious. I had managed to catch *Le Seigneur des Anneaux* (*The Lord of the Rings*) in St-Jean-de-Luz, but had been forced to go by myself to enjoy the spectacle of Christopher Lee whirling furiously around on his computer-generated crag, snarling, '*Qu'est-ce qu'on peut faire avec ces 'obbits?*' ('What can you do with these hobbits?'). The hobbit family of Baggins had been renamed Saccin, which was understandable, since *sac* means 'bag', but Bilbo Saccin just didn't sound as intrinsically loveable as Bilbo Baggins.

My next project was the stylized musical by François Ozon, *8 Femmes*. I tried to sell this to Margaret, an artist I had met at the French class. Everyone liked Margaret. She was warm, genuine, clever and a conscientious student. I liked her especially because she was about the same height, colouring and age as me, and had the air of someone who might have gone to the Paris Pullman when it was the best art-house in Chelsea. I mentioned that *8 Femmes* had had rave reviews and that, with Catherine Deneuve, Fanny Ardant, Isabelle Huppert, Emmanuelle Béart, Virginie Ledoyen and Danielle Darrieux in the cast, added to an award-winning costume designer, if we didn't understand every word then at least we'd be able to enjoy the gorgeous frocks. We were on the point of going when her husband had to go into hospital for an operation which immobilized him for some weeks.

Then the cinema in St-Palais proposed a midsummer night's dream, a free open-air screening of the comedy *Le Dîner de Cons* in the municipal stadium. *Le Dîner de Cons*, a satire on over-sophisticated city living in the spirit of *Frasier*, was originally a hit on the Paris stage and is probably the funniest film I've ever seen. I laughed so much at it when I first saw it that Chloe nearly ordered me out of the cinema because I was embarrassing her with my uncontrolled shrieks of mirth. However, nobody could be persuaded to come to see it in St-Palais, even for free with the added attraction of a non-stop bar.

With Chloe to amuse, I decided on a final throw. This time *Gosford Park* was coming to St-Palais. I'd already seen it in London and could vouch for its entertainment value. Persuading my regular companions to venture out was still tricky. I dared not ask Annabel and Gerald, since I suspected the film's setting, in a grand English country house of the thirties, would look to them like a patronizing American attempt to rewrite their own childhoods. Margaret's husband had recovered enough to get back to his daily walk in the forest, but had found a pair of abandoned puppies who were occupying all her attention.

I tried in vain to interest others in the English-speaking community. I began on the wrong tack. 'It's a film by Robert Altman,' I said. Blank stares. 'You know, the totally brilliant director who made *The Player* and *Short Cuts* and *Prêt-à-Porter*.' Blank stares. My heart broke a little. Altman is my all-time movie hero. The high spot of my early career as a journalist was going to interview him one day when the *Evening Standard*'s venerable critic, Alexander Walker, was otherwise engaged. It was one of those thrilling last-second assignments you get the day you come back from holiday, and the only clean thing I had to wear was a dress much like the one awarded to the character of the irritating journalist in Altman's masterwork, *Nashville*. I can still remember almost every golden word of the interview.

'It's an *hommage* to classic 1930s country house murder mysteries,' I tried again. Blank stares. Never, ever, use a word like *hommage* to a non-buff. 'It's got everyone in the world in it – Helen Mirren, Maggie Smith, Eileen Atkins, Alan Bates, Richard E. Grant, Kristin Scott Thomas, Camilla Rutherford, Michael Gambon, Charles Dance, Jeremy Northam . . . just a cast to die for.' Blank stares. In London, nine out of ten girlfriends would have been queuing at the box office with fibrillating credit cards at the mere words 'Jeremy Northam'.

'It's been nominated for eight Oscars,' I said. No response. 'I've seen it already and it's really good. And the tickets are only five euros. I thought we could go round the corner for a *steak-frites* afterwards.'

Eventually, Andrew, Geoff and *les Écossais* were persuaded, along with the ex-treasurer of the International Club, his wife, her brother and some house-hunting people from London she had met on the plane.

'Oh! You don't need the subtitles! You can understand what they're saying!' gasped the girl in the box-office, astonished to sell tickets to people speaking VO themselves. The cinema was small, comfortable and almost empty, apart from us. The party liked the film, although the print was so underlit that it seemed to be projected through a bath of plankton, but the evening went downhill fast after the closing titles. There were so few English-speaking people in the region that there was often a lifeboat spirit of camaraderie among them. The need for company often over-rode all kinds of social, cultural or political differences. But no British community can ever leave class-consciousness behind. *Gosford Park*, with its parallel narratives among masters and servants, sensitized everyone to the things that divided them, and the conversation languished.

We united, briefly, in an attempt to persuade the house-hunting couple to buy a holiday home in the more elegant Gers, where sophisticated Kensington types would be far happier than in the ramshackle Béarn, but the evening was nothing like the jolly gatherings over pizza that I had enjoyed in London.

Gosford Park turned out to be the only VO film in English to play all summer, just as *Mulholland Drive* had been the English-language choice in the winter. Andrew and Geoff soon felt confident enough of the French cinema to see it twice more, in Saliès, and I saw it for the third time with Annabel and Gerald, who loved it. Chloe was so inspired she agreed to come to see *Spiderman*, dubbed into in French, the following week; Tobey McGuire seemed to do for her generation what Jeremy Northam did for mine.

Spiderman, when dubbed, became only Speederman, which she found disappointing because she'd been expecting him to be translated, hobbit-style into something like Arain'homme. However, behind us in the tiny auditorium sat Lesley from Dublin, now the new owner of Sandy-and-Annie's house, who led us confidently to a *bar des sports* (rugby, rugby and rugby, of course) that didn't close until 2 a.m. I had no idea that St-Palais possessed such a treasure. Life started to look up. Lesley seemed to be my kind of girl. She'd already been to Spain to watch the World Cup in the bosom of a really great soccer nation, and she was going rafting on the Gave the following Friday.

'They say they'll take anyone from four to seventy,' she said. 'Would you like to come?' It sounded good to us.

Trial by Ordeal

The stories of the three good eggs tells you a lot about what it took for a woman to earn herself a place in history hereabouts. Queen Jeanne, always known as Jeanne d'Albret, is much appreciated. A Parisian couturier once named a fragrance after her. In the Béarn, streets, squares, restaurants and hotels are named after her and in Saliès the building which is now the Crédit Agricole proudly bears a plaque claiming that she once stayed there. All this acclaim she earned by being a ruthless, pig-headed dogmatist. The atrocities which she sanctioned in converting her kingdom to the Protestant faith would put her on trial for genocide nowadays. In 1571 she torched the town of Tarbes – perhaps not completely beyond comprehension to those who know it today as an ugly grey sprawl with pretensions to becoming a conurbation – and slaughtered over a thousand people who refused to abandon the Catholic faith. Giving birth to Henri IV was the only good thing Jeanne ever did. Her father, according to legend, made her sing a Béarnais song while she was in labour to make her baby brave and strong.

Corisande was of the next generation, which was destined to suffer years of religious war. She was a princess who loved reading the chivalric romances that were the chick-lit of the sixteenth century, full of questing knights, languishing troubadours and beautiful princesses just like her. Her real name was Diane d'Andouis, Comtesse de Guiche, but she called herself Corisande because it sounded more romantic. Her father was the royal seneschal of the Béarn, and at court in Paris her good looks made her popular with the sinister Queen Mother, Catherine de Médicis, who tried to add her to her 'flying battalion' of seductive girls employed to persuade important noblemen to support her devious schemes.

Corisande loathed the idea, and all the excesses of the court. She rebelled, and, after her husband was killed in the Wars of Religion, retreated to the safety of her castle at Bidache, which is now an imposing ruin.

Henri of Navarre, at that time raising support for his campaign to become King of France, couldn't resist the challenge of a beautiful, wealthy and powerful widow spurning all suitors in her impregnable castle. He came to Bidache and fell passionately in love with her, as his letters and poetry still witness. Corisande became his lover and ally, and backed his campaign for the throne. She also gets the credit for teaching the rough and ready Gascon warrior some manners and grooming. However, for being clever, honest and adored, Countess Corisande gets no streets named after her.

Nor does Queen Sancie; her story is the legend attached to the Pont de la Légende, the half-ruined medieval bridge at Sauveterre, the same over which the town squabbled for so long that they lost the pilgrim trade, but it does not reflect much honour on the town either. Sancie was the widow of Gaston V, the Viscount of the Béarn, and she lived in one of the most stable and contented periods of the region's history. The Béarn had enjoyed a century of peace and independence as a self-governing province. It was ruled by its viscounts, minted its own money and paid homage to no one. It was supposed to be the best governed, freest and happiest region in all of France at that time. This was not Sancie's experience.

Unlike Corisande, this unhappy queen had not kept her name free of scandal. In 1170, Sancie was charged with what is euphemistically described as the infanticide of her new-born son. The child was deformed, and had most likely died a natural death anyway. If he had survived, Sancie could have become regent, and ruled the province until he came of age, the custom which was to give the Béarn several brilliant female rulers as well as Jeanne d'Albret. Sancie thus had no motive to kill her son . . . unless the child had been conceived outside her marriage, after her husband's death. Sancie's real crime, therefore, was to have been suspected of having a lover.

The Béarn was governed according to an ancient body of laws called '*fors*', which apparently allowed for trial by ordeal. Sancie protested her innocence. To test her claim, she was tied hand and foot and thrown off the bridge into the river, on the theory that God knew if she was guilty and would intervene to save her if she wasn't. As it happened, Sancie did not drown nor was she dashed to pieces on the rocks. The river carried her downstream for a distance equivalent to three arrows' flights, and then washed her up on the bank, alive and well. History does not record that her accusers apologized. To this day, however, the majestic panorama of the river gorge, crowned by the silhouette of the church tower and the grey stone mass of the castle, has a strange air of melancholy, as if the cruelty of a bygone age still lingers in the air.

A Day on the River

Besides the two shuttered hotels which overlook the bridge, Sauveterre has three cafes; one, which says it has a terrace that also fronts the river, is always shut. Another, on the main square, is one of those elegant art deco cafes often found in remote French villages, but it's always empty. The third, which shows signs of life, is known as the cafe with the yellow chairs, because of its ugly plastic furniture. We met there, and gave the rafting staff €50 each. They ordered us to leave everything but a towel and a T-shirt behind, and I had to make a special case for Chloe's suncream. Our belongings were stuffed into two plastic barrels, which were loaded with us on to a coach, and driven up the valley to Oloron Sainte-Marie, the town from which the Gave d'Oloron gets its name.

Below the Renaissance battlements of grey stone there was a warehouse containing more wetsuits than anyone has ever seen hanging on rails. We were ordered to take a wet-suit, a life jacket and a paddle each, and to climb onto a yellow rubber raft. 'Thanks to our qualified team, our activities are accessible to everyone in complete safety,' promised the brochure.

Two boats were pushed out in the swirling waters of the Gave. The first was weighed down by fourteen French police cadets on holiday. Ours contained two French couples, an Irish family of two adults and two children, Lesley, her friend Kevin, Chloe and me, plus the raft captain, tanned to a dark cinnamon, who yelled 'Pa – dell!' as we approached each set of rapids. He needed the boat to get up as much speed as possible, he explained, otherwise he couldn't steer it.

The first stretch of the trip was miserable, since the young cops assumed that we were just longing to be soaked with water, and used their baling buckets and paddles to drench us as soon as they got within range. The weather wasn't anywhere near hot enough for this to be fun. The French, normally so repressed and orderly, have the propensity to go clear over the top when a window of relaxation is allowed. My dreams of drifting peacefully downriver, watching the herons and the dragonflies, were shattered. 'What did you expect?' sniffed Chloe. It wasn't until one of the young French women burst into tears that the management intervened.

By the end of June, the Gave was no longer a raging torrent, just a forceful body of dark green water swirling majestically westwards to the Atlantic. The rapids were plentiful, just foamy enough to be fun but not fast enough to be frightening. Having negotiated some peace, we glided happily downstream between curtains of trees. The raft captain pointed to the flotsam and driftwood high in the branches, marking the level of the river that the river had reached only a couple of weeks ago, when storms had combined with the meltwater from the Pyrenees. In a few days, he predicted, the Gave authorities would send a cleaning party down to get rid of all the plastic bags and other rubbish brought down by the floods, restoring the river banks to a picture of green innocence.

We did not see any of the disturbing sights about which Margaret, who lives in a riverside village nearby, had warned us. No bags of drowned puppies, no thickets of tomato plants flourishing on the sandbanks. The tomato plants betray the presence in the river of untreated human waste. Tomato seeds pass through the gut without being digested, but like nothing better than to put down roots on a sunny sandbank.

Medieval plumbing standards prevailed in many of the old houses in these riverside villages. Those built near the banks had only short pipes leading directly from the lavatories to Mother Nature's own original sewers. As an ecosystem, the Gave d'Oloron must work pretty well; the river was teeming with fish, and with fishermen, after the season opened in April. Near the towns, it also teemed with canoeists, swimmers and rafters like us, from whom I heard no reports of vile infections.

The northern river, the Gave de Pau, is a different kettle of bacteria. This body of water is a brilliant turquoise whatever the colour of the sky; in its defence, it must be said that the water in all the rivers gushing down from the Pyrenees was the same astonishing colour from high up in the mountains, and that the hot springs bore witness to quite enough deposits of copper, iron and chromium to make the colour naturally possible. However, the Gave de Pau runs from Lourdes, up in the mountains, through Pau and then past the chemical works at Mourenx and on through Orthez.

Whatever goes on at Mourenx, so many local jobs depend on it that no questions are asked. Here, a few kilometres from Pau, is the largest natural-gas deposit in Europe, which earned the region the name of 'le Texas Béarnais'. The lights of the vast plant which extracts and processes this precious fuel give an orange tinge to the eastern night sky which is visible from Orriule, and when the wind was in the right direction — which it rarely was — I could smell its chemical fumes in my garden.

The gas will soon be used up, and the plant is switching to process chemical waste which will be stored in the underground chambers that once held the gas. 'No risk to the environment is posed by the injection of liquid industrial effluent at a depth of 4,000 metres,' the departmental newsletter reassured us. Thus the alpine colours of the Gave de Pau were much admired, but nobody actually swam in it.

The two Gaves meet at Peyrohrade, a small town with a huge intact medieval castle whose four towers dominate the valley. They flow on towards Bayonne as a single stream called les Gaves Réunis, where they join the mighty, meandering Adour, which, with its tributaries, drains the entire midsection of the chain of the Pyrenees and sweeps over the plain of the Chalosse before turning south to Bayonne. The Nive, which runs down from the mountains through Cambo-les-Bains as a chattering torrent, is the last of the lesser rivers to join what by then is a swirling grey waterway about 800 metres wide. The pleasure of sitting in the riverside cafes in Bayonne can be seriously spoiled by the antics of the rats playing by the waterside when the tide is low.

Where we were paddling, the Gave d'Oloron was a relatively innocent river and we enjoyed it as much as you can when paddling for your life in a cut-off wetsuit. Between the rapids, we cruised serenely between the green walls of woodland, stopping occasionally to enjoy a swim or to squelch into a muddy inlet to admire a waterfall. By lunchtime, we had reached a little beach by the wooded foreshore below the chateau at Laàs. The captains made a fire and barbecued lamb chops and sausages, then offered us some *gâteau Basque* for dessert.

I blame what followed on that *gâteau Basque*, the only classic of the local cuisine which I regard as a complete waste of space. It's a heavy cake, like a Bakewell tart with an extra layer of custard, sometimes cheered up with some of the semi-sweet black cherries which are unique to the Basque Country. Freshly baked with the finest ingredients, a *gâteau Basque* can be memorable, but you rarely find one in that condition. Usually it is as it was on this occasion, leaden and boring, one up from eating a carpet tile. But we were hungry, so they were eaten, and the boat was definitely lower in the water as we approached what seemed to me to be quite a small waterfall. I thought the smooth green cascade was only about four feet high. Chloe says it was about eight feet high.

We paddled towards the edge of the falls like good galley slaves, the raft tipped up as it slithered over the rocks and I was thrown off its upper side into the bottom. My left foot was tangled in a strap and twisted at an ominously unnatural angle. It was also agony, agony of the precise quality I remembered from the last time I broke my leg.

My view of what happened next was from the rubbery floor of our boat. It seemed that a pile of people fell on top of me, though Chloe says they were trying to help me up.

The mother of the Irish family kindly poured arnica tablets down my throat. The raft captain called his base camp on his mobile. The most annoying of the hooligan policemen turned out to be the first aider, and climbed over to our raft to lay my ankle tenderly over his ham-like thigh, and agree with me that there was a fracture and it should be moved as little as possible.

We sailed on for a while, until the raft put in at a spit of pebbles, where the company owner and one of the land staff were waiting in a 4x4 to take Chloe and me to the hospital in St-Palais.

ER à la Basque

The Clinique Sokorri had a special door for casualties arriving by ambulance, but it had no ER. Nor did it have any of the things I would have expected to find in a London A&E department: no crammed waiting area, no drunks, no nutters, no dead people lying abandoned, no frazzled and guilty nurses, no warning notices about violence to NHS staff and no medical tourists, unless I counted as one.

A nurse appeared to assess my injury at the door as soon as I arrived. She also asked about my insurance status and accepted on trust that I had the '*feuille E cent-onze*' (form E111) confirming my entitlement to state health care in the EU. Then she found me a wheelchair, and I was wheeled straight into the waiting area for the orthopaedic consultant.

Dr Suleiman, I learned later, was Moroccan. He was a man of few words. He sent me down the corridor for an X-ray, which took about twenty minutes including the developing time, then showed me my shattered fibula and chipped tibia, and said, 'You could go home, but I'd prefer to keep you in hospital for a few days.' He was expecting me to protest. I was expecting him to do what an NHS doctor would have been forced to do – everything possible to keep me out of hospital. The doctor, mistaking my amazement for a protest, explained that my ankle was swollen and he considered there was a risk of thrombosis, so he wanted to keep me in hospital until the injury could be plastered safely. I burst into tears and agreed.

The main problem we had to solve was that Chloe had to go back to London the next day, to be ready for a chance-of-a-lifetime work-experience placement with a leading London casting agency. Before she could make any generous offers, I insisted that she stick to this plan, and then called Annabel to see if she could help. It was then that I discovered just what wonderful neighbours I had.

The room upstairs was a spotless two-bed ward in which there was already one patient, a young woman who was getting ready to go home after a minor operation. Gerald and Annabel arrived in a couple of hours, bringing me nightclothes, my washbag and a couple of books. 'Thank God this happened to you in France!' they said, and whisked Chloe away, promising me that she would catch her train without fail the next morning.

I passed a quiet weekend, except for the nurses, who, whether they were French or Basque, just pampered me. In fact, I hadn't felt so pestered to need something since the last time I stayed in a five-star hotel in Marrakesh. 'How are you this morning? Did you sleep well? Because if you didn't we can give you something. You must ask us. And have you got any pain? No, please, you must tell us if it's still hurting. No, really, we can give you stronger pain killers, just ring the bell. Let me show you how the bell works . . .' They also explained every procedure very carefully, making sure that I'd understood in spite of my flawed French.

The room lacked those tidemarks of grime that a London hospital room seems to get within months of being built. The whole building, which fairly glowed with cleanliness, was over thirty years old, and all its equipment, some of which was far from new, seemed to be dusted and polished daily. 'It's so *clean*,' marvelled Andrew when he came to visit.

None of the staff ever seemed stressed, either, nor did they have that sad, guilty air that I'd seen so often in British hospitals, on people who knew they weren't going to be able to treat their patients as they wished but couldn't do anything about it. The only experience of rudeness I had while I was there was from the English 'advisers' working for my insurers, who clearly felt I was trying to defraud them because I didn't want to be helicoptered to Bordeaux and repatriated by air ambulance immediately. In one unforgettable conversation, the 'adviser' accused me of trying to cheat them by claiming I had a broken ankle when their records used the term 'fracture'. She would not accept my assurance that these words had the same meaning. Remembering the few but traumatic visits to hospital I'd had with Chloe, I realized that to be ill or injured in Britain now often means feeling frightened, defensive and mistrustful, knowing you will have a fight on your hands just for basic necessities.

Then there was the hospital food. It was very simple, always fresh, and delicious. Four meals a day, four courses with a little plastic glass of wine at lunch and dinner. On Sunday, we had duck *à l'orange*. The portions were, by French standards, ample. One day I wrote down the menus. Breakfast was fresh bread with butter and jam. Lunch was melon or soup, followed by chicken or hamburger with gravy, potatoes, *petits pois* and carrots with lardons, then green salad, cream cheese and bread and cassis and lemon sorbet. At tea time, they offered me a yoghurt or fruit. Dinner always started with alphabet soup, then it was fish pie and broccoli with two poached pears for dessert.

When I'd finished the books, I watched some television, a luxury which cost me an extra few euros a day. A contestant on the French version of *Who Wants to be a Millionaire?* was asked a €200 question: what is the plural form of the expression for self-service, '*libre-service*'? Again, something bubbled up from the sludge at the bottom of my memory, and I got this right. The contestant did not. The right answer was 'libres-services' – with a compound adjective, you see, you have to add an s to both parts of it for the plural. Such a logical language, but so exacting that even native speakers make mistakes. Once a year, a professor delivers a dictation test on national television. Renée had been encouraging us to try it. Her own score, of which she was very proud, was only ten mistakes.

By the time it was Monday, and I was lying on a trolley feeling floaty with a pre-med injection with the operating theatre lights in my eyes, trying to summon up enough vocabulary to respond to the nurse's questions about allergies and earlier operations, I really didn't feel too bad.

Recipes

Merlu Koskera

This is one of several Basque recipes which put fish together with the new vegetables of early summer. With the white fish, green peas and shellfish, it looks extremely pretty, particularly if you can find the carpet-shell clams, called *palourdes* in French, which open up to look like big striped butterflies.

Hake is probably the most popular white fish on the Côte Basque and the north Spanish coast, perhaps because cod, whose flesh is equally firm and creamy, could be preserved by drying and salting, and so was a valuable commodity to trade inland and use to provision ships for long voyages. Now of course cod is an endangered species.

Wash and scrape the mussels and clams well so they don't add sand to the dish. Don't use any with broken shells or shells which refuse to shut tightly.

Serves 6

500 g (1 lb 2 oz) asparagus
500 g (1 lb 2 oz) fresh peas, in their shells
300 g (11 oz) mussels
300 g (11 oz) clams
6 hake steaks, about 115 g each
salt and pepper
flour for dusting the fish

vegetable oil
2 bay leaves
small piece of *espelette* pepper or a half a red chilli,
    finely chopped
200 ml (7 fl oz) dry white wine
200 ml (7 fl oz) fish stock or water
3 hardboiled eggs
3 cloves of garlic
a handful of parsley, chopped
olive oil

First trim the asparagus and cut into 1cm pieces. Blanch the peas in boiling water for 5 minutes, setting the asparagus in a sieve over the water to steam. Drain and keep these vegetables aside.

Dust the fish with seasoned flour. If you prefer it in small pieces, slice the steaks into chunks before coating. In a sauté pan or large frying pan, fry the fish on both sides until pale gold. Add the bay leaves, the *espelette* or chilli, the wine and the stock or water, and allow to come to a gentle simmer. Then add the mussels and clams, and continue to simmer until they are all open. Add the peas and asparagus and allow another 10 minutes of simmering. Cut the eggs into quarters lengthways. Pick out the bay leaves and add the parsley. Serve in soup plates, decorated with the egg. Some good crusty bread or plain new potatoes are all you need to go with it.

Stuffed Courgette Flowers

For this, you need breadcrumbs, and for breadcrumbs you need a hearty *pain de campagne*. Gascon cooking has no truck with an urban frivolity like the *baguette*, which, when it's made properly, will be stale in two hours. People who have work to do in the fields can't be leaping off to the baker in the village twice a day. In a traditional household, the baking was done once a week, and included country loaves which weighed in at about 2 kg each, with plenty of soft insides and good keeping qualities.

For this recipe, the best way to get breadcrumbs is my mother's traditional method: letting the bread become slightly stale – overnight can be enough – then grating it or rubbing it through a sieve. Result – dry, fluffy breadcrumbs. The easier way, soaking the bread in milk or water then squeezing it out, tends to make the stuffing mixture too wet.

If you examine your courgette plants, you will see that some flowers are on long thin stalks and some aren't. Those which are on long stems are the male flowers, whose role is to pollinate the female flowers. Since one male flower produces ample pollen for a whole row, you can pick as many of them as you like without robbing yourself of courgettes for the following week.

For each person, as a starter

a little olive oil
crumbs from a good thick slice of bread
1 heaped tbsp fresh goat's cheese
1 tbsp toasted pine nuts
1 tbsp mixed chopped parsley and chives
salt and pepper
3 fine, dry courgette flowers

Preheat the oven to 180°C/350°F/Gas 4. Use the oil to grease an ovenproof dish. Mix all the rest of the ingredients, except the flowers, gently together.

Pick up a courgette flower and hold it in your hand with

the open end upwards. With a dessert spoon, gently pack
the interior with the stuffing – very gently, or the fragile
orange petals will tear. Fold the petals around the mixture,
then lay the little parcel gently down on the oiled dish.
Repeat with the rest of the flowers.

Drizzle over a little more oil and put into the oven for
just long enough to warm the parcels through and cook the
tiny area of stem at the base of each flower – about 15 minutes. Serve in the dish, if you can, to avoid the risk of the
delicate things collapsing when they're moved.

Pastis Landais (Raion-des-Landes method)

When you first cut into this large, light dessert cake it
releases the full aroma of the liqueurs with which it is
flavoured. The other ingredients are simple to the point of
innocence – flour, eggs, sugar, butter, vanilla; it's these
flavourings and the lightness of the mixture that gives the
confection a luxurious feel.

In texture, a *pastis landais* is halfway between a sponge
cake and a *brioche*, traditionally made in a deep *brioche* tin,
lightly glazed and given a crunchy topping of sugar crystals. Sometimes, a few stoned Agen prunes are added to the
mixture. Classically, the *pastis* is served as a dessert with
fruit and *crème anglaise*, which is real custard, made with
fresh eggs. It keeps well and doesn't even mind spending
time in the freezer. Willingly, it will adapt to all kinds of
dishes from elsewhere in the world, such as trifle or tiramisu.
If you have some left over, it makes a decadent treat for
breakfast and an elegant cake to enjoy with a cup of tea
anytime.

Pastis landais is always made in a paper case inside the
deep *brioche* mould that causes it to rise into a luscious dome

like the breast of a goddess. If you haven't got a traditional tin, it adapts happily to an 18 cm (7 in) or 20 cm (8 in) cake tin, with a lining of foil to encourage it to turn out easily. The other essential piece of equipment for this recipe is a really large mixing bowl.

Making the *pastis* before electric beaters were invented must have been a real workout for the cook's right arm. Perhaps the fact that most Landais families prefer to buy a professionally made *pastis* is a hangover from these labour-intensive days. I searched for months to find a recipe that worked; eventually Tony used his charm on Lucienne Dupouy, a friend of Marie's, who remembers her mother Marguerite making thirty *pastis* at a time on high days and holidays. She would give them away to her neighbours. Very kindly, Lucienne reduced the original recipe for a modern cook.

The entire process will take about 6 hours, but for most of that period the mixture requires no attention as it's just sitting in a bowl while the yeast works. So this is a fun recipe to try on a day when you have to be at home most of the time – I tried it while I was correcting the manuscript of *Wild Weekend*. Don't worry if you're not used to working with yeast. Although the process seems elaborate, it's almost idiot-proof. The only thing that can go wrong is that the cook may get impatient and rush the cakes into the oven before they have had time to rise to their full glory.

A word about ingredients: I've specified 'strong' flour, which is the high-protein flour used to make bread. If you use ordinary flour, the result is a bit heartless. The liquid vanilla extract is not the same thing as vanilla flavouring; it's more expensive but essential for its rich aroma. Amazingly, I managed to buy a vial of it in Tesco. And baker's yeast – well, you need to buy it from a real baker. In London, I found mine at Clarke's in Kensington Church Street. It will keep in a plastic bag in the fridge for about a fortnight. The dried yeast in sachets is much easier to find and works pretty well, but doesn't impart the same fresh flavour. If you go with dried yeast, follow the directions and use the quantity recommended on the packet.

Makes 3 cakes

For the yeast mixture

100 ml (4 fl oz) milk
50 g (2 oz) flour
30–40 g (1–1½ oz) fresh baker's yeast

For the dough

350 g (12 oz) caster sugar
half a wine glass of milk
half a wine glass of dark rum
half a wine glass of anisette (Lucienne specified Marie Brizard)
a third of a wine glass of liquid vanilla extract
1 vanilla pod
350 g (12 oz) unsalted butter
8 whole eggs
1 kg (2¼ lb) strong white flour

For decoration

sugar crystals or crushed cube sugar

First, start the yeast working. Put the milk into a small bowl and mix the flour into it until you have a smooth paste. Crumble the yeast into this and stir briefly to mix it in. Put the bowl in a warm place – a radiator shelf or the back of an Aga is ideal – and leave for half an hour for it to start 'working' – which means fermenting, so that bubbles appear and the volume of the mixture increases.

Put the sugar, milk, rum, anisette, vanilla extract and

vanilla pod into a small saucepan, and warm over a low heat until almost at boiling point. Turn off the heat and leave to infuse. In another small saucepan, or a bowl in the microwave, melt the butter.

Crack the eggs into a really large bowl and beat them briefly. Withdraw 1 tbsp beaten egg, add 1 tbsp of water to it, and keep aside for glazing. Then beat the rest of the egg mixture fast with an electric beater, until it is a pale yellow froth honeycombed with small bubbles.

Slowly pour the melted butter into the egg mixture, beating all the time. Pick the vanilla pod out of the sugar–alcohol mixture, and add the mixture to the eggs and butter in the same way. Then add three-quarters of the flour, sifting it into the mixture a few tablespoons at a time and beating continuously. By the end of this process, the electric beater may be struggling. Switch to dough hooks or a wooden spoon.

Finally add the yeast mixture, with the last of the flour, while continuing to beat to obtain a smooth, homogeneous dough. Cover the bowl with a clean dry cloth and leave it in a warm place to rise until it has doubled in volume. The exact time will depend on how warm the environment is and how feisty the yeast – 'feisty' being originally a Yiddish word describing the general ebullience of a yeast mix.

Butter the 3 *brioche* or cake tins generously and line the bottom of each with buttered foil. Divide the dough between the tins, pouring it or using a large spoon. Tap each tin smartly on the work surface to settle the dough, then return them to the warm place and leave, uncovered, to rise again for about the same period. In the traditional tin, the *pastis* is ready for baking when the mixture has risen up to the edge.

When the mixture is almost ready, turn on the oven to pre-heat at 200°C/350°F/Gas 6. Put in the tins and leave to bake for half an hour. Take a pastry brush and quickly glaze the tops of the *pastis* with the reserved egg mixture, then sprinkle with the sugar crystals. Return to the oven to finish baking for 15–30 minutes – test with a skewer to make sure the cakes are cooked through.

Take the *pastis* out of the oven and let them rest for 5 minutes before turning them out of their tins. Put them to cool – right side up – on a wire rack. When they are cool, pick one to eat now and two to freeze or give away. Serve in slices, with *crème anglaise* or red-fruit coulis.

Crème Anglaise

575 ml (1 pint) milk – full fat, or half milk and half cream
    if you're feeling really indulgent
4 eggs
90 g (3 oz) sugar

Scald the milk. Beat the eggs and sugar briefly in a mixing bowl, and pour the hot milk slowly into this mixture, beating all the time. Either set the bowl over a saucepan of simmering water, or pour the mixture into the top of a double saucepan, or heat very gently over a tiny flame, stirring frequently to keep the mixture smooth, until it thickens into a custard. The anxious cook can blend in 1 tsp cornflour to be absolutely sure the sauce will be thick and smooth. *Crème anglaise* is usually flavoured with vanilla, but it's a bit too much of a good thing when the *pastis* is already redolent with this spice.

July

St-Jean-de-Luz: le Port des Pecheurs

Despair

I had been doing fine in hospital. It was after Annabel and Gerald drove me home that things suddenly looked black. Dr Suleiman issued stern instructions not to put any weight on the injured leg: no walking, no driving. Hopping about on crutches only. For at least five weeks. The plaster came just below my knee. I had a pair of crutches, on which I could get about slowly and awkwardly, at the price of total exhaustion after half an hour. Orriule might as well have been a tiny island in the Pacific Ocean. I was marooned.

Maison Bergez was suddenly nothing but a hundred more accidents waiting to happen. The tiled floor downstairs was like a skating rink. The polished floorboards upstairs were just as bad. I had to scramble up the high, uneven front steps on my knees, and it took me a quarter of an hour to crawl upstairs. The bathroom, and the loo, were upstairs. Given that all the wooden floors sloped, in places quite steeply, it was the easiest thing in the world for one of the crutches to skid and pitch you over in a heap. I spent a night in tears, wondering how I was going to cope.

Annabel drove me into Saliès to see the man who would now be my GP, a young doctor with an Italian name and long curly hair like a Botticelli portrait. He listened carefully, wrote prescriptions in a blur of speed, and explained that he wanted me to have a daily visit from the district nurse, to take anti-coagulants and calcium-fixing enzymes, and to have a wheelchair. I was also entitled to apply to the *mairie* for a home help; I was grateful that Annabel had already sent me her own cleaner, a young girl called Amandine from Burgaronne who stormed about the house like the white tornado of the TV commercials, pausing only to admire Piglet.

People rushed to my assistance. Annabel lent me her old office chair on castors, then disappeared to welcome Zoe and the first party of school children. Willow lent me her camping toilet. Gordon came over to cut the grass and stayed to help me make up the bed in the downstairs bedroom, 'boy style', he said, apologizing for being psychologically incapable of tucking in the sheets. Even Piglet, after watching me hobbling around with an expression of dismay, rushed into the garden and came back half an hour later with a dead mouse, which he dropped generously in front of me, obviously hoping it would build me up.

Bernadette, the senior of the two nurses who made house calls in the area, swooped in and organized me with the blatant joy of a woman who loves to run other people's lives for them. She banned the camping toilet, announcing that it was dangerous, and whisked the doctor's prescriptions away to the chemist in Sauveterre, returning with the officially approved commode. The next day she came by with her son, a trainee physiotherapist, who helped her deliver and assemble a gleaming new wheelchair, which I would be able to hire as long as I needed it.

Florists began to telephone, asking with obvious irritation where exactly Orriule was, where exactly was my house. I discovered that the conventional way to identify a house in a rambling village is to specify the colour of the shutters – dark green, and the orientation to the *mairie* – facing uphill. To a Gascon florist, no work of nature is so lovely that it cannot be improved with cellophane printed with bows of custard yellow and knicker pink, or ribbons of Day-Glo green and orange. However, with her killer style-radar, Tara, my editor at Time Warner Books, found an establishment at Orthez that could not only source sunflowers and delphiniums but wrap them up prettily. The bouquet was over a metre high, and cheered me up considerably. Another well-wisher sent an arrangement in a basket, which the florist had watered so enthusiastically that about five litres spilled all over the floor as soon as I took off the wrapping. This gave me a very nervous morning, slipping on the wet tiles as I hopped around with a mop in one hand and a crutch in the other.

Margaret rushed over with a wonderful basket of vegetables from her garden, and stayed to repaint my toenails in Chanel's most cheerful red. Finally Roger, having heard of my plight, drove over in his Mercedes with another wheelchair. This he had found abandoned at the town dump. It was a 1950s model with a red leather seat, and handy side pockets; just what I needed to get around the garden.

Roger's speciality is painting panoramas, very large, very precise views of famous towns, full of witty details, which are designed to be exhibited in the round. His best-known work is the panorama of Bath. The wheelchair he had used while painting the panorama of Saliès, which was at that time housed in a special circular gallery in the little garden with a bandstand near the Thermes. The wheelchair had allowed him to whiz up and down the giant canvas all day without getting exhausted. It allowed me to struggle around the garden, and keep up with picking the tomatoes, the sweet peas and now the dahlias. Dahlias, I had noticed, were as popular with my neighbours as they are with English allotment gardeners. Every row of tomatoes ended in a flourish of red and yellow sunbursts.

My day quickly settled into a new rhythm. I could get a morning's work done before Bernadette, or her colleague, Noelle, called in. Being a temporary cripple couldn't break my habit of lunching off bread and cheese at my desk, after which, if it wasn't raining, I allowed myself a couple of hours outside, to do some laborious pruning and weeding, or to sit in a deckchair and read. Then it was back to the office, to work through until the evening, when I could expect a kind visitor. Often it was Zoe, calling in at the end of her day, on her way to a head-clearing walk between the maize fields. I envied her hopelessly. No strolling through the fields for me, nor any of those long days I'd planned to spend roaming in the mountains. The walking, like the chickens, was never going to happen.

After visiting time, I made for the kitchen and worked my way through the recipes in this book to test them. Cooking from the wheelchair turned out to be easy, as long as I remembered to cover a frying pan before it spat in my eye. At some point in the evening I would also call Chloe, who was staying in a friend's flat in the centre of London while she worked for the casting director, whose office was nearby.

She was worrying about me, and I was worrying about her. Talking to a daughter – or a son – who's living in central London for the first time is guaranteed to wring any mother's nerves. Every morning, she found a new deposit of used hypodermics in the flat's window boxes. Of course, when I had heard the 'don't touch that, you don't know where it's been' warning from my own mother, I had never imagined that the day would come when I would say it myself. Nor had I foreseen that the object not to be touched would be a drug addict's discarded needle, implying the risk of Aids. But then, I had never envisaged Aids, let alone the need to explain it to my daughter when she was five years old and terrified by the first public service TV commercials about the disease.

Another evening, when I called, she answered in obvious distress, having just spoken to a friend who had gone out to buy milk from a corner shop around 10 p.m. The friend had found a male-on-male gang rape in progress outside her front door, and turned back in a state of shock. On another occasion, Chloe called me unexpectedly, having suddenly got time on her hands because her date for the evening had cancelled. The reason? His parents had imposed a 10 p.m. curfew on their children after coming home from a weekend away to find that their younger son, a boy of fifteen, had been kidnapped by drug dealers, robbed and locked in the bathroom of their flat in Bethnal Green for twenty-four hours.

In this month two young girls were abducted in the Cambridgeshire village of Soham. In my year away, this was the only event in Britain which caught the attention of the French media. It was reported with an appalled dignity, in sharp contrast to the cynical breast-beating of the British tabloids. Crimes against children certainly happen in France, but in the media the desire to shield the people from these horrors tends to override any ghoulish impulses to exploit them as an audience-building opportunity.

In London, I used to feel oppressed by the inescapable knowledge of the evil abroad in the city. Living in Orriule, where life was shaped by the desire to honour the seasons, the Christian year and the processes of nature, I felt guilty for having escaped the nastiness of British life and left others behind with no choice but to endure it.

The Singing Sisters

On Thursdays, Andrew came over, with a selection of visitors who'd been regaled with the quaint charm of the market in Saliès. Maysounabe was welcoming a steady stream of house guests now; one London fashionisto, having failed to spot the basic difference between the Béarn and St Tropez, arrived with a choice of four Rolex watches with which to impress the locals.

Andrew also brought with him a selection of fish from the Otranto sisters, two Basque fish merchants who brought the cream of the catch from St-Jean-de-Luz up to the markets in Orthez and Saliès every week. No lurid salmon or limp sea bass from fish farms for them, but rubbery tangles of octopus, a rattling heap of scallops, buckets of *petite friture* and whatever the sea had provided that morning – once it was a brill as big as a cushion. Their pitch in the market at Saliès was next to the music stall, which gave them the opportunity to air their fine Basque voices and sing along with their favourite songs while they scaled and gutted their wares, only drawing breath to pass down cooking advice with the goods.

Andrew's new favourite dish was one that he had to resign himself to buying ready-prepared, because the Otranto sisters made it a thousand times better, not to mention faster, than any of us. This was *piquillos farcis*, small sweet red peppers stuffed with a mixture of salt cod and mashed potato. It took us half an hour just to peel the peppers, let alone soak the cod for a day in several changes of water, peel and mash the potatoes, put the whole thing together and make a tomato sauce for it. The tinned *piquillos* in the shops were revolting. There was nothing to do but keep the Otranto sisters busy. I could see Andrew beginning to fizz with frustration because when he asked how to peel the peppers they told him, willingly and at length, but his French was not yet good enough to understand and I was a prisoner at home and couldn't translate for him. It didn't help that they naturally used a lot of Basque words. Some were easy to guess – like *atuna* for tuna and *xardinak* for sardines, but

others, like *ezkirak*, which turned out to be prawns, sent us
diving for the dictionary as soon as we got home.

Many of the recipes the Otranto sisters parted with so
gaily bore the name of *kaskarota*, meaning it was attributed
to the *kaskarotes*, the women who used to sell fish from the
ports of the Basque coast, Hendaye, St-Jean-de-Luz and
especially Ciboure, where the composer Maurice Ravel was
born. Their ancestors were partly the gypsy boatmen of the
Spanish border towns and part *cagot*, the lost Gascon race
of untouchables. In the old photographs they appear as tall
strong-featured beauties with smouldering black eyes, and
the firm chins and noses which are characteristic of the
Basque face. The legend is that the young women stripped
naked and plunged into the waves to greet the fishing boats
as they returned to port. They did the deal for the catch on
the spot, and no doubt the most beautiful got the best price.
Then the *kaskarotes* loaded the fish into their baskets and
climbed ashore, where they jumped back into their flounced
skirts and espadrilles and raced off to the markets with the
baskets on their heads. The *kaskarotes* could cover forty kilometres in a day, carrying thirty kilos of fish, and could easily
reach Bayonne with the fish still fresh. The Otranto sisters,
being small-boned, red-haired and fully dressed, and travelling in a white van on the motorway, were obviously their
heirs in spirit only.

Las Hestas deu Vilatge

The invitation was written in Béarnais first and French
second. The village *fête* would take place on the 6th and 7th
of July. The meal would be at midday on Sunday. *Que'vs
demandan d'emplea lo paperot acieu devath*. Fill in the coupon
below. €13 a head. Annabel and I agreed that it would be

good form to go, and she called for me in her car to save me struggling down the steep, gritty hill on my crutches.

Our big mistake was forgetting the Béarnais quarter of an hour, which on this occasion stretched to about two and a half hours, to allow the absolute maximum amount of chatting and drinking aperitifs before the party was invited to sit down at the long trestle tables in the *salle multiactivités*. The former mayor, a jolly, grizzled farmer whose house overlooks the fish pond, insisted on buying us drinks and refused to be fobbed off with requests for a couple of orange juices. Our choice was port or whisky.

Almost every village has a summer *fête* whose sole purpose is to bring past and present neighbours together to share some drinks, a meal and some dancing. If the patronal festival of the village church – the day awarded to its patron saint in the Catholic calendar – falls in the summer, the two events will be combined, with a processional mass on Sunday morning.

This is what happens in Ossages, where last year I was woken at 5 a.m. by a van from a florist in Orthez delivering a red, white and blue wreath to the church door. It sat on the church-yard wall by the dustbins all morning, until about two hundred people filed out of the church at 11.30. This Marie bewailed as a really sad sight, since in her youth there would have been about two thousand in the congregation. They gathered around the war memorial, and a man with an accordion suddenly appeared beside it. He played the 'Marseillaise' as the mayor stepped up to collect the wreath and lay it on the memorial step. A Course Landaise took place in the afternoon, in a temporary arena erected on the car park of the sports hall. At the end of the day, a mobile disco drove into town and parked on the roundabout in front of the church. A bar opened in somebody's garage, and a handful of citizens passed the night pleasantly, drinking and reminiscing as they watched a few couples dancing under the street lights.

Orriule did things in a more Béarnais style, with two live bands which delighted the revellers with non-stop folk songs. In England, the mere expression 'folk song' conjures up pictures of sad blokes in beards and sandals wailing lewd ballads at an audience who can't understand a word. Between urbanization, American cultural imperialism and the demands of multiculturalism, our own native music has been almost obliterated, along with the communities which cherished it. Only a micro-minority of musical anchorites are concerned to keep this despised heritage alive, and they get very little encouragement from sniffy civil servants, whose concern to promote 'diversity' has led to a suppression of our native culture. Ninety-five per cent of the English population probably couldn't sing one song that was known to their great-grandparents.

The Béarnais, on the other hand, have a great and living musical tradition. Not a tradition as renowned and profoundly nationalistic as that of the Basques, whose stupendous voices are acclaimed all over the world, but a great tradition all the same. The deep, resonant Béarnais voice is also a gift of the mountains, created by generations of people calling to each other, and to their livestock, across the steep valleys.

In recent years, Béarnais music has received firm official support, but it would have been a vital part of everyday life without that. An old man pottering around his garden or a young man setting off for work will let rip a few verses just for the joy of living. In the churches, any member of the congregation with a good voice is welcome to get up and improvise a solo with the choir. There are songs for every occasion, haunting or spirited, with poetic lyrics or hearty choruses. At a family celebration or a public festival a high spot of the event is the singing. So the citizens of Orriule were soon in full cry, with their arms around each other's shoulders and tears in quite a few eyes.

The meal proceeded slowly, especially after the dancing began. I could see it would be my fate to pass the summer smiling over my plastered leg at other people enjoying themselves more energetically. The men did the serving, giving the women a rare few hours of relaxation. The main dish which had been chosen, apparently after much discussion, was a Basque one: *axoa* – it sounds like a sneeze, because the 'x' is pronounced like a slightly forceful 'ch' – is a ragout of veal and peppers.

Worrying about Gerald, who had been left resting alone at the house, Annabel decided to leave at about 5 p.m. Since Maison Bergez was only a few hundred yards from the *salle multiactivités*, it was impossible not to know that the festivities didn't stop until 2 a.m.

An Ill Wind

By the end of the month, I had something like the beginning of a book in my computer. My injury, coupled with relentlessly sulky weather, had grounded me so effectively that I wrote over ten thousand words in the last two weeks of July alone. I wasn't completely happy with them; I was still struggling between the two languages and my writing seemed to have taken on a stiff, nineteenth-century tone instead of the clean, contemporary zip on which I had been able to pride myself before now.

On the plus side, many of the elements in the story which had been fuzzy and troublesome were clearing like clouds blown away by the wind. *Wild Weekend* is about the English countryside, and I had been casting about for the kind of threat which the seriously misguided Minister of Agriculture might pose to the landscape in the near future. It wasn't difficult, since the novel's scenario was overtaken by reality almost every day. If I wrote about an urban fox, suddenly reports of fox infestation in London were everywhere. If I created a farm which employed illegal immigrants to pick potatoes, suddenly the media were full of stories about the very same phenomenon. My minister, I decided, as the row about building on the green belt built up, was going to be in charge of turning Suffolk into a giant patio. The major problem with this scenario was that the way things were going, there was a real danger that it would be a reality before the book was due to be published in May 2004. The minor problem was the language which this harpy should use to make her speeches. I was too far away from Westminster to be able to catch the echo of the government's hideous circumlocutions.

I took heart from John Frankenheimer, quoted in his obituary: 'Keep putting one foot in front of the other, keep showing up, and you can turn it around.' At least, unlike Frankenheimer, I wasn't a drunk. My fear of degenerating into a sozzled ex-pat faded; surely if I had the ability to take to the bottle, it would have shown itself while I was dragging myself around on crutches for eight weeks straight.

Margaret invited me to dinner, having persuaded Roger to come too, and to drive through Orriule to collect me on his way. She and her husband lived in a gorgeous house in a village on the Gave, a few doors away from the French friend who introduced them to the region. The main building is painted a rich, peachy pink, very like the colour of the Beverley Hills Hotel, and the LA theme is strengthened by the giant palms in the courtyard on either side of the front door.

Peter, her husband, is a sculptor, and was an art teacher. They've lived in the Béarn for ten years, very successfully.

One of their barns has become his studio. Peter gets up late, and takes their dogs for a long walk in the nearby forest, then comes home for an early supper and starts work in the evening, finishing in the small hours. Their daughter lives in London, and their household is completed by a shifting population of dogs and cats, mostly abandoned, like the new puppies which Peter rescued while out walking. Henri Cat was probably a survivor of the same custom.

Sometimes, Peter and Margaret take a day off to walk in the high mountains, or even drive over the Spanish border for a change of scenery. Margaret is an animation artist, and occasionally goes home to London for a few weeks when a well-paid job comes in. They have a few close friends, which is all they want, and, apart from Margaret's attendance at the French class, they avoid the ex-pat community.

Peter seemed to want to talk about the creative process, something I hate doing because I never feel comfortable at the level of self-importance you need to reach to have this conversation. Also, I feel superstitious about examining my own mind too closely, in case too much analysis kills the whole system. Plus, I lack the requisite tradition. Writers don't often talk about their work that way. In fact, writers, as Douglas Adams once observed, are a bit like rare birds who're going extinct because they never meet members of the same species. Perhaps this is why so many of my friends are visual artists, whose culture is much more sociable. As a conversational hostage, I mentioned the difficulty I was having in getting the politicians' jargon right.

'Which politician do you hate most?' Peter demanded. Spoiled for choice, I thought for a while, realizing that I didn't actually hate the politicians, just what they were allowing to happen to our country. Finally, I nominated Robin Cook. Loftily, Peter announced that I obviously didn't know enough about New Labour to write about them. Ten seconds later, he revealed that he'd never heard of Alistair Darling, which was ironic since he bore him a slight resemblance.

Later, Peter brought down his work in progress. He works in found metal, making animals out of oil drums, sardine tins, paint cans, typewriter spares and old tractor panels. They're strong, witty pieces, and sell steadily through a couple of galleries in America. He was working on a stork with a blue body and red wings, another piece full of energy and humour. It had been devised so that it could be disassembled, by separating the long neck and head from the body, and fitted into the largest standard box which the French post office would accept. Thus packed, it would be posted to San Antonio. Margaret would write instructions, complete with Ikea-style diagrams, to help the gallery reassemble the sculpture when it arrived.

More Visitors

Since I wasn't fully mobile, I had to accept some animal company. Henri Cat was in the kitchen every day, so in the end I gave him his own dinner dish on the window sill. Taking my cue from the Birdman of Alcatraz, I became the Catwoman of Orriule. First I got him to take a titbit from my hand. Then I threw a little caress in with the titbit. Then I persuaded him to walk cautiously onto my lap. Finally, he allowed me to pick him up. It took about three weeks.

At dusk the garden was still alive with crickets, and Piglet delighted in bringing them in to chase them all over the sitting room in the evening, which meant that when I hopped sleepily towards the coffee in the morning, a large grasshopper would often leap out from under the sofa and cling to one of my legs. This was fine when they grabbed the plaster cast, but on the good leg, their grip could be as painful as a scratch from the cat's claws.

One evening a bat flew into the house, got confused in the narrow hallway and couldn't find its way out. Normally, my plan for bats involves catching them with a fishing net or a swimming-pool skimmer and ejecting them gently, but with only one leg to stand on that was impossible.

Hopefully, I left the front door open until midnight, and thought I saw the bat fly out. Wrong. Next morning, I noticed something hanging from a beam in the hall. It looked like a seed pod or a giant beetle, but when I examined it more closely I saw that it was the bat, hanging upside down with the claws on its wings neatly hooked on a groove in the wood. It was sound asleep. The leathery wings enfolded its head and body completely. Later in the day, it woke up and had a wash, grooming its little furry front like a very tiny inverted cat. Amandine said she had never seen a bat at such close quarters. The housework went to hell for half an hour while we watched it.

The bat stayed for two days, by which time somebody had told me that it was a young one looking for a place to found a new colony. I was getting worried I would soon find twenty of its friends hanging from the beams in the hall. However, when Roger dropped me home after dinner with Margaret and Peter, it was zooming around the hall and up and down the stairs so indignantly that it seemed as if it had only just realized its mistake. After a couple of false starts it managed to fly over my head and out into the night.

High Culture

By the end of the month, la Maysou was empty again, having given almost a hundred London school children the

chance to have extra French tuition not just in France, but
in their teacher's family home. They had had lessons in the
morning, then spent the afternoon enjoying themselves on
the river, on the beach or in the mountains. The donkeys had
been pampered and the village had rung with curious young
English voices.

Zoe has a new boyfriend. He is a young banker, the
nephew of Babi who stages concerts at her house in the hills.
The announcement threw Annabel into a quandary. She
was ecstatic that her daughter seemed to be serious, not just
about a Frenchman, but about a Béarnais, but anxious that
the seriousness might lead to a wedding, and the wedding
to a reception and a wedding reception to a party of such
proportions it would bankrupt the bride's family.

Matthieu, Zoe's new boyfriend, is tall, brown-haired and
fair-skinned; he looks more English than Zoe herself, who
is as dark, slim and Mediterranean in looks as her mother is
fair, rounded and an English rose. Matthieu's mother is one
of twelve brothers and sisters, and his grandmother, who
lives in an imposing chateau overlooking the Gave, is also
one of twelve. When all the cousins are counted, it could be
a big wedding. If a wedding is on the cards. Zoe is giving
nothing away, but she seems to have a plan. I pretended I
knew nothing and tried to think of soothing things to say.

With the wheelchair in the back of Annabel's car, we
went to see a Russian folk ensemble perform at Babi's rustic
concert hall, which is at a place called Tilh, high in the hills
to the east. It was here that Zoe and Matthieu met. Babi is
a tall, elegant woman, the only person I saw all year wearing
kitten heels. Until recently she was a music agent in Paris.
Now, with her husband and the help of their six children,
she runs an arts and music society from Tilh, putting on
concerts several times a year. 'The happiest and most daring
of initiatives,' according to a local writer.

The concert hall is a huge former barn, attached to the house in which Babi and her family live. The situation is stunning, almost at the edge of an escarpment which projects south from the main mass of hills. One of the local people described it to me as a *'grande bastide'*. Strictly speaking, a *bastide* is something fortified, usually a town, so perhaps there was once a military building here, and soldiers patrolled the level ground in front of the house, now a neat lawn, bordered with roses, with a breathtaking view.

The concert hall is like something in a glossy magazine, with its exposed beams, whitewashed walls and eccentric stone staircases. An audience of about three hundred can fit in there, and after the performance the children and their cousins run in to set up trestle tables. Everyone turns around their chairs and a supper is served. That night, Babi had booked a group of Russian performers who were on their way home from the annual music festival at Oloron-Ste-Marie.

The stage in the bar wasn't big enough for the dancers, so a bigger stage was built on the lawn, the chairs were brought outside and everyone prayed for the rain to hold off. It was more than a little bizarre to watch the standard export package of Russian culture, the dancers leaping into their *gopak* and *trepak*, the singers with their scarlet lipstick and false plaits, the musicians strumming their balalaikas, all with a background of grey clouds swirling over the distant Pyrenees. The swallows were flying so low their wings almost brushed the grass. Annabel was nervous, knowing that half the audience were probably Matthieu's relatives, and were assessing us critically, wondering what sort of people were threatening to join their family.

A Leg to Stand On

The following week, Roger took me to the first great celebration in Saliès, the Piperadère. Impressive as this is, it is only a dress-rehearsal for the town's main festival, the Fête du Sel in September. In the spring, Saliès had woken up from its genteel hibernation with a will and was now gay with window boxes full of flowers and bustling with tourists.

The Piperadère lasts only one evening, when a giant frying pan, so heavy that six men are needed to lift it, is dragged out of storage and used to make enough *piperade* for four hundred people. Marquees are put up in the main square and its nearby streets, sheltering long tables, a live band and a dance floor. A bar and a serving point had been set up on every corner, and the revellers all collected their five-course dinners, slapped into plastic trays like giant airline meals, and managed to buy their wine, all in about half an hour. At least, it seemed like no time to me, grounded on the sidelines by my plaster.

Since the streets are pretty narrow, people were soon standing on their chairs to dance, and finally dancing on the tables. This embarrassed Roger severely. 'I'm glad you've got a broken leg,' he joked. 'You'd join them otherwise, wouldn't you?'

One of the most popular rugby songs was about *piper-ade*, but not because it is supposed to be the breakfast of champions. The song concerns a man who's been out drinking and who comes home and wakes his wife up and asks her to make him a *piperade*. Well, that's the polite way to read the lyrics. '*Fais moi un piperade!*' goes the first line of the chorus. The next few lines of the chorus are all the same and a bit shorter, '*Fais moi un pipe!*' This means 'Give me a blow job!'

I guessed that Roger had not appreciated this dimension of regional culture. It seemed best to let sleeping *piperades* lie.

By the end of the month, there were a lot of long faces among the International Club. The stock market had nosedived, and although every day brought more pundits predicting that the bear market had bottomed out, every new dawn brought tidings of fresh losses. Since many of the British ex-pats were retired people whose savings had been invested in stocks and shares, a mood of utter despair settled in as their pensions began to dwindle below subsistence levels. Those who still had pensions. There were many who had joyfully taken early retirement a few years ago, only to fall victim to the Equitable Life collapse. Now they commiserated grimly with the neighbours who had seemed so much luckier only a year before but had been made as destitute as they were. Having very few shares, I could maintain a philosophical attitude.

Recipes

Piperade

Piperade is one of the keynote dishes of Basque cuisine, a redolent amalgam of eggs and peppers served as a supper dish or a starter. It is absolutely nothing like scrambled egg. I hate to disagree with Elizabeth David, who first put this notion about and thereby turned generations off the dish, but it isn't. In fact, most of what she has to say about *piperade* is regrettably characteristic of many British food writers who typically spend a weekend in Biarritz in a hurry and think they've done enough to touch base with one of the world's great cuisines. If you make a *piperade* in lumpy, scrambled-egg style, it just turns watery and unpleasant. The other great lie about piperade is that it's like ratatouille. Not really.

Piperade should be smooth and rich, like thick, dark-red cream with shreds of sweet pepper. It's almost always served over a thick slice of Bayonne ham, but is almost equally good, and acceptable to vegetarians, poured over a chunk of bread which has been drizzled with olive oil and lightly toasted. The choice of peppers is up to you; personally, I like an all-red or red-and-yellow piperade, because it's sweeter and prettier, but if you prefer the spicy combination of red and green peppers, you have tradition on your side. There is even a version made only with the sweet green *piments* of the Landes.

Serves 4 as a starter

1 onion
olive oil or fat from some ham or bacon
1 red pepper
1 pepper of another colour
1 clove of garlic
500 g (1 lb 2 oz) fresh, skinned tomatoes or *chair de tomates*,
    finely chopped
6 large fresh eggs
salt and pepper
4 slices Bayonne ham, or toast

Peel and chop the onion – you want it finely chopped, and if you're feeling lazy you can shred it in your blender. Put the oil or fat into a heavy-bottomed frying pan over a low heat, and let the onion sweat until it's transparent. Definitely no browning.

Deseed the peppers, slice and reserve some slices for decoration if you like. Chop the rest into fine dice about the same size as the pieces of onion. Add the chopped peppers to the pan and continue to cook on a low heat until they are soft.

Crush the clove of garlic, add to the pan and cook another 5 minutes. Then add the tomato, and continue to cook until you have a red mush with no visible liquid.

Beat the eggs well and pour them into the pan. Keep the heat low, and keep stirring the whole mixture until the eggs are completely blended with the pepper and tomato mush, and cooked to a smooth, creamy consistency. Season to taste with salt and pepper. Place a slice of ham or toast on each plate and pour the piperade over it. Some cooks like to grill the ham first, some prefer it cold.

Axoa

I swear this spicy meat stew was the forerunner of chilli con carne. Think about it. The Basques got to the new world first. They grabbed the exotic hot peppers and added them to their traditional meat stews; then the Mexicans added the beans and created a one-pot meal ideal for cowboys. Subtract the beans, and there's your *axoa*.

Axoa is usually made with meat from a shoulder of veal. The better the cut you use, the tenderer the *axoa* will be. If you have to use ready-chopped stewing veal (a last resort) it may include tougher meat from the shin, in which case it will need to cook for longer.

Serves 8

2 large white onions
3 cloves of garlic
2 red peppers
2 green peppers, or 10 *piments*
1 *espelette* pepper, or fresh red chilli to taste
1.5 kg (3½ lb) veal
2 tbsp olive oil or duck fat
1 *bouquet garni*, or bay leaf, thyme and parsley

Peel and chop the onion and the garlic. Deseed and chop the peppers. Cut the meat into small cubes, about the size of sugar cubes.

In a heavy-bottomed casserole, heat the oil or fat over a medium flame and brown the meat quickly, stirring to make sure it is sealed on all sides. Then add the onion, garlic and peppers and mix with the meat. If you have used a good cut of veal, then add the *bouquet garni* and allow to cook briskly for 7 minutes, then slowly for another 7 minutes, then cover and leave to simmer for a final 7 minutes more. If you're using stewing veal, don't try this; cook for 5 minutes, then add the herbs and enough stock or water to cover the meat and simmer, uncovered, for an hour, stirring occasionally.

Axoa shouldn't be watery, so if there is too much liquid in the casserole when the meat is cooked, carefully pour it off. Transfer the red-white-and-green stew to a serving dish. Traditionally *axoa* is served with boiled or sautéed potatoes. You can also cook the potatoes in the same pot, adding them, cut into 1in chunks, for the last 15 minutes of cooking.

Tuna *Kaskarote*

Serves 6

700 g (1 lb 9 oz) ripe tomatoes
7 piments or 1 green pepper
2 red peppers
2 onions
2 cloves garlic
olive oil for frying
salt and pepper
a handful of parsley
1 bay leaf
2 branches of thyme
1 tsp *espelette* purée, or a good pinch of dried *espelette* or chili
6 steaks of fresh tuna
flour for dusting

Skin the tomatoes, discard the seeds and chop into quarters. Deseed the peppers and slice across into strips. Peel and chop the onion and garlic. Put a little oil in a large sauté pan and gently cook the onions, garlic and peppers for about

15 minutes, until they are soft and the onion is transparent. Add the tomatoes, the seasoning and the herbs and spices, and cook for another 5 minutes.

Dust the tuna steaks with flour and sauté them gently in oil in another pan, turning to make sure both surfaces are sealed. When the fish is nearly cooked – probably in about 15 minutes – slide the steaks into the pan with the vegetables and allow them to cook together for 15 minutes more, until the fish and sauce have thoroughly exchanged flavours. Pick out the herbs, and transfer to a serving dish, or serve from the sauté pan.

August

Empress Eugénie – perfect
Romantic icon

La Mer

No race on earth caricatures itself as magnificently as the French on the beach in August. Those who know only the international meat rack of the Riviera have never seen the full, adorable absurdity of a French family enjoying their *grandes vacances*, complete with candy-striped beach huts, shrimping nets, muscular lifeguards, yelping lap dogs, daft beach games and matelot sweaters for everyone.

The phenomenon reaches perfection on the Atlantic coast, all the way from Brittany to the Côte Basque, where the great ocean rollers crash on the endless silver sands and the whole scene sparkles with magical pale light reflected from the ocean. In the normal way, I would have been right there jumping the surf with them, but this year, with my ankle in plaster, I had to sit the summer out in various beach bars and watch the fun.

The fathers lead the way, striding out for the sand with the same show of authority as they had put on in their offices only the day before. On that first weekend of summer holidays, which the French have designated *le grand exit*, the breadwinners haven't yet slowed down. The fathers, strutting determinedly towards the beach, irresistibly recall Jacques Tati in *M. Hulot's Holiday*. Even if they're short, fat and bossy, whereas the great comic actor of the Fifties was tall, gangling and apologetic, you know they are all equally vulnerable to the slapstick accidents of a day at the seaside, and in the fullness of time their dignity will be punctured by the nip of a crab or the unwary step on a slimy bit of sea-weed.

After the father come the children, skipping with excite-ment at the multiple treats ahead: swimming! ice-cream! Papa! Finally, the mothers dawdle at the rear with the designer towels, the coordinated beach mats, the bats and balls, the fishing nets, the suncream and the rest of the family impedimenta. While the children scamper off to the water's edge, the mothers stare around disdainfully, flicking sand off their T-shirts, fiddling with the straps of their costumes, thinking up a morning's worth of little services which they can ask their husbands to perform for them.

The French beach is, of course, regulated. The lifeguards assess the sea each morning and stick their flags into the sand to mark out the safe swimming area. Swim only between the flags, please. We cannot be responsible for people swimming outside the flags, and at the first breath of wind we'll be out there with our whistles, calling in any offenders. What is the point of being a lifeguard if you can't puff out your chest like a Michelin man and blast antisocial elements out of the water with your whistle?

One scorching Sunday at the height of summer in Biar-ritz, when the tide was in and the narrow strip of beach not under water was already so crowded you could hardly open a copy of *Elle* without casting a shadow on the next-door sunbather, all the lifeguards suddenly ran down to the sea and whistled every swimmer ashore. We crowded fearfully onto the sand, wondering what drama was unfolding.

It was, of course, the drama of the French nanny state. A helicopter flew into the bay and hovered over the sea about a hundred metres out. A man in a red wetsuit jumped from the helicopter into the water. A loudspeaker crackled into life, informing the crammed beach that there would now be a life-saving demonstration. Two men in black wetsuits jumped from the helicopter into the water. The helicopter lowered a cradle, and the man in the red wet suit was manoeuvred into it, after which all three men were winched aboard. In the doorway of the helicopter, the men in black mimed a resuscitation drill. Then the helicopter flew away and the lifeguards informed the bathers that they could go back into the water. Instead of being annoyed that their afternoon's pleasure had been spoiled, the swimmers and the sunbathers nodded to each other with appreciation.

Lifeguarding is a regular summer job for medical students and police cadets. Every beach has its Baywatch station, usually a concrete bunker not unlike the lookout points built in World War II. Outside is a blackboard displaying the weather forecast and the water temperature, and a flagpole on which the official status of the sea that day is signified by the colour of the flag. Green flag – the sea is calm, bathing is permitted. Yellow flag – the sea is a bit rough, bathing may be undertaken with caution. Red flag – the sea is definitely rough and bathing is not advised.

There is some point to this on the coast to the north of Biarritz, where the long straight sweep of golden sand runs for miles where the Landes meets the sea. This may be one of the best surf beaches in the world, but it has lethal rip-tides and when the wind rises suddenly it whips the waves up to a gigantic size. In the same afternoon you can wade out into friendly breakers which are hardly bigger than Shetland ponies and, a couple of hours later, stagger ashore in terror leaving rollers the size of houses thundering at your heels.

There are other reasons why a beach on the Côte Basque might be glad of a lifeguard. One day in an earlier summer my friend Gill and I had been enjoying my favourite beach in Biarritz, called the Plage de Port-Vieux. It's also the smallest, a little crescent of sand between two spurs of rock, where the waves are always tame and the water usually crystal clear. If you want some excitement, you can swim out around to the little islet called the Rocher de la Vierge or take a mask and watch the fish darting around the caves hollowed out of the red-brown cliffs. When the tide is right, the most daring can dive off the rocks into the turquoise depths. Port-Vieux also has a nice little bar, overlooking the water from a headland.

Tiny as the beach was, we noticed that it had three life-guards. It's too small for a proper Baywatch station, so the guards were hard to miss, three muscular young men lolling on their towels with their flippers stuck blade-first into the sand in front of them.

'Why do they need three of them?' Gill wondered. I looked around at the other people on the beach. Apart from us, the average age of the swimmers – even the swimmers who were 800 metres out, braving the open sea – was about seventy. Since Port-Vieux slopes a bit too steeply for small children, it's also the beach which the local people prefer, and the local people in the South-West enjoy the greatest longevity of the whole country. Nutritionists call this the 'French paradox' and do not understand how longevity is compatible with a lifetime diet of confit and red wine.

Sometimes, however, the French take their respect for the sea to levels that the British find ridiculous. One day, at a small beach south of Biarritz at the end of the season, the lifeguards had decided to work short hours and posted a notice informing the kind clientele that they would not be on duty until 11 a.m. It was a cool morning, but not breezy and the sea was calm. Up strode a French father, his striped sweater tossed around his shoulders, all ready to supervise the swimming of his two sons of ten or so. Where was the lifeguard? he demanded of the owner of the cafe near the flagpole. She pointed to the notice. No lifeguard until 11 a.m. But the flag wasn't flying, he protested. They'd put the flag up at eleven, she promised him. The father looked anxiously at the sea. What was one supposed to do about swimming, with no flag flying? The cafe owner shrugged. 'What do you think?' he asked her at last. 'If there *was* a lifeguard on duty, what colour flag would he run up?' Clearly, swimming without a flag was an impossibility.

Fortunately for me, there were plenty of beach bars. There's hardly an inch of the Côte Basque which isn't overlooked by some appealing establishment offering tapas and cocktails, or, if it's oriented to the surfing clientele, *frites* and beer. Our favourites were Txamara, overlooking the tiny port at Guéthary, and the Blue Cargo, just south of Biarritz at a one-time village called Ilbarritz. We liked it because it was modern and stylish, with a big canvas canopy, like a sail, shading rough wooden tables.

In the daytime, Blue Cargo was just a nicely chilled beach bar. By night, it was one of the most popular gay bars on the coast. This was not saying much, but since Andrew and Geoff had been more than ready to leave the London gay scene behind, they weren't disappointed to find that Biarritz had little to offer beyond a whiff of nostalgia. Inland, gay life was rare. Willow introduced them to a gay friend who lived in the Chalosse, and somebody knew two former airline stewards over near Orthez. That was it.

On the landward side, Ilbarritz is now less of a village than a golf course, which has the pleasant side effect of leaving the foreshore almost unravaged by building and the beach in a natural condition. The curve of the bay is shallow, but enough to break the surf down from majestic rollers as high as a car to waves of more jumpable proportions. The sand when dry is fine and silvery; when wet, it's firm, greyish and ridged by the sucking tide. Rising here and there are just enough red rocks to lend drama to the eternal horizontal of sea and sky, and keep children amused all day hunting for crabs.

I know I played on beaches like this in England as a child; I know that those beaches are now mobbed all summer, littered with plastic and almost devoid of marine life. Geoff's parents, who had come over from Somerset to visit him, said the same about the countryside around Maysounabe, with its flowering meadows and woodland. It reminded them of England, twenty years ago.

The It-Girl Who Owed It All To Her Dentist

The seaside holiday was invented, or at least perfected, at Biarritz, in the middle of the nineteenth century. The new-hatched holiday industry swiftly transformed what was once a small whaling port into the most glamorous resort in Europe. The town owes its status, its grand buildings and its decades of prosperity to the Empress Eugénie, a Victorian It-girl who spent the happiest days of her life playing on its golden sands as a child.

'Empress of France!' wrote a seriously biased historian. 'What a dazzling dream for this Spanish woman, with her generous heart and a soul burning with noble and refined feelings, always irreproachable in spite of living in outrageous times!'

Eugénie was born a countess, the daughter of a minor Spanish nobleman, the Count of Montijo. Her family lived in Andalucía, and to save their children from the burning heat of summer there, they sent Eugénie, her siblings and her duenna, north to the green hills and cool breezes of the Côte Basque.

Beautiful, stylish, well connected among Catholic royal houses but scarcely rich, Eugénie was pretty much on the shelf by her mid-twenties, by which time she, and her ambitious mother, had moved to Paris. Eugénie had an American dentist, who introduced her to another of his patients, the Emperor Napoleon III. Just then the Emperor was desperate for a suitably noble and Catholic wife.

When they married in 1853, Napoleon III was nearly forty-five, and, despite being short, tubby and disfigured by a goatee, a confirmed philanderer. The product of Napoleon I's relentless nepotism, he was the son of the first emperor's younger brother and his step-daughter Hortense, child of the Empress Josephine from her first marriage. He went into politics, was elected President of the French Republic, then gambled on France's lingering nostalgia for imperial glory and called a referendum, as a result of which he too was adopted as Emperor.

Napoleon III found himself ruling a prosperous but unstable country, and was in urgent need of a wife and heirs, especially after Queen Victoria scotched his attempt to marry one of her nieces.

Eugénie was not, at first, a popular choice. In London, *The Times* reported sarcastically: 'We learn with some amusement that this romantic event in the annals of the French Empire has called forth the strongest opposition, and provoked the utmost irritation. The Imperial family, the Council of Ministers, and even the lower coteries of the palace or its purlieus, all affect to regard this marriage as an amazing humiliation.' The *Thunderer* then went on to point out, in Eugénie's defence, that Napoleon III probably wasn't even a real Bonaparte, but the son of one of his mother's lovers.

Eugénie, however, was a star. She was born to be an empress, and if she had lived in modern times her genius for being fabulous in public would have gone over well with *Hello!* magazine. Not until Jacqueline Kennedy would the world see a consort who expressed the spirit of her age so confidently as a public figure and a patron of all the decorative arts.

With her smooth dark hair, centre-parted under her diamond crown, her large eyes, oval face and pale complexion, Eugénie was a perfect icon for the Romantic era, and she set about imposing her opulent style on the world. Having a tiny waist and pale, sloping shoulders, she looked wonderful in a crinoline and was an ideal clothes horse for the couturier Worth, whom she soon appointed court designer.

She lost no time in dragging her husband down to Biarritz, where he too fell in love with its rugged red cliffs and golden beaches. They built a magnificent palace on the point of the largest bay, which was soon surrounded by the Victorian-Gothic fantasy villas of the nobility and gentry. The humble whalers' cottages almost disappeared under new terraces and shops. The child who once paddled in the rock pools below the cliffs had grown into a woman whose nostalgia for those innocent pleasures created the modern concept of fun in the sun.

However magnificent their summer residence, the Imperial couple were restless and travelled constantly, perhaps inspired by the romance of the Three Musketeers. The fact that Biarritz was a long way from the actresses of the Comédie-Française, and from her husband's official mistress in Paris, was an added attraction for Eugénie. She was a fine horsewoman, and as athletic as her husband was fat and lazy. The medicinal hot springs of the Pyrenees soon lured them inland, where they went on mountain excursions guided by local smugglers and revelled in a landscape as dramatic as the dreams of the romantic poets.

As a result, the grand hand of Eugénie can be seen all over

the South-West corner of France. The court doctor took charge of the salt springs in Saliès-de-Béarn, and raised a candy-striped Moorish-style spa building above them. The tiny mountain village of Eaux-Bonnes is almost swamped in grand Victorian villas and the formal gardens designed by the imperial landscaper. The lovely hamlet of Sare dedicated a chapel to Eugénie, and on the little peak of La Rhune, a sacred mountain to the Basques, a special trail was laid down for her visit in 1859.

Pau was almost completely redeveloped in the Imperial era, when the great sweep of the Boulevard du Pyrénées was thrown over the town's huddled hills, leading around a line of grand new villas to the foot of the revamped chateau. Up in the Landes, another village blessed with hot springs renamed itself Eugénie-les-Bains and laid out a formal garden, with fountains and waterfalls, to restore the energies of the Imperial couple on their long trek to and from Paris.

The legacy of spacious villas at Eugénie-les-Bains was eventually taken over by one of the great French chefs, Michel Guérard, and his wife, Christine, pioneers of the *cuisine minceur*, who developed the entire village as a shrine to health-conscious gastronomy. All the same, it looks just another little Landais village, and as you approach down a meandering lane between the maize fields it is not until you're almost at the first house that you notice that instead of the normal sleepy dilapidation, every building is a shop, a restaurant or a fitness centre, painted up to the eaves and wired for credit-card transactions.

When she was a child, a gypsy fortune-teller told Eugénie that 'an eagle will carry you to the heavens, then drop you'. For all its brilliance, her life was scarred with the trials and tragedies that nowadays seem to add that essential note of poignancy to a diva's CV. Eugénie met them all head-on with persistent courage.

Napoleon III's rule lasted less than twenty years. He was deposed towards the end of the Franco-Prussian War and the couple fled to England, where he died shortly afterwards, in 1873. Eugénie's pregnancies were difficult, and the couple had only one child, a son, called Napoléon Eugène. He went to South Africa as an observer with the British army, and was killed in a battle with the Zulus in 1879.

Eugénie's palace in Biarritz burned down, and the ruin was demolished by the government of the Third Republic of France in 1881, which also sold off the palace grounds for building land. A new edifice was built, and was gutted by fire in its turn. The present Hôtel du Palais, a low-rise pink building whose resemblance to a slab of cake is only enhanced by its white Gothic stonework, was built on the site in 1905 and was never anything but a commercial establishment, though it is an elegant spot for cocktails.

Biarritz was all the rage in the Belle Époque, or the Naughty Nineties as the British called the sunset of the century. The town heaved with English pleasure-seekers, Russian émigrés and Italian aristocracy, and many exotic villas in the fin de siècle and art nouveau style were built on the grounds of the former palace. While the resort she had created continued to be Europe's most fashionable summer destination, Eugénie lived quietly in Farnborough in Hampshire. At the age of ninety-four, she decided she wanted to see Spain again before she died, and passed away during the trip, in Madrid. She is buried with her husband and son at St Michael's Abbey in Farnborough.

A Girl's Best Friend Is Her Best Friend

Finally, Gill came out, just for a week. She gets three weeks holiday a year. When we've spoken on the phone over the past nine months, she's been yelping with stress if she's in the office, and catatonic with exhaustion if she's at home. She runs the finance department of a group of health clubs, a glossy business which has grown fast. Her department is where all the bucks stop. She came alone, because her partner, a musician, couldn't be persuaded to leave London in case he was booked for a session, and her company immediately cheered me.

Dr Suleiman was not pleased with my ankle; the fibula which he set so carefully has moved a millimetre out of alignment, probably because I've been kidding myself that I really can garden on one leg. He swapped the plaster for a splint, which makes me a bit more mobile, but no way, he said, can I walk on the injury before the end of August. So Willow and Tony fetched Gill from the airport, Amandine made her bed and Annabel took me shopping.

Being helpless is an experience I haven't had for a long time. Not since Chloe was a new-born baby, and I was wondering how we were going to live on my salary of £125 a week, in a damp basement flat from which the landlady was trying to evict us, with no help from either of our families. Cometh the hour, cometh the friends — thank Heaven. Andrew looks at me sometimes and mutters 'so brave' but when I compare these days with those, a broken ankle in a strange land doesn't seem so bad.

We had planned a party for my birthday. It seems I know forty people who're prepared to come to Orriule if promised drinks, dinner and the chance to meet new friends, though for the antisocial the last of those was no incentive. With time on my hands, I had hand-painted invitations and, with Annabel and Margaret to help me, I had photocopied maps. I had also begun to marinate the ingredients for Marie's sangria. This is nothing like the watery thirst-quencher served up beside Spanish swimming pools. A Béarnais sangria is a dark, spicy drink with a kick like a cow, and it's a favourite to start a big celebration.

However, nobody could fix the weather, and they certainly would have done if they could by then. Each day seemed to be more dismal than the last. Grey was as good as it got, most of the time. Every now and then, I called the recorded forecast from the weather station at Pau, on which the meteorologists had been getting increasingly desperate. '*Bonjour.* This is François at the weather station at Pau with the forecast for the region for the next twenty-four hours. *Nouvelle désolation . . .*' The question was now not whether it would rain, but only how much.

If it rained on the day of the party, forty people would not fit into Maison Bergez. I made phone calls to people who had those little plastic pavilions which are meant to keep the sun off a garden picnic, but would surely be just as good at keeping the rain off a buffet. For the big day, however, François's forecast was cautiously optimistic. Possibility of a clear spell. Wow.

Yes, I am a total Mrs Dalloway, I love giving a party, even in the rain with a broken ankle. This doesn't always go down well in the world of books, where a party is a networking opportunity or nothing. People like me, who're always ready to put on a new dress and go out shining just for the sake of it, don't fit the mould.

Nor does liking a party fit well with long-hours London life. I had not been able to celebrate my birthday this way for years. In August, most of my friends are away, and those who aren't are simply too busy to get anywhere before 9 p.m., by which time they would be too shattered to enjoy themselves. The city is huge and travelling around it gets more demanding and more dangerous all the time. Relaxing in good company is a challenge in London; mostly, the best you get are occasional opportunities to apply alcohol to the pain of living.

Then I have all these theories about parties. One of them is that it is actually easier to give a buffet for forty than a dinner party for eight, because you simply cook large quantities of simple food and let people get on with it, instead of messing about with garnishes and cooking times and changes of plates and the possibility of people offending each other and the whole event going pear-shaped. For a larger party, all you need to do is organize yourself to cook ahead.

I made a big tomato tart – my vegetable plot, by now, was heaving with tomatoes and the challenge was to pick them before the giant brown slugs got them. These slugs look like mobile turds, decorated with orange frills around their flanges. They're so monstrous that they frighten Piglet, who cautiously tiptoes round them when they meet. The hedgehog, who appears from behind the catalpa trees to trundle about at dusk, doesn't even attempt to eat them. Since I had started writing about Suffolk for *Wild Weekend*, I had discovered that the population of hedgehogs in East Anglia has declined by 50 per cent since 1991, due to the destruction of their habitat by intensive farming.

Before the party, I also made a red onion *tarte Tatin*, a salad of green beans and yellow peppers and a dish of lentils with mint and garlic. I ordered cakes from M. Charrier, including his *Mediaevale*; this is pretty much like a paving slab made of rich dark chocolate mousse, and it had become an instant legend in Ossages since I had taken one to Tony's birthday dinner a few weeks earlier. Finally, with Gill's help, I added cold spit-roasted chicken with tarragon, an oriental salad with marinated pork and a big dish of prawns. With potatoes, green salad, bread and cheese, the menu was sorted.

Gordon came over to spruce up the garden. He had been
a really great friend, despite having spent the summer going
from one *fête* to another and doing justice to the aperitifs.
He was still living in a caravan, with electricity at last, and
the purchase of the property at Bellocq had finally come
through, but Fiona and the children went home in June,
and he was angry about it. Every now and then, I floated
the suggestion that she had crashed into a depression, and
that this wasn't an unreasonable reaction to having no roof
over her head, no table to put the children's food on and
no chance of getting back their life savings from the tree-
fern disaster, all in a non-stop downpour of rain. Since
Fiona could only speak a few words of French, professional
help wasn't an option. I didn't blame her for baling, but
he did.

While they were living in the caravan, the children were
out on the street every night, which Gordon saw as a good,
healthy way of life. Fiona, for all her language skills were
limited, could see that the only other children on the street
in a law-abiding village like Bellocq were the ones from
other marginalized families. Cam's constant companions
were two much older boys. One of them looked after his
mother, who was a paraplegic. She had been abandoned by
her family and shunned by the villagers, who left the child
to care for her and his younger sister as best he could. The
three of them either hung about by the river side in Orthez
with young toughs of almost twenty, or sat in and played
violent video games all night. When their home was only a
tiny caravan, it was impossible to keep the children off the
street.

Gordon had a new French friend, another *marginalisé*, a
big, good-natured, open-faced man who had been promised
a job as a bouncer at a casino in Dax, but it was always going
to start the next week. Meanwhile, the two of them were

making short work of small building jobs in the foreign community, and the owner of the little *bar-auberge* in Bellocq was thinking of getting them to manage the place when she went over to Montpellier to see her family. Gordon was trying to talk himself into seeing this as a great business opportunity.

Amazingly, François in Pau was right about the weather. The day of the party was dry. Willow came to lend a hand, and my two good mates transformed the garden of Maison Bergez into an open-air pleasure dome. Remembering the lobster challenge at Christmas, they set up tables covered in lacy cloths under the trees. Cushions were tucked invitingly into the hammock and the bar was set up outside the kitchen window.

Roger arrived with his French girlfriend, Reine, who was slim, blonde and sparky. The widow of an artist, she lived in St-Jean-de-Luz and spent the weekends with Roger, either at his house in Saliès or his studio on the sea at the surf resort of Hossegor. She regarded me as a threat to be seen off – in the most charming possible way, of course. This she tried to accomplish by darting to my side every time an unaccompanied man arrived at the party and demanding to know if this was my *petit ami*. Each time I explained that I had no *petit ami* and didn't actually want one at this point in my life, but she seemed not to understand. Reine was seventysomething, so from her viewpoint a luscious young fiftysomething like myself was obviously on the pull.

It must have been a good party. We encouraged the stragglers to leave sometime around 2 a.m. The next day the friend who stayed over staggered down to the bottle bank by the pottery and was there for half an hour, disposing of the evidence.

Meanwhile, I had the childish pleasure of opening

presents and the adult satisfaction of receiving compliments. People rang to say thank you, then casually asked for a recipe. The most popular dish was the sticky pork salad, which had simply vanished. 'I'm so glad you did all that,' said one English woman. 'That'll show the French, always going on about how we can't cook.' Marie flattered me by asking how I had cooked the potatoes, but I suspect she was just choosing safe ground on which to be nice.

Pining Away

Andy wanted to find more beaches, to show the fashion editors and photographers among his non-stop guests at Maysounabe exactly what stupendous locations they would be able to use next year. We had explored the chic, urbanized strands at St-Jean-de-Luz and Biarritz, so now it was time to venture further north, and check out the surf beaches of the Landes.

Once again, the unearthly flatness of the land and the endless kilometres of bracken, gorse and pine trees made us feel first tranquil, then sad, then peculiarly detached from the world. The coast was another kind of hallucination, with golden sand stretching to the horizon in both directions and the waves rolling in so uniformly they seemed unreal.

The Landes, just as much as Manhattan, is a monument to human ambition. It's hard to believe, since the trees and the dunes seem to stretch away to infinity without any sign of human life on them, but the landscape is entirely man-made. The name, *landes*, means simply 'moors', but don't think *Wuthering Heights*. The sense is of a desolate kind of a place overgrown with scrubby heather and gorse, but no altitude is implied. The Landes is flat. Absolutely flat. Flat as far as the eye can see. Most of the ground is covered with pine forest, and as you pass through it in a train or car the flickering light between the great tree trunks puts you in a trance. This is a man-made landscape. In fact, it's a reclaimed swamp, which explains the strange character of the endless golden beach and the endless dark forest behind it.

The River Adour was the first force to shape the Landes. In prehistoric times, dozens of mountain torrents gushed down from the Pyrenees and joined to run to the coast in a single deep channel. As the centuries passed, the river began to silt up and choke itself. Then it started to meander across the flat plain of the Landes, changing course every couple of hundred years.

The Adour was always a huge waterway and easily navigable, so it was a valuable resource to the people of the region, especially those who lived near the point where it reached the ocean. However, the river mouth was moving constantly, so no sooner was a port established and in business than the docks turned to sandbanks and the river wandered off. The towns of Bayonne, Cap Breton and Vieux Boucau all enjoyed a burst of prosperity when the Adour was flowing their way. The boats came down from the interior bringing brandy, wine, wool and salt for export, and the boats from the ocean brought cloth, fish and the treasures of the New World. Then the Adour changed its course and these flourishing ports suffered a miserable decline.

The vast plain of the Landes was nothing but a swamp and not a healthy environment. Epidemics of malaria and fevers added to the misery of the inhabitants. The region was impassable, and so became a refuge for outlaws, criminals and Protestants making for the port of La Rochelle, from which they sailed to America, no doubt feeling right at home when they got to the bayous of Louisiana. Eventually the central government decided to intervene and try to reclaim the land. In 1569, the King, Charles IX, ordered that the Adour should be tamed and Louis de Foix, the architect of the Escorial in Madrid, was hired to begin the operation.

The first phase was to fix the river mouth and stabilize the port at Bayonne. To do this, a sea wall was planned and the sand dunes, which shifted easily, were turned into solid ground. A dyke twelve metres high was built, and the dunes were anchored by sowing marram grass, known in French as '*gourbet*', which has thick, mat-forming roots. The engineer in charge, Bremontier, also ordered the inland ground to be stabilized. Seedlings of the pines, broom and gorse which are now so characteristic of the region were imported and raised under cover of brushwood. The sandy ground was perfect for these hardy species and in two years the gorse was two metres high.

It took generations of toil, but by 1867, three thousand hectares of sand dunes on the coast were covered with *gourbet*, and eighty thousand hectares of inland ground were planted with pines. The Landes problem wasn't fixed, however. There was still a large area of marsh inland.

A geological survey revealed that about fifty metres below the swamp water and the reed beds was a layer of brown limestone, material from the Pyrenees which had been washed down by the river millions of years earlier and compacted into an impermeable layer that prevented water from draining away and formed a barrier to the roots of plants.

In the days of Napoleon III and the Empress Eugénie, an engineer called Chambrelent came up with a plan to drain the marshes and plant a mixed woodland – pine again, alternated with shallow-rooted cork oaks and holm oaks. He succeeded, and the Landes was finally converted to dry land.

The conversion isn't complete, however. There are still dozens of lakes and a labyrinth of little waterways left, a unique environment which is extremely rich in wildlife. There is a little terrapin found nowhere else in the world, masses of birds and freshwater fish including eels, pike and shad.

The pines became the Landes' fortune, making the department at one time the richest in all France. They are grown not only for their timber, but also for their resin. In modern times the sap is gathered from each tree every twelve days by a process involving sulphuric acid, which doesn't damage the bark too badly. In Eugénie's time the foresters still milked the pines by slashing deep cuts in the bark, and letting the sap bleed out into a little conical pot. Théophile Gaultier found the sight so upsetting that he wrote a poem about it.

The Pine in the Landes

The only tree you see, travelling through the desert of
   the Landes
The French Sahara, dusted with white sand
Springing suddenly with dry grass and puddles of
   green water,
Is the pine, with its wounded side,
To drain it of its tears of resin,
Man, that avaricious torturer of creation
Who lives on the blood of his victims,
Has opened a great crack in its grieving trunk
Without complaint, its blood running drop by drop
The pine pours out its balm and its seething sap
And holds itself straight at the edge of the road
Like a wounded soldier who wants to die standing up.
The poet is in the Landes of the world
Even though he is unwounded and can keep his treasure
He must have a deep cut in his heart
To pour out his words, his precious golden tears.

Recipes

Sangria

Serves between 20 and 60, according to taste

6 lemons
6 oranges
2 cinnamon sticks
10 cloves
small piece – about a quarter – of a nutmeg
1 bottle of rum
1 bottle of Cointreau or Grand Marnier
1 bottle of Armagnac
6 bottles of light red wine
soda water or lemonade and sugar to taste
fruit to decorate

Two weeks before you want to drink the sangria, marinate the fruits and spices in the spirits. Cut up the lemons and oranges, pour the spirits onto them, and leave them to steep in a covered jug or jar.

When you want to make the sangria, strain the infused spirits into a large jug or bowl, add the wine and dilute to taste with soda or lemonade. It must be said that the Béarnais host may not dilute the mixture significantly at all. If your guests have a sweet tooth, stir in some sugar. Decorate with sliced red apples, orange, lemon and strawberries if you must, but all that fruit salad takes up an awful lot of room in the glass.

Tomato Tart with a Polenta Crust

This is a wonderful celebration of the tomato glut of high summer. If you're lucky enough to have the great bulging tomatoes found in gardens and markets all over southern Europe, you can make a rustic, lumpy tart with thick slices of them piled deep. If you'd like something more elegant, you can make individual tarts packed with whole cherry tomatoes, or a big tart filled with halved plum tomatoes.

This recipe is adapted from one in *Cuisine Grand-Mère*, Marie-Pierre Moine's affectionate book of traditional French home cooking. The essential principle of the dish is that the grated cheese under the tomatoes makes a barrier between the tomatoes and the pastry, and so keeps the crust crisp in spite of the juicy filling.

Polenta, or maize semolina, is every bit as typical of Gascon cooking as it is of Italian, if not more so. The maize, after all, must have travelled from Spain and through France before it reached Italy. Along with the peppers, tomatoes and chocolate, it is an integral part of the New World heritage in the cooking of the South-West.

Serves 6 as a starter, 4 as a main course

For the filling

about 800 g (1 lb 12 oz) big tasty tomatoes
salt and sugar to taste
60 g (2 oz) grated Parmesan
60 g (2 oz) grated Gruyère or other hard cheese
sprigs of thyme
olive oil

For the pastry

150 g (5 oz) plain flour, sifted
75 g (2½ oz) fine polenta
1 tsp thyme leaves
1 tbsp grated Parmesan
120 g (4 oz) cold diced butter
1 large egg
olive oil

To serve

rocket leaves
parsley and basil, or ready-made pesto

Preheat the oven to 200°C / 400°F / Gas 6. Slice the tomatoes, sprinkle lightly with salt and leave to drain in a colander.

Start the pastry either by mixing the dry ingredients, including the Parmesan, in a bowl, then rubbing in the butter, or by processing the dry ingredients briefly in a food mixer and adding the butter in small pieces. Next beat the egg and work all but a little of it into the mixture, then add enough oil to get a stiff, workable dough. Wrap in clingfilm and rest in the fridge for a short while. Butter a 28 cm (11 in) tart tin, or some small tins.

Roll out the pastry and fit it into the tart tin at about 5 mm (¼ in) thickness. The pastry will be very crumbly but don't worry if you make a bit of a bodge of getting it into the tin, it will all bond nicely in the cooking. When the tin is lined, rest it in the fridge again.

Pat the tomato slices dry on kitchen paper. Take out the chilled pastry in the tin, brush with the remaining beaten egg and prick the base with a fork, leaving a border of 1 cm (½ in) round the edge. Then sprinkle the grated cheeses evenly over the bottom, and add the sprigs of thyme. Arrange the tomato slices on top, sprinkle with sugar and a little salt, then bake for about 20 minutes, until the pastry is cooked, the cheese melted and the edges of the tomatoes slightly caramelized. If too much juice has run out of the tomatoes in cooking, carefully tip it out of the finished tart before it causes sogginess.

While the tart is cooking, whiz the rocket and parsley, mixed with the basil, in a food processor, or chop and pound in a mortar. Dribble in enough olive oil, or, if you're using ready-made pesto, dilute it with a little oil, to get a green sauce that will just pour. Drizzle the sauce over the cooked tart, and serve warm or cold.

Sticky Pork Salad with Lime Dressing

This is a Gascon take on a modern fusion dish, using local ingredients instead of some oriental ones. It also works beautifully with *magret* of duck instead of pork. The contrast between the rich, spiced, sweetish meat and the cool, crisp, aromatic salad is an unexpected delight.

Serves 6–8

For the pork

500 g (1 lb 2 oz) pork fillet
3 tsp *quatre épices* or five-spice powder
salt and pepper
2 tbsp soft brown sugar
1 tbsp lemon thyme leaves
3 shallots, peeled and finely chopped
1 *espelette* pepper or 3 large mild red chillies, deseeded and chopped
3 tbsp soy sauce
3 cloves of garlic, peeled and crushed
3 tbsp oil

Marinate the pork fillet whole in all the remaining ingredients, for at least an hour and preferably overnight. Rub the marinade in well and turn the fillet several times.

Preheat the oven to a high temperature. Put the pork on a piece of foil in a roasting tin, anoint with marinade and cook on maximum heat for 5 minutes. Then baste again, and turn down to 190°C/375°F/Gas 5. Roast the pork for a further 15 minutes, basting and turning twice. Take out of the oven, baste again and allow to cool. The outside of the meat should be a deep glossy brown. Slice into medallions when it's cold.

For the salad

2 limes
1 tsp sesame oil, plus 2 tbsp light olive, sunflower or
    grapeseed oil
2 tsp caster sugar
a pinch of salt
1 Little Gem lettuce (or half a cos or a romaine)
1 medium cucumber, peeled, seeded and sliced into fine
    batons
handful each of mint, basil and coriander leaves, left whole
4 spring onions, halved and shredded into strips
2 tbsp toasted peanuts

Juice 1 lime, and mix the juice with the oils, sugar and salt. (If you have to use salted peanuts, the salt may not be necessary.)

Slice the peel off the other lime and cut the flesh off the pith in segments. Tear up the lettuce and put in a flat salad bowl. Mix in the cucumber batons, lime segments, aromatic leaves and spring onion strips. Chill the salad until just before serving.

Toss the chilled leaves with the lime dressing. Pile the

slices of pork in the middle of the salad and glaze with a little of the leftover marinade. Sprinkle over the peanuts and serve – the meat and salad will naturally mix in the serving process.

Roast New Potatoes

Simply take a large piece of foil, lay it in a roasting tin, smear it with olive oil and sprinkle with a little sea salt. Add several branches of fresh thyme. Pile new potatoes into the centre and spread them out in an even layer. Drizzle with more oil, sprinkle with more salt and add more thyme. Seal the foil to make a cushion-shaped packet, and roast in a medium oven for about 45 minutes, until the potatoes are cooked and coloured on the under-side. To serve, simply slide the potatoes out into a serving dish, glaze with the warm oil, pick out the cooked herbs and garnish with a bunch of fresh thyme.

September

La Fête du Sel – and the *bandas* play on

Back to Normality

My leg was free at last. Dr Suleiman took off the splint and told me I could walk, drive and do whatever I liked. 'Naughty little injury, isn't it?' he said, looking at me diagonally through his half-glasses. He also ordered a new visitor to Maison Bergez, the physiotherapist, M. Duclos, who arrived with a jar of some wonderful gel that smelled of lavender which he ordered from a herbal pharmacy in Paris, and started to massage my foot back into action. It took a while. All the bones, from ankle to toe, seemed to be completely fused and the blood vessels had not appreciated two months of inactivity. To walk, I still needed the help of one of the crutches.

I had been prescribed twenty-five physiotherapy sessions. Later I discovered that in the UK the NHS would have allowed me only six. '*Petit à petit*,' warned M. Duclos. 'This will take six months for you to walk normally and it will be a year before you can forget you ever did it.' He was exactly right.

Suddenly I wished that I hadn't taken quite such a satirical view of one of the characters in *Heartswap*, the New Age con artist who hypocritically lectures the main character about her lack of spirituality while all the time trying to seduce her fiancé. M. Duclos, spotting one of the French editions of the book about the house, asked if he could borrow

it, read it in two days, but then accused me, with a pained
look in his eye, of being a sceptic about alternative therapies.
But at least he was interested to read the book. Even some
of my long-standing friends in England had never felt it
necessary to read a book just because they knew the author.

Chloe was due back for a final three weeks of fun and revision before the university term started. She still preferred
the TGV to flying, even if the journey from Edinburgh by
train took nearly eighteen hours. I found a train that would
take her as close as Orthez, and was able to drive over and
collect her from the station. She was shocked to see me
hobbling along with a crutch, but a month of working flat
out as a front-of-house theatre manager at the Edinburgh
Festival had left her in much better shape than her end-of-
year exams, and she was ready to enjoy herself.

A few days later, one of our cousins also arrived. Nicola
was born in Toronto and went to university in Quebec, so
she speaks Canadian French. I felt slightly validated in
front of my neighbours, being able to produce more than
one member of my family. Since moving to London, Nicola
had become an enthusiastically urban creature, favouring
all-black minimal everything. She looked wonderingly out
of the car window at the medieval landscape around us.

The Béarn had suddenly returned to its normal, smiling,
sun-kissed, sleepy self. The rain stopped and the rich,
golden sun of early autumn blazed down every day. We had
misty mornings full of birdsong and glorious sunsets with
churring crickets and whooping toads. The mountains
reappeared as if some perverse magician had hidden them
on purpose for the holiday season.

The garden was bursting with food. Finally, the vegetable
world was winning, and producing fruit faster than the
birds could eat it. On the three big fig trees overhanging
the front hedge, dozens of figs ripened every day, to the utter

delight of thousands of tiny birds who twittered ecstatically in the treetops as they stuffed their tiny beaks. They also left copious purple droppings on my car. Henri Cat, now almost perfectly tame, had taken to sleeping on the car bonnet in the sun, and did not approve of this development, which forced him to pick his spot with care before settling down for his morning nap.

The walnut tree, from which the hammock hung, started to blanket-bomb us with nuts. They were huge, some of them as big as small apples, with a blackened soft skin over the hard shells, so they really hurt when they fell on your head from a great height – the tree, neglected for decades, had soared away to something like ten metres. The squirrel couldn't keep up with the bounty; not that I saw him, but I found dozens of scrapes in the lawn where he had frantically tried to bury some of the nuts before getting distracted by a fresh fall.

At the back of the house, the hazel bushes sprinkled the lawn with cobnuts and the apple tree, a puny, wizened, little thing of which I had had no hope of fruit at all, suddenly began to blush with delicious red-skinned apples. We didn't get to these fast enough, however. As with the cherries, the tree was stripped by canny birds, or maybe by my neighbours, the instant the fruit was ripe.

Only my potager was less than the picture of abundance. The last tomatoes had rotted from the rain and fallen prey to the giant brown slugs. The courgettes were still flowering, but their leaves were mildewed. Within a few days of the sun's return, however, the mildew disappeared, and the plants began to set courgettes again.

The sweet peas were shrivelled and at the end of their tether, but my old-fashioned orange-pot marigolds were unstoppable and the dahlias were still luxuriant, though M. Lavie's were better. The last artichoke plant was finally

bearing flowers. Should I ever be lucky enough to grow artichokes again, I will remember to pinch off some plants to
prolong the flowering season. As a tribute, I decided to leave
them to grow purple on their stems. The real triumph, however, were the Jerusalem artichokes, now huge green plants
that were taller than I was, bearing starry yellow flowers.

In Saliès, most of the tourists, with their terrible shorts
and even uglier insistence on immediate pleasure, had gone,
leaving a handful of steadfast walkers strolling curiously
around the town centre. These are the kind of visitors that
Saliès seems to like. The crass invaders of high summer
had simply filled everyone with irritation, and now they
were gone half the town slumped gratefully back into its
enchanted slumber.

The underwear shop, which in June had suddenly pulled
up its embroidered linen blinds and taken down the faded
notice promising that it would reopen in April, decided to
have an end-of-season sale, and hung handwritten signs in
its window proclaiming 50 per cent reductions on what
remained of its stock. Where this stock came from, I could
never imagine. The pink net bra with the sequinned lotus
blossoms on the cups, the green Tactel string bikini with the
matching skirt, the orange lace boxers . . . no threat of a leading brand, no decorous lace from Lejaby, no neat little bras
from Cacharel, no workaday knickers from Dim. Obviously,
the women of Saliès had a far more exotic intimate life than
outsiders imagined. The sale was over in forty-eight hours
and the modest linen blinds came down again.

Most of the commercial enterprises now focused on 'la
Rentrée', the start of the new school year. They took the
souvenir mugs and bad-taste postcards out of their windows
and filled them instead with notebooks and geometry sets.

In the garden centres and the outdoor shops, however,
the main event was the start of the hunting season on

1 September. Geraniums and grass seed were swept off the
shelves and their places taken by camouflage-print gun
sheaths and thorn-proof jackets. Behind the till in Saliès'
favourite garden shop appeared a locked, glass-fronted
cabinet selling cartridges, flanked by a shiny new notice
warning that ammunition could be sold only to adults over
the age of eighteen and possessing an up-to-date hunting
permit.

Everyone seemed to be obsessed either with hunting or
with mushrooms. Benoit, the potter's son, leaned out of his
office doorway and promised to bring me some ceps.
M. Duclos, the physio, while he was massaging my ankle,
told me about his trips into the mountains at the weekends,
looking for mushrooms in all the secret places only he knew
about. Since the weather was now glorious, the mushroom
hunters set off early every Saturday and Sunday, just as the
skiers would as soon as the first snow was announced.

Catching the mushrooming spirit, I limped around my
garden to see what might be springing up there, and found
four or five inedible species and a group of white death-caps.
This, the most deadly mushroom in Europe, is a pretty little
thing that looks like a fairy parasol, and I'd given it a cameo
role in one of my earlier novels, *Harvest*, which has a long
and lovingly researched mushrooming chapter and a villain
in need of a good death scene. Annabel was the only person
in the department not suddenly fascinated by fungi. Having
once left a cep in a plastic bag too long, she was afraid of
finding worms in them.

September 11

Andrew and I felt we would like to do something to mark
the first anniversary of 9/11. We decided to go to the

pilgrim church of St André in Sauveterre. There we found only a man and a woman washing the floor beneath the twelfth-century portal, which is carved with figures of Christ and the evangelists. There was no sign of any special ceremony planned for later. Geoff, meanwhile, walked slowly with Otto towards the cafe with the yellow chairs, where we joined him after a few minutes. It was a very beautiful day, with brilliant sunshine and clear blue sky reflected in the surging Gave. 'I can't believe I'm allowed to live anywhere so gorgeous,' said Andrew.

Chloe and Nicola had gone to Bayonne, and reported that no special observances seemed to be planned there. The television showed us the ceremonies in New York, and the *Figaro* carried the story as its second lead. It was good to be far away from the sanctimonious empathy that seemed to be the official line in London, but also ominous. Even here, the aftershocks of 9/11 touched our lives in all kinds of ways. Most of us were quite literally poorer for it.

So much, perhaps, was to be expected. What made us sad were the signs that the integrity of our host community in France, that quality whose loss we mourned in England and which, more than any pleasure, made us feel happy to live here, would soon be threatened by international political correctness. The Béarn had been a diverse society for centuries, but not in the flashy, shallow, global manner that governments were now trying to impose. The Béarnais had no guilt to bear for the racial tensions of other regions of France. The community was kind to foreigners, even if there were far fewer of them here than in the big cities.

Except for the two Moroccan women in Orthez and perhaps Dr Suleiman (I never asked), there probably wasn't a Muslim within miles of Sauveterre. When the *Sud-Ouest* interviewed the conductor of the departmental orchestra in Pau they asked him about music, not how he felt as an

African Frenchman. Nevertheless there were straws in the wind, small signs that official thinking would soon be trying to cow this innocent community into feeling guilty just for being white and Christian.

We looked on these developments with alarm, because by now we'd worked out that the sense that life in our corner of France was somehow more real and authentic than our lives in London derived partly from the elements of shared European heritage that had been preserved here. It felt almost as if we were living in the gene bank of our ancestors' culture, a Noah's Ark of our own vernacular traditions.

The landscape, created over centuries of harmony between people and nature, allowed us to feel both the power of the elements and the reassurance that man could harness them. The architecture, from the ruined castles to the tumbledown cottages, evoked the fairy stories that were part of our identity. The cycle of the year, marked by ancient festivals and by the Christian calendar, left us feeling more comfortable with life than the undifferentiated days of toil in the city. The songs, the dances, the legends and the mythology which we enjoyed were all continuing traditions, forces which connected people to each other, to their past and to their environment.

We had discovered in ourselves a buried nostalgia for this culture, which our own country had once shared but had long ago destroyed. I remembered, sadly, a conversation with a gifted arts administrator working in the West Country, who bemoaned the 'monocultural' nature of her region and saw no benefit in supporting anything rural. Andrew identified a real sense of envy for the traditions and pastimes of the Béarnais. 'I don't care about hunting,' he said once, when the debate was hotting up in Westminster again. 'I don't care about foxes or toffs in red coats or any of it. But I do care that people want to ban it, because it's part

of my heritage and my past and I don't like people thinking
they can just take that away.'

La Heste de la Sau

The season of *fêtes* continued without a break. The big one
came in the middle of September, le Fête du Sel, or, in Béarnais, la Heste de la Sau, the salt festival in Saliès, the Béarn's
event of the season. It was to last four days.

From the Thursday, the cafes on the market square began
to put up extra bars on the street. Workmen appeared with
pick-up trucks loaded with small acacia trunks; it's a very
hard and dense wood that burns badly but the branches
grow very straight and an acacia sapling or six make the
perfect framework for a temporary bar. In a few hours,
the bars had been roofed with pine and plastic, then decorated with palm leaves or green bamboo, ready for the first
gathering, a low-key soirée in one of the public rooms, followed by a concert of Béarnais songs. The transformation
reminded me of my home town of Hammersmith getting
ready for the Boat Race. Suddenly this decorous, sleepy little
place was turning into a major party venue.

Every householder had apparently been gardening by
stealth in his or her back yard, because suddenly every balcony and window sill was gaudy with begonias and busy
lizzies as the residents brought their brightest blooms out to
the public side of their houses. The shops and cafes were
hung with medieval banners and paper flowers. Small
groups of young people sat around the ancient bridge and
the municipal fountain and practised strange musical
instruments, a mandolin, a hurdy-gurdy and a set of
bagpipes.

On the first big day, the Saturday, a market of regional

produce took place and stallholders from all over the department arrived at dawn, set up their tables and their canopies
and laid out their wares. You could buy anything from a
hand-loomed, hand-dyed, pure mohair stole to a damn fine
sausage. The cafes lowered the steel shutters which we'd
never seen before and had probably been installed during
World War II, and transferred their service to the temporary
bars outside.

The amateur troubadours started strolling through the
alleys, stopping frequently to rehearse or retune. A band
of young men in black-velvet doublets paid homage to the
Gipsy Kings on guitars and mandolin, while four nervous
maidens, squeezed into brightly coloured taffeta dresses,
strolled around with the bagpipes and the hurdy-gurdy.

All the restaurants were suddenly booked solid, even la
Terrasse, which, as far as I knew, never took bookings.
La Terrasse is my favourite place to eat in Saliès. It's the
complete Elizabeth David dream, a simple, genuine, everyday restaurant where you'll find yourself eating next to the
postmaster and the florist, and the young waiter is nervous
about serving foreigners. It also has a stunning situation,
right on the river, by a pretty stone bridge, opposite the
church. But no, La Terrasse was full.

How could we contemplate this festival without a festive
lunch? It was particularly bad news for Willow, who suddenly found herself with a large party of friends from way
back staying with her while they looked for a house. Being
an adopted Chalossoise, she'd never got into this Béarnais
rave and found it hard to understand that this gentle town
of discreet middle-aged divorcees had suddenly turned
itself into the St Tropez of Gascony, even if *seulement pour le
weekend*.

Eventually, we ran into Gordon, who advised a place he'd
discovered the year before, a sea-food bar in a little garden

near the bridge over the river. Here, under a couple of luxuriant mulberry trees, a fish merchant who'd come all the way from Arcachon set up a bank of griddles and was getting ready to shuck oysters, and grill sardines, prawns and baby squid, straight out of the fishermen's crates. Wine could be bought from the stall of a local vineyard, cunningly pitched nearby, and I sent Chloe to buy a loaf of country bread from a craftsman baker around the corner. It was the size of a computer monitor and slightly charred on the bottom from the wood-fired oven, but the interior was warm, soft and fragrant, exactly what we needed to clean our fingers and mop our plates. Fifteen of us eventually sat down to eat together, seven English, two Scottish, one Australian, one New Zealander, one Canadian and three French – Françoise and her children.

Sunday was the really big day, beginning with a sung mass in Béarnais in the church of St Vincent, which dominates the centre of the town from its position on a rocky outcrop overlooking the river. It's an extraordinary building, very simple inside but with wonderful acoustics, and asymmetrical, because of its natural foundations. Grandeur was something it grew into, because originally it was nothing but a little chapel of rough stones built to serve the spiritual needs of the soldiers who guarded the salt spring.

Saliès has every reason to celebrate its salt, because it owes its beauty and its past prosperity to the geographical accident which, millions of years ago, created a salt marsh miles from the sea. Rain which falls in the mountains is channelled down towards the earth's core, and is then pushed up through a freak conformation of rock strata containing the mineral deposits left by an ancient ocean. The water emerges here, in the middle of the flat and fertile Béarnais plain, as a hot spring redolent with dissolved minerals. The legend which is passed down tells that the marshes of Saliès were

so salty that they sparkled in the sun with the salt that
crystallized on every blade of grass.

The whole history of Saliès is of the ownership, defence
and exploitation of this resource. Early in the Middle Ages,
the marshes were drained and the River Saleys, thus created,
diverted into a stone storm drain through the centre of the
town. There it could be dammed, the water extracted in
huge vats which came to be called *samaux*, and evaporated
in salt pans, from which the crystals were brushed into tidy
piles, dissolved again, purified, bagged up and sold all over
France and Spain.

Since salt was a highly valuable commodity in past times,
and Saliès was blessed with a spring whose water was five
times saltier than the sea, this industry made Saliès-de-
Béarn rich for centuries. Where any other small market
town of comparable size in France would now boast nothing
but a ring road and a half-ruined rampart, Saliès is a half-
timbered, droopy-eaved dream, a townscape which looks
as if it was mocked up for some 1930s fairy-story book
plates. The perfectly preserved medieval centre is made up
of handsome merchants' houses, several old water mills,
the unique church of St Vincent and several less eccentric,
later churches, a massive underground cistern and countless
other architectural treasures. Not to mention the spa, called
les Thermes, and the bandstand in front of it.

It is also an immensely stable community, in which many
families can trace their ancestry back to the Middle Ages.
In all its history, Saliès suffered only a tiny blip of depriva-
tion, between the Revolution, when the salt business was
nationalized, and the arrival of the Empress Eugénie in the
mid-nineteenth century, when the town was reborn as a
fashionable spa and les Thermes were built. Over the next
seventy years, a new phase of building added a clutch of

imposing art nouveau villas and fin de siècle hotels, including the Hôtel du Parc.

Saliès became a fashionable must-see for the Biarritz set.
Marcel Proust arrived in 1885, as a boy of fourteen, coming
with his mother to take the waters. He was, his letters to
his grandmother reveal, extremely bored, a great tribute
to the soothing properties of the elements of the South-
West, which easily overcame the future master of ennui. He
was saved by the conversation of a certain Mme Catusse, the
wife of a future senator, who apparently added 'the essential
grain of poetry' which was necessary for the young genius's
existence. He reported that she was also very beautiful,
physically and morally.

Saliès was probably still enjoying the twilight of its
heyday in 1926, when Scott Fitzgerald, accompanied by his
wife Zelda and their five-year-old daughter Scottie, fled the
severity of January in Paris to enjoy a couple of months here.
He hadn't picked the best time to visit the Béarn. The only
hotel which was open was out in the low-lying meadows of
the Bellevue quarter and the only other guests were seven
invalids taking a cure at les Thermes.

They had a simple, pine-panelled room, filled with light
from the Pyrenees, and embellished with a bronze bust of
Henri IV. The great novelist believed that Henri's mother
had been born there, whereas every Béarnais knows that
Jeanne d'Albret was born in St Germain-en-Laye, now a
suburb of Paris. Zelda herself was suffering from a colic con-
tracted from 'the abuse of champagne', but Scott bought
himself a beret, a pair of knickerbockers and a walking
stick, and took the family on trips to Biarritz, Pau and
Lourdes. He did a bit of journalism, and wandered down
the misty alleys buying Scottie sweets, but they too were
basically bored. But then, a jazz-age writer had to be bored
by everything.

Saliès has drifted gently into lean times, which continue
to this day. Many remarkable buildings that should be open
to the public are closed, because there's no money to restore
them. The largest hotel, an imposing wedding cake of white
stucco and wrought-iron balconies, had been gutted by fire
and was nothing but a burned-out facade with soot stains
streaking upwards from the glassless windows and lingering
whiff of corruption.

The town should have been a perfect candidate for those
Euro-funds earmarked for preserving our heritage, but
Annie-Claire told me the story of how anti-rural prejudice
had scuppered their chances.

Her husband, and les Amis de Vieux Saliès, worked long
and hard on a restoration plan. Annie-Claire was entrusted
with taking their application to become a UNESCO World
Heritage Site to Brussels, because her husband couldn't
leave his nursery. When a man owns the only serious plant
centre in the department, he has his anxieties. Or perhaps
he suddenly became aware that a big man in a small town
may not feel too comfortable as an obscure stranger in an
international capital.

Unfortunately, les Amis de Vieux Saliès had overlooked
the box on the form which needed to be filled with the name
of the restoration project. The bureaucrat to whom Annie
handed the application pointed this out. Annie borrowed his
telephone to call her husband, who was out in the nursery
inspecting his plants.

'Sorry to take so long,' she said, jokingly to the official,
while she waited for him to be fetched. 'We're in *la France
profonde*, you know – he's out in the fields!' At this admis-
sion of peasant origins, the bureaucrat barely suppressed a
shudder. Annie-Claire spoke to her husband and completed
the form, but as she left the office she saw the official
shoving it disdainfully in a lower drawer, from which, she is

sure, it was never to be rescued. So Saliès, betrayed by the
Gascon sense of humour, continues to crumble in charming
obscurity.

By midday on Sunday things became even more serious.
The marquees and the long tables reappeared in the square,
and lunch for a thousand people was laid on, with more
music, more singing, more dancing on tables and a huge
pile of dirty plates in the washing-up tent that was set up in
a little square out of sight of the revels.

The more circumspect party-goers arrived later and dug
in at the bars. At three thirty plus the Béarnais quarter of
an hour, a procession of floats began to form up outside les
Thermes, a long line of hand-made marvels pulled by tractors, which moved slowly through the crowd. The theme
was the '*riches heures*' of the Béarn, from prehistory to the
present, and every nearby village had been given one era to
depict. They were cheered on their way by at least four
bandas, belting out the old favourites on cornet, trumpet,
hunting horn and tuba, and reinforced by music from musicians in the crowd.

At the rear of some of the floats, boxes and barrels of
wine had been mounted, and whenever the parade halted
the followers energetically poured plastic cups of wine for
the crowd, while giggling schoolgirls tossed out handfuls of
confetti, the user-friendly modern substitute for the ancient
custom of hurling salt at the onlookers.

All the usual suspects were presented: Gaston Fébus
hunting the boar, Henri IV in his tortoiseshell cradle, a team
of Aztec maidens honouring the maize, a man in a chicken
suit capering around the *poule au pot*, a tableau featuring a
giant Bayonne ham, a lorry draped with vines and dispens-
ing wine and a giant black beret, about five metres in diameter. Every village in the neighbourhood was represented,
plus some of the town social clubs, the cycle club, the rugby

club and les Amis de Vieux Saliès. Geoff and Andrew were
not amused to find that Castagnède had chosen to depict
what in heartless English would be called the village idiots.
In ancient time the '*cagots*', the programme explained, were
originally the marginalized folk of the village, who lived
like the untouchables of India. Perhaps the offspring of
outcast lepers, their origins were lost to history, and they
disappeared when the Revolutionary government granted
them equal rights.

A Nazi tank ('Mum, it's just a drainpipe on a tractor
painted khaki,' said Chloe, eager to deflate my sense of
wonder) signified World War II, when the demarcation line
dividing the German-occupied zone from the region ruled
by the collaborationist Vichy regime ran right through
Saliès in the Cout quarter, slicing off the east side of the
town for the enemy. Nobody ever refers to the agony that
this innocent country town must have suffered when it was
ripped apart by the Nazi army, but the wounds must have
been deep. No doubt the hundreds of Allied fugitives
following the secret Resistance route over the border to
Spain found a warm welcome in Saliès. Annabel's house, La
Maysou, was then the home of a Vichy governor. When it
was clear that the Germans were losing, he fled by night,
but was hunted down to Nancy, in the north, where he was
found in possession of a vast sum of money and jewellery
worth 850,000 francs. He was arrested, tried and executed.

The modern floats were the most inventive. The 1950s
were represented by masses of silver pipes for the gas plant
at Mourenx, while the present day was symbolized by the
tunnel through the mountains at Somport. This was almost
my favourite float. Its builders had erected a five-metre
chunk of cardboard mountain, thickly decorated with pine
branches and heather, and embellished it with borrowed
taxidermist's masterpieces, a stuffed fox, a pine marten, an

eagle and a stag's head. At the back of the float was mounted a bright blue Peugeot, as if it was emerging from the tunnel to be greeted by the tableau of a family picnicking in the middle of the road, being noisily admonished by a gendarme in full uniform. The tunnel at Somport runs under a mountain pass that was given its name by the Romans.

After the parade, and another Béarnaise quarter-hour, and more beer, and more 'selgria' and more music, the *samau* races began. By this time the town square was completely packed, apart from the race course running from the old salt works, past the fountain and the Crédit Agricole, up almost to the bridge, round a barrel which marked the halfway point, and back.

One after another, a pair of young men ran up and down the course, carrying on a wooden yoke a huge tub of salt water. The fastest time would win. The *samaux* were tall wooden pots made of oak, bound with iron hoops, wide and flat at the bottom to keep them upright even on uneven ground. A *samau* could contain up to 100 litres of water, so even for two strong rugby-playing lads, running over the cobbles was a challenge.

The trick was not merely to win, but to get around the treacherous corner by the Crédit Agricole without the swinging weight of the water bringing down the runners and causing the whole kit and caboodle to hit the deck, thus spilling salt water over the track and making it even more slippery for the later racers. The very first team managed to do this, to a roar of disapproval from the crowd. Feeling sensitive to the prospect of somebody else breaking a leg, I decided it was time to head home.

The Real Spa Experience

Fountain, waterfall, geyser, swans' necks, power jets, the boiling banquette, jacuzzi, jet shower, *hammam* . . . there was absolutely nothing you couldn't do with salt water at les Thermes. I dragged every one of my guests there, and took huge pleasure in watching them step tentatively into the distinctly 1970s swimming pool and suddenly beam with pleasure as they felt the magic of the spring water. Now that I was a genuine convalescent, I sent myself there to swim as often as I could and give my recovering ankle the full benefit of the medicinal waters.

Now until I went to les Thermes, I was sceptical about hot springs. All those legends about the old boar and the old dog – well, they were just folk tales. Nothing could get through skin, the epidermis was designed to be impermeable, and swimming in water in which all sorts of odd minerals had been dissolved couldn't possibly make any difference to your metabolism.

Well, incredible as it is, it does make a difference. You feel fantastic. Even with a hangover. And it takes about five minutes. Les Thermes are a complex of pools, some of which are specifically designed for remedial treatments, but the one to which I was addicted was simply a swimming pool with lots of fancy massage jets to pound your shoulders, tickle your back and wobble your cellulite. The water was the natural spring water, maintained at 32°C, the pleasant warmth at which the spring comes out of the ground.

Of course, people have analysed the spring water. Its really heavy on sodium and chlorine, of course (NaCl, the salt, right?) and also in bromium and magnesium. But there's lots of calcium, chromium, cobalt, iron, lithium, manganese, nickel, phosphorus, potassium, selenium, silicone, vanadium

and zinc in it, too. All those jolly trace elements that nutritionists are always waffling about, just naturally bubbling
out of the ground, and then cunningly piped into les
Thermes. The waters are meant to be particularly beneficial
to gynaecological problems and children's illnesses. This is as
may be. All I know is that I always came out pink-cheeked,
ultra-relaxed and distinctly euphoric.

There was probably some kind of spa here when Eugénie
and Napoleon arrived, but as soon as they felt the amazing
tingle, the instant zest, the supernatural sparkle that the hot
spring water gives you, they delegated their own doctor to
supervise the development of the station into something
appropriately luxurious. Hot springs are a nationalized
resource in France, so nobody can develop them without
government backing, and in the case of les Thermes at
Saliès, the Emperor himself supervised the process. A new
spa building was erected, a fantasy palace of pink and white
brick, with Venetian crenellations around its decorative tower.
It looks like a little sister of Kuala Lumpur railway station.

From the old photographs, the inside hasn't changed
much. There is still a wide marble-floored central corridor,
with park-type benches for the weary *curiste* to rest on. The
public pool was obviously redesigned in the 1970s, though
given the lingering fascination which the French have for
the bad-taste decade it could be much later.

Outside, there is a little park, shaded by blue cedars,
containing the bandstand and the little circular gallery
where Roger's panorama was exhibited until he got bored
and turned the building into a studio. After 1870, there was
also a statue of the silent, bare-breasted spirit of the spring
and a group of gambolling infants whom she had cured, but
between erosion and vandalism, *La Mude* was disfigured and
removed to a less prominent spot.

Everybody goes to les Thermes. The Salisiens use it just

like any other pool; in fact, they probably use it more. Fathers bring their children at the weekend, mothers bring their children after school, groups of giggling office girls come in after work, pairs of lovers enjoy a relaxing hour together, old people come in the evening when it's quiet and the curious from out of town come any time the pool is open, from 10 a.m. to 7 p.m., seven days a week, but not, obviously, at lunch time.

There are concessions to modern ideas about fitness, a small cardiovascular conditioning suite and some weights which occasionally get lifted, always by men. There's a studio where the supernaturally patient young men who supervise the pool take aerobics classes. These were not well attended, though the handful of women in the advanced class looked as stringy as marathon runners.

It may be different in the cities, but in the South-West, French women do not seem greatly enthusiastic about exercise. When I visited the big sports hypermarkets, Decathlon and Sportner, there would be just a couple of racks of limp pink Lycra leotards hiding coyly behind rows and rows of clothing for men and boys. Even finding trainers in a woman's fitting was a challenge. I never saw women out jogging, cycling or snowboarding. For a woman of my age, a decorous promenade up a not-too-steep hill, preferably with someone to chat to, was considered a real workout.

Yoga was also permissible; Denise, the elegant young Englishwoman who taught Andrew and Geoff French, was one of the yoga instructors, as was Kathy, the French partner in McGuire's Irish Pub. Chatting was an important feature of the yoga class, too, and doing the tree pose on my recovering ankle was a strain. But popping into les Thermes for a few lengths a couple of times a week was just what the doctor ordered.

Recipes

There is probably a different *garbure* recipe for every citizen of Gascony, since every woman, and quite a few of the men, make it and most people have at least two versions, one for a simple, hearty family supper and one for a festive one-pot meal. It can be a very simple dish of meat, cabbage and potato or a very elaborate one with every winter vegetable and several kinds of meat.

People who aren't part of the *garbure* tradition — like, say, a British ex-pat — tell you that it's just a soup made of boiled-up leftovers. Perhaps on a Monday night, when the weary stand-in cook at a run-down *auberge* looks out of the kitchen and sees a large party of British heaving through the door to put an end to his hopes of an early night, the *garbure* may be padded out with cold second-hand vegetables and any old bit of whiffy sausage, but in a private home it is always freshly made. For public consumption, it's the sort of dish that's done best at simple main-square restaurants like La Terrasse in Saliès or the Auberge du Foirail in St-Palais, where almost every single diner will order it.

Chloe tried several recipes and they came out a bit watery. Renée had given us the best part of an entire lesson on *garbure*, when the textbook challenged her Béarnais nationalism by mentioning such infinitely inferior dishes as Quiche Lorraine and Gratin Dauphinois. She had emphasized quite passionately that it was absolutely essential to include a piece of *confit*, of pork, goose or duck, whatever you had, but *confit* was essential. This Marie confirmed. You started with fresh water, never stock or bouillon, she said, and you added a piece of *confit*. If there were only a few of you, it was the way to use all those odds and ends which were preserved, like the wing tips and the spare ribs.

Finally, we worked out the magic formula. For a *garbure* to be what it ought to be, silky but chunky, and delicately savoury, so that the steam off the dish brings the most appetizing aromas to your nose before you even pick up your spoon, you need to use a little *confit* fat early in the cooking, and then add the meat *en confit* at the end. The *confit* process imbues the fat with the flavour of the meat and so, in an age before the curse of monosodium glutamate, the fat then adds its meaty savour to the whole soup. So, should you want to try this recipe when you haven't got any *confit* of anything in the cupboard, you could cheat by using some meat stock and a bit of good dripping. It'll be quite good, but it won't be the same.

Simple *Garbure*

Serves 8

20 g (¾ oz) *confit* fat
5 cloves of garlic, chopped
1 kg (2¼ lb) potatoes
3 nice purple turnips
a chunk of green cabbage, about 250 g (9 oz)
1 piece of *confit*, preferably pork or goose, of about
    200 g (7 oz)
salt and pepper

Bring 3 litres (5¼ pints) of water to the boil in a large saucepan and add the *confit* fat and the garlic. Peel the potatoes, cut in halves or, if they're huge, into quarters, and add to the pan.

Let the potatoes simmer while you quarter two of the turnips and cut the cabbage into strips as fine as you can. Discard the tops, tails and cabbage stalk. Keep back a couple of cabbage leaves, and add the rest of the cabbage and turnips to the pot. Simmer for a further 40 minutes.

Slice the third turnip into thin sections – these will be used to make the dish look pretty, something few Gascon cooks would feel necessary. By this time the potatoes will be starting to break up in the pot. Add the meat *en confit*, and the reserved cabbage and turnip slices. Simmer for a further 5 minutes, breaking up the meat gently as you stir.

Some people serve their *garbure* with the potato mashed into it, so you can stand up a spoon in the thick mixture, and some people like to leave the broth clear and the vegetables whole. The choice is yours.

Garbure de Fête

Serves at least 8, as a whole meal

100 g (3½ oz) *confit* fat
2 large onions, quartered
100 g (3½ oz) Bayonne ham, cut into lardons
100 g (3½ oz) salt pork or streaky bacon, cut into pieces
2 bay leaves
2 branches of thyme
4 stalks of parsley
1 clove and 10 peppercorns, tied in a scrap of muslin
10 cloves of garlic
100 g (3½ oz) dried haricot beans, soaked for at least
    2 hours
3 carrots, peeled and chopped

3 turnips, quartered
2 leeks, sliced
about 300 g (11 oz) green cabbage, shredded
1 kg (2¼ lb) potatoes, peeled and halved
2 large or 4 small Toulouse sausages
2 good pieces of pork or goose *en confit*
a good slice of pumpkin, without peel or pips, cut into
   chunks

Put the *confit* fat into a heavy-bottomed saucepan over a low
heat, and sweat the onions until they start to get soft, then
add 3 litres (5¼ pints) of water, the Bayonne ham, salt pork
or bacon, herbs, garlic and dried beans. Simmer for 2 hours,
which gives you plenty of time to prepare the other vegetables. Top up the water so the ingredients are always covered.

Add all the vegetables except the pumpkin and a few
shredded cabbage leaves, and simmer for a further 10
minutes. Then add the sausages, and simmer for 10 minutes
more, then add the meat *en confit*, and simmer for another 10
minutes. Add the pumpkin chunks and shreds of cabbage
last, and simmer the whole thing for a final 5 minutes. Taste
the soup before you serve it – it will probably not need salt.
Pick out the bay leaves, thyme, parsley and spices. Extract
the cooked sausages, slice them and return them to the pan.

A hearty *garbure* like this is served heaped in shallow soup
plates. Salt, pepper, vinaigrette dressing, country bread and
gherkins – the little sweet *cornichons* – are the traditional
accompaniment.

Tarte aux Noix

We discovered that fresh walnuts are absolutely delicious,
quite unlike the sour, dusty things you buy in shops. Nicola

collected a small mountain of them which we dried off in the sun and heaped up on a tray by the fireplace. Cracking them became compulsive, and soon a big dish of kernels was begging to be employed. I bottled a large quantity with honey. The walnuts bleed a little oil into the honey, thinning it and giving a smoky flavour. The result is delicious spooned into yoghurt or poured over ice cream, vanilla or coffee.

This is another of Pierre Koffmann's recipes, for a deliciously rich and crunchy nut tart that rounds off a winter meal to perfection.

While the full-sized tart is sumptuous, the mixture also works wonderfully in very small moulds, which results in exquisitely luscious bite-sized morsels. You can vary the flavour by using Armagnac instead of rum, or with a strong-flavoured honey like heather or pine. If you're condemned to using store-bought walnuts, rinse them in milk while the pastry is resting and leave them wet to regain the shadow of their youthful plumpness.

For the sweet tart pastry

250 g (9 oz) plain flour, sifted
100 g (4 oz) icing sugar
pinch of salt
1 whole egg and 2 egg yolks
100 g (4 oz) butter, warmed almost to melting

For the filling

120 g (4½ oz) softened butter
150 g (5 oz) honey
300 g (11 oz) shelled walnuts in pieces
150 g (5 oz) sugar
5 egg yolks
100 ml (4 fl oz) double cream
50 ml (2 fl oz) rum
a spoonful of icing sugar to decorate

Make the pastry by mixing the dry ingredients, heaping them on a work surface and making a well in the centre, into which put the eggs and butter. Draw the flour mixture into the wet ingredients and gradually mix to a soft dough (or chuck the lot into a food processor and blend briefly). Move the dough to a floured board and knead briefly with the heel of your hand. Roll into a ball, wrap in clingfilm or a cloth and leave to rest in the fridge for an hour before rolling out and using to line a well-buttered 22 cm (9 in) flan tin.

Preheat the oven to 190°C / 375°F / Gas 5.

Warm the butter and the honey. Gently mix all the filling ingredients together in a bowl, pour into the flan case and bake for 40 minutes. Leave to cool, sprinkle with icing sugar and serve.

October

Ahetze – *brocanteurs* at lunch

It was time to get going. I picked a date, 2 November. I called the moving firm; they were a bit startled to be asked to move somebody back. People didn't come back from France, as a rule. The human traffic was definitely one-way. I could have my pick of collection dates, and chose one just a couple of days before I planned to leave.

I began to pack Chloe's room first; the summer clothes, the old school books, the even older cuddly toys, the bag of baby shoes. After that, my own souvenirs: the Ossie Clark mini-dress from the sixties, the sequinned bustier from the seventies, the striped blazer from the eighties that I'm wearing in Glynn's portrait. Did I need these things? No. Did I want them? Yes. I had examined my past lives and chosen my memories. Some unswept corner of my character had been aired and accepted.

The boxes which had contained my books were still in the *abri*, the lean-to with a tiled roof which was originally designed to store firewood – those I hadn't given to Fiona to take back to New Zealand or to Sandy-and-Annie to help them with their move. Thus there were ninety-eight coming out, and there were going to be seventy-nine going back. Fortunately the last *vide grenier* of the season was looming, and it was going to be right on my doorstep, in the *salle multiactivités* in Orriule, sponsored by the Club International de Saliès-de-Béarn.

With so many British people involved, this event

inevitably took on the feel of an English village fete, an institution that endures even in the London suburbs, like Chiswick, which are famous for their 'village atmosphere' and take care to replicate a few events of a rural community calendar. Annabel, who had accepted responsibility for the catering, had dutifully researched the lower links of the antiques food chain and visited several *vides greniers* over the summer. Nothing, however, could persuade her that it was necessary to offer alcohol and bacon sandwiches. She had issued an appeal for home-made cakes, and I, still enjoying a barrage of walnuts, dutifully cooked Margaret's wonderful walnut sponge and took it over in the glass croissant-keeper which I'd bought at a sale earlier in the season.

It was a roasting hot day, especially out on the *fronton*, where there was no shade. Inside the hall I found Annabel installed at the serving counter behind a tea urn, already drawing startled glances from the handful of villagers who had ventured into the hall to witness their new amenity being colonized by foreigners for a Sunday. There is no tradition of *noblesse oblige* in France. The lady of the *manoir* is not required to go slumming for the good of the community. Aristocrats are expected to stay in their chateaux – or, more often, in Paris – and get on with their lives of unearned luxury, not descend from their great height of privilege to rub shoulders with ordinary people and perform ritual acts of humility, like an archbishop washing the feet of the poor on Maundy Thursday.

Gracienne, the prime mover in the event, was perhaps as much of a foreigner as any of us. She tripped about with her metropolitan poise, collecting the exhibitors' fees of €6 per metre of stall frontage, and then retiring to preside over her own stall, where she was selling off the least desirable stock from her antique shop.

Roger arrived in his Mini Moke, loyally accompanied by Reine, who helped him set out an enticing array of items he has scavenged from the town dump over the years. Having a surprisingly fine eye for bric-a-brac, he saw his stall picked bare by the dealers in an hour. However, right opposite his pitch was a young man from a strange religious community in the valley, who did his bit to support himself there by buying up army-surplus goods and selling them in the markets. He also sold old electrical fitments. Roger's eye was irresistibly drawn to the flak jackets, the camouflage nets and the spools of brightly coloured electrical wire. It seemed likely he would go home with more stuff than he'd brought.

Reine seemed to have relaxed about me. I noticed her circling my stall with a discreet expression of amazement in her eyes while I was selling half a rack of size-sixteen clothes to a well-built young woman from Orthez; perhaps that was what finally reassured her that I had no designs on her *petit ami*.

Apart from the Club's members, the event was not well attended. The Mayor looked in, stood about awkwardly for ten minutes, then made her excuses and fluttered back to her own house. The jolly farmer with the fish pond planted himself in front of the tea urn and was resolutely gallant about the non-availability of aperitifs. Most of the rest of Orriule stayed away. All the same, I managed to sell all my surplus English books and magazines, and all my out-of-style clothes.

The dealer next to me, a woman about my own age who was selling antique textiles from some old trunks, struck a bargain with me to watch her stall while she went outside to chat. She had not bothered to unpack most of her goods. At the bottom of one of the trunks, under a pile of old lace curtains and ragged tablecloths, was a huge and perfect wolf-skin rug, the sort of accessory which might be seen in a picture in *Elle Decoration* for a price tag of about £600. I sold it to Annie for the price the dealer had marked on it – €60.

The Future of Henri Cat

Would a Béarnais wild cat enjoy chasing sewer rats around Hammersmith? I didn't think so. Not for all the Whiskas in Tesco. Besides, the pet-passport regulations required any animal being imported into Britain to have been micro chipped and vaccinated six months before passing through customs. Six months ago, Henri Cat was so wild he wouldn't come within two metres of a human.

Now, however, he was a sleek, well-covered, affectionate young cat. The nights were getting nippy, and he was getting used to curling up on the sofa after I'd gone to bed, and strolling into the kitchen in time to have his breakfast biscuits on the window sill. Piglet, having been thoroughly bribed by me with duck scraps and extra cuddles, had decided to tolerate him. The Duchess, on Planet Pedigree as usual, was barely aware that he'd become part of the household.

Henri Cat was on my conscience. True, he still vanished for two or three days at a time, but he never went far. I could usually find him lying comfortably on a patch of dead oak leaves by the washing line, surrounded now by a sprinkling of wild cyclamen flowers and purple autumn crocuses. Gerald was issuing daily sermons about the unfairness of getting an animal used to love, food and comfort and then letting it down. There was such an emotional edge to his lectures that I began to wonder what had occurred in his own life to make him empathize so passionately with a seduced and abandoned house pet.

However, when he was a kitten, Gerald had tried to catch Henri Cat, who scratched him and, in his frail state of health at the time, caused a nasty wound. So Annabel had set her face against Henri, and wouldn't consider adopting him. Instead, they had a new kitten of their own, an adorable young Birman who was doing a fine job of being a surrogate grandchild.

I confessed my guilt to Andrew, who immediately offered to adopt Henri. He was now a born-again cat lover, having been converted by the two ginger kittens he acquired shortly after moving into Maysounabe. They were called Patsy and Edina, and they made short work of their owners' intentions that they should sleep in the kitchen and be seen and not heard. However, the Béarn wasn't going to be enough for Andrew and Geoff for twelve months of the year. They planned all sorts of migrations – to Spain, to Florida, to anywhere there isn't snow in the winter. Earlier in the year, when they took off to Bordeaux for the weekend, Sandy-and-Annie were left in charge of the livestock; Edina immediately left home and set herself up in the woods above the house. I doubted not that if Henri went to Maysounabe, he would join her there almost immediately. Better he should stay on his own turf.

One morning, Henri let me off the hook. He was snoozing on the car bonnet at usual, and as usual I went to talk to him before I shooed him off and started the engine. He was tame enough to pick up by now, but as I took him into my arms I caught a strong whiff of scent. It was not my scent. It was Guerlain's Shalimar, a great classic fragrance which I can't wear. Henri Cat had found himself another admirer. I felt I could leave him in Orriule with a clean conscience.

La Vie en Mince

Zoe had announced her engagement to Matthieu. La Maysou was in a state of exalted rapture and high anxiety. The date! The invitations! The ceremony! The reception! The cousins! The caterers! The dress! The photographs! Oh my God, the photographs!

Annabel decided that, as the mother of the bride to be, whose image would be immortalized in the photographs for generations to come, it was time for her to lose weight. I had come to the same conclusion on my own behalf, since spending six weeks in a wheelchair testing recipes had done nothing for my figure. Furthermore, it is a sad truth of a writer's life that a new novel will put anything between ten and twenty pounds on the writer's frame, unless he or she is a chain-smoker. And even then, the combination of anxiety and inactivity can obliterate a waistline in fifty thousand words. *Wild Weekend* was up to that size already. I'd gained weight in proportion, and I had been quite big enough before I even left England. In London, I had been steadily shedding the stubborn deposits left by unhappiness, HRT, literature and the love of cooking with the help of Weight Watchers.

I started with Weight Watchers after Chloe was born, and dropped thirty-six pounds in six months. I also learned more about self-motivation than I learned in the whole of the rest of my life; back then, the basic diet, which is totally flexible unless you want to flex it in the direction of a cream-cheese Danish every morning, was supported by a motivational programme devised by a genius. Nowadays, the psycho-dynamic element disappeared, and a dreary emphasis on selling diet products replaced it. It's a shame. I still use some of the tricks to get me through writing a book, since a curious, butterfly-brain such as mine isn't naturally inclined to sit still and concentrate for months on end.

Surely this excellent organization would have a branch in France? A quick search on the Internet confirmed the fact. We could choose between a class in Saliès, a class in Orthez and several classes in Pau. Amandine, I had discovered, went to the meeting in Orthez, and we didn't want to embarrass her by pitching up at the same weighing machine. Saliès, we guessed, would be a bitchy little gathering and not our style. So, although it meant a forty-minute drive through the autumns mists once a week, we decided to go to Pau. The most highly recommended wedding-dress couturier in the department had her salon in Pau, so Annabel hoped to kill several birds with one stone.

The meeting took place in the Kyriad Hotel, an exquisitely vulgar edifice of pink concrete which, in proper Béarnais style, was almost empty of staff despite the fact that several hundred women would be ready for a *cappucino-lite* by the time the day was over. We wandered about the corridors and eventually found the low-ceilinged room in the basement where the familiar set-up had been installed. With a few French embellishments.

For the uninitiated, a Weight Watchers meeting will comprise the following essentials: a registration desk, at which the member presents her membership card for the sticker of the week; a weighing machine, on which the member then steps to find out how much she's lost that week; a table displaying Weight Watchers products for sale; a row of chairs on which the members will sit while the group leader gives her talk; and the before-and-after pictures of the leader to prove that you really can get thinner here.

In France, two things were different. One was that you

were weighed with your shoes on, for 'hygienic reasons'. In Britain, you take your shoes off in order to weigh as little as possible, and think nothing of stepping on another member's verruca viruses.

The other difference was that the weighing machine was discreetly screened, in what looked like the cardboard box that had once housed a big fridge, carefully covered with coloured crêpe paper and plastic flowers. Thus you could step on the scales and nobody but the meeting clerk would know how much you weighed. Nobody mentioned the figure; the clerk wrote it down on your card in silence and handed the card back to you closed, so nobody would know the awful truth.

Our leader was another Françoise. She was divinely tall, which reassured me, since I wasn't looking forward to being lectured by some Edith Piaf clone of 4 ft 11 in who would, inevitably, have been jealous of anyone taller. She was also very pretty and only about twenty-one; she too had joined Weight Watchers to lose weight after having her first baby. She was a sparkling performer, and soon her group engaged in an animated sharing session about their dieting experiences of the past week.

It was far more about boasting than sharing. 'I don't snack any more,' announced a grey-haired lady, rattling her gold necklace with self-satisfaction. 'I've simply stopped. I don't nibble at all.'

'Nor do I,' responded a bouncy young woman next to me. 'I eat exactly what it says on the sheet. Four meals a day. Not a scrap of food passes my lips except what I'm allowed. No more nibbling for me. I've given it up forever.' There was much preening from the speakers, fortified by much nodding and muttering of approval from the listeners.

'They must be lying,' whispered Annabel.

When it came to following the diets, another major difference in style was obvious. There was a huge emphasis on
the pleasure of food. The cover of the welcome booklet bore
a picture of nine fruit tarts and the booklet for week two
featured the cork of a wine bottle suggestively speared on a
corkscrew. Inside, however, we discovered the unpalatable
truth. Instead of encouraging members to live on skinless
chicken breast and Quorn-burgers with unlimited vegetables, like the British food plans, the French menus were
simply scaled-down versions of the full meal. A tiny veal
chop with four green beans, a microscopic piece of bread
with a half-portion of Camembert. A spoonful of beetroot
salad, a tiny wing of skate in yoghurt and dill sauce, six
prunes poached in tea. Half a stuffed quail.

The recipe which had Annabel in hysterics for a morning
was for stuffed roasted lamb's kidneys. It was excruciat-
ingly fiddly to prepare and it was not until she pulled the
dish triumphantly out of the oven that she realized that her
portion was to be one single kidney.

It was then that I understood the real secret of French
women's figures. Their food-labelling regulations are not the
same as ours. It's very rare to find the energy value printed
on the label of anything. The label on meat will tell you
exactly who raised the animal and at which abattoir it was
killed, but nothing on a pot of yoghurt will tell you how
many calories it contains.

The French disdain calories. Their secret is portion control, enforced with a rigour that Chairman Mao might have
approved. I had had an inkling, when Reine sweetly offered
to fetch me a plate from my own buffet at my birthday
party. I thought she was just being bitchy when she reappeared with a carefully composed artwork including three
green beans, one scrap of chicken and a lone tiny potato.
Now I realized she had just served me as she would have

served herself. Thus may one remain thin from the cradle to the grave, without ever having to raise the pulse rate. I tried to learn, really I did, but spending an hour preparing a courgette quiche with a single courgette and the white of an egg seemed like a great waste of life.

Corny but Essential

The harvests which were celebrated in October were of the humblest and most central foods – the beans, which must have been the staple starch food in the region for centuries, and the maize, now a heavily subsidised export crop, which has transformed the agricultural profile of the whole of the South-West.

The most famous haricots were from Tarbes, introduced into the valley of the Adour in 1712 by the Bishop of Poudenx, a hamlet in the Gers which must have been considerably grander in those days. The city of Tarbes, for all its urban pretensions, laid on a grand celebration of its beans, but it wasn't enough to persuade us over there. In any case, the *haricots maïs du Béarn*, smaller, sweeter, with thin, satiny skins, were obviously superior.

The maize festivities were inescapable, and since everyone was fed up with the damn stuff by then they seemed highly appropriate. By this time the maize plants were three metres high, dried out and brown. When a strong wind blew the stems rattled against each other, making a sound like ghostly skeletons clattering their bones. Everyone was sick of the ugly sight of the maize fields, and fed up with the huge bugs of every shape and colour which seemed to hide out in there by day.

In the evenings, which were getting longer and darker now, they flew out in squadrons to bomb the villagers' lighted windows with such force that in Maison Bergez it sounded as if someone had thrown a tennis ball at the glass. When I went out to investigate I found one of the copper-coloured beetles, as big as a small apple, lying dazed in the border, feebly waving his legs. I wasn't woman enough to turn him over and the next morning, thank the hedgehog, he was gone.

The village of Laàs went maize-crazy, with a three-day festival for the harvest. The music and singing and the shrieks of the children floated up from the bottom of the valley on the humid autumn air. The local schoolchildren were all invited to help with the festival cutting of the first hectares, and rewarded with a distribution of popcorn. The major enterprise, the felling of the labyrinth, or the maze of maize, was left for Sunday, after the festival mass and the second *grand répas toutenmais*, for those still fit to lift a fork after Saturday night's dance.

At the Auberge de la Fontaine, Alain Darroze put his *milhassou* back on the menu. Darroze is an ambitious young chef who's determined to reinvent the classic dishes of his childhood for a sophisticated clientele. The Auberge has a pretty terrace on the square, and an attractive dining room with an open fire in winter.

It was when I tried *milhassou* that I realized that maize dishes are the comfort food of Gascon cooking. They play the same role as suet puddings in Edwardian England or oatmeal in Scotland, a warm, substantial end to a winter meal for hungry people who've been out in the cold all day.

The maize flour specified in the old Gascon dishes is the same product as fine polenta used in fashionable 'Tuscan' cuisine. Maize dumplings made with finely chopped ham, liver or herbs can enrich any soup you like. In Gascony, *milhas*, a maize porridge or soft polenta, was traditionally served with the *poule au pot* or the *pot au feu*. It inherited the name from millet – called the same in French – which was the staple cereal eaten in the region before the maize was imported.

Milhassou, a cross between a cake and a custard, made with milk and eggs, is a traditional dessert, a beautiful rich gold in colour, served with anything from chocolate sauce to a simple sprinkling of sugar.

Le Milhassou

4 medium eggs
500 ml (16 fl oz) milk
120 g (4 oz) maize flour or fine polenta. Pre-cooked is fine.
120 g (4 oz) butter, left in a warm place to melt
120 g (4 oz) sugar
a pinch of salt
1 tbsp orange-flower water

Preheat the oven to 180°C/350°F/Gas 4 and butter a 23 cm (9 in) cake mould or deep tart tin.

Break the eggs into a bowl and beat them briefly to mix yolks and whites well.

In a medium-sized saucepan, bring the milk to the boil and sprinkle in the maize flour or polenta. Add the butter and sugar, and whisk energetically, so the polenta doesn't form lumps.

Add the beaten eggs, salt and orange-flower water, and mix well.

Pour into the mould and cook for three-quarters of an hour, checking to see that the top isn't blackening. If it starts to turn dark, protect with a piece of foil while the rest of the cake cooks. It's definitely done when the sides are starting to pull away from the tin and, if you stab the centre with a skewer, the skewer will come out clean, without any smears of half-cooked mixture on it.

Remove from the oven and allow to cool for 10 minutes before unmoulding onto a plate. Serve warm or cold, by itself, sprinkled with a little caster sugar, or with the sauce, ice-cream or fruit of your choice. Alain Darroze makes a mini-*milhassou* in a dariole mould (a small individual dessert mould, a little bigger than a ramekin) and serves it warm, with a chocolate sauce and a scoop of supercooled ice cream nestled in the centre.

Aztec Gold

In honouring the origins of the crop that changed the face of their region, the Béarnais firmly identify it as a gift of the Aztecs, whereas we in the Anglophone world regard the Native Americans as the first cultivators of what my mother called 'Indian Corn'. So the French discreetly express their disdain for the United States in a bag of popcorn. At every celebration of the crop, there are colourful reminders of the grain's origins: an Aztec-style idol in papier mâché, a photo on the poster, or a tableau vivant of an emperor and his handmaidens on the float in the Fête du Sel.

The maize suits the soil and climate of the South-West perfectly. It's a coarse, grown-anywhere crop, equally happy in the poor soil of the Basque valleys and the rich land of the Adour valley. I've even seen it growing on traffic islands in Croatia. It's perfectly happy in a deluge. In fact, it's such a thirsty crop that there is an issue with local environmental groups about the effect of its cultivation on the water table. Many farmers, particularly in the less rainy regions like the Gers, have built reservoirs to conserve rainwater.

In the wet summer of 2002, maize was probably the only crop in south-west France which didn't fall prey to mildew, though the crop of 2003, ironically the driest year in living memory, was useless and by July the farmers were ripping it out of the baked soil.

On a small farm, the maize cobs are dried in tall, narrow racks walled in chicken wire and roofed with wood or corrugated iron, which give the grain the maximum exposure to sun and air. They're used principally as animal feed over the winter months, and are the staple food for the chickens and ducks. Perhaps as a consequence of Henri IV's famous promise, the South-West is considered the premier poultry region of France, and the Landes the absolute centre of barnyard excellence.

The total dominance of the duck in Gascon cooking is probably due to the fact that, for a smallholder's wife, rearing around a hundred birds every year, ducks were much more profitable than chickens or geese. The preferred breed is the French Muscovy duck, a much beefier bird than any of our British fowl. From one of these magnificent creatures, the breast, called the *magret de canard*, and the *aiguillettes*, which are simply *magret* sliced longways to make it go further, can be as tender and meaty as fillet steak.

A small-time poultry keeper would also fatten her own ducks to produce one of the ultimate delicacies of France, the *foie gras*. The name literally means 'fat liver', and it is obtained by selecting mature ducks, cooping them up in a warm barn for the last three weeks of their lives and overfeeding them with maize two or three times a day. By the end of this period, they are so fat they can hardly walk, and their livers have become pale and enlarged.

To eat, *foie gras* is less like liver and more like butter; to the unaccustomed digestion, a bilious attack on toast, but to its devotees, one of the ultimate gastronomic luxuries. In the days before industrial agriculture, the feeding – called *gavage*, which means stuffing – was a skilled art. Every duck was individually and very gently hand fed with a small funnel, while the feeder stroked the bird's neck to make sure it was swallowing comfortably. The old cartoons of knowing-looking poultry maids embracing their ducks always featured old hags with nutcracker faces because the skill took half a lifetime to learn.

Today, with the large-scale *foie gras* producers, the *gavage* is a semi-mechanized and undoubtedly cruel process. It also results in inferior *foie gras*. The livers produced by the old method were smaller and fleshier; the livers produced by modern methods are so fatty that they often disintegrate if you try the old ways of cooking them by roasting or poaching. You can still buy hand-reared *foie gras*, directly from hundreds of small farms all over the South-West, and if you really can't live without this controversial delicacy, that would be the most civilized thing to do.

The maize is also fed to the cattle, and the butchers shamelessly advertise 'Traditional Corn-Fed Beef' when, of course, traditional beef would have been fed nothing but the long green grass. Feeding corn, however, is seen as a much safer alternative than fattening cattle on the high-protein nuts that carried the prion proteins which are thought to have caused BSE.

Nobody in *la France profonde* gives any credence whatever to the official line that the country is not at risk from mad-cow disease, and everybody believes that feed made from infected carcasses from Britain has entered the food chain. This does not stop anyone enjoying a good dish of *tête de veau* with *sauce Ravigote*. The only thing that could possibly put the Béarnais off this classic dish of well-presented offal is the revelation that the President, Jacques Chirac, likes it.

This was revealed in a cunning little book which was published that month called *A Table Avec Les Politiques*. Two astute young women writers flattered the wives of a string of prominent politicians and took them out to lunch. In the course of idle conversation, these overlooked consorts of the peacock males of Paris happily divulged all the secrets of their husbands' gastronomic preferences. This was considered the most telling information possible about the morals of the men running the country.

The fact that Chirac was said to like *tête de veau* and that the Prime Minister, Jean-Pierre Raffarin, formerly described as the man nobody was waiting for, revealed a homely liking for snails, suggests that both their wives were on to the authors. Nothing was more likely to convince the cynical electorate that these unloved public figures were really honest men of the people than the claim that they enjoyed these down-home classics. I was ashamed to see that a senior political commentator at *The Times* described *tête de veau* as 'cow's brain', when in fact it's what traditional British cooking would call brawn, the poached meat from the head of a calf, including the tongue, but not the brains. Brawn was a staple dinner dish for a poor family in my parents' day. Being cheap, provocative and quintessentially French, *Tête de Veau, Sauce Ravigote* was also Roger's favourite dish at La Terrasse.

How To Spend €100 on a Coffee

Andrew and I planned a final day of bargain hunting, at the Foire des Antiquaires at Pau, a grand occasion in that grand little city. With us came a new friend, Penny, who, with her husband, had forsaken an Elizabethan mansion in Shropshire for a house in the Chalosse with a stunning view due west over the lush green hills. Penny is blonde, square-shouldered, athletic-looking and tall. When she stands beside Andrew, at six foot something, Geoff at six foot even more, and me, at only five foot ten, we look like half a veteran basketball team.

The Foire was a serious event, held in a convention centre in the centre of the town, and in the sports ground and the car park and the warehouses adjoining it. Maysounabe was still fairly bare, and next year they planned to start work restoring a ruined barn in the garden to add five extra bedrooms to their spread, so furniture was still needed.

By now, we had worked out a bargain-hunting routine. First, we cruised through the whole event, checking out likely items which caught our eye. This we did twice, because you always miss things the first time when you're still getting oriented. At this point, it was a good idea to buy any item which was utterly desirable or seriously under-priced, because it would sure as hell be sold to somebody in the next half-hour.

We would then go for a coffee. Then we went back to look over the things that had interested us, and checked the prices. Then we did another sweep, and had another coffee, and talked over the merits and demerits of the pieces we fancied. Then, as lunch time began to loom, we made our final choices and went shopping.

At first, Andrew was not enthusiastic about the cornucopia on offer. The dealers were too professional for him to get the thrill of finding a real bargain, and the French taste in antiques, for anything twiddly, frilly, gilded, encrusted with carved rosebuds and looking as if Mme Pompadour once sat on it, was too much in evidence. He drifted grumpily up and down the aisles, complaining that all the furniture was over-restored.

Then he found a painting. It was big, about eight feet by

six, late-Impressionist-going-on-Modernist, definitely from the early 1900s, mostly chalky beige and light olive green, and its subject was the Moulin Rouge in Paris. Not framed, but prominently signed. It had been carelessly propped against the side of a stall, and the dealer wanted €600 for it.

We considered it for some time. On the plus side, it was a really nice painting and we liked it. Also, thanks to Baz Luhrmann, every air-head model in London would be able to recognize the Moulin Rouge. No damage and a signature – these were also good. On the minus side, Andrew didn't know enough about paintings from the period to feel confident that the price was right, and I wondered if the dominance of neutral colours on the canvas might not mean that the whole thing blurred into the middle distance when it was hung on the stone wall of the studio at Maysounabe, which was the only place with space to hang it.

We went for a coffee and discussed these matters. On balance, it was a great painting, €600 was a good price for a painting of that quality and size, and the subject would make it easy to sell on if it turned out to be a mistake. Andrew wasn't 100 per cent convinced, but we decided to go back and take another look.

The painting had gone. Utterly desirable and seriously underpriced, of course it had gone. Andrew was peeved. Now that the painting had vanished, he was 100 per cent convinced that he wanted it.

We made a final sweep, bought some sexy little water-colours (me) and some massive stone urns (Penny), and intended to meet up on the steps of the hall before going to lunch. As I approached the main doors, I saw the painting, now more respectfully displayed, on another stall.

'The Moulin Rouge hasn't left the building,' I said to Andrew. 'It's on another stall, just inside the doors.'

The three of us went back inside. The Moulin Rouge

looked better than ever. We asked the price. It was €1,000. Andrew offered €700. The seller, a slightly built man with thinning hair, dismissed the offer immediately. It was a really nice painting, he didn't really want to sell it, he wanted to enjoy it himself for a while. Anyway he'd only just bought it.

'We know you've only just bought it,' Andrew explained, his French now up to the task. 'We looked at it with the man you bought it from, and he only wanted €600. You probably got it for €500. If you take €700 now, you've made €200 in half an hour. That's not bad.'

The seller looked stricken, possibly because the three of us were looming over him from our superior height. He could see our point. We could see his point. Since he had a mobile, sympathetic kind of face, I decided a bigger guilt trip might swing the deal.

'Look,' I said, 'if we'd bought that painting when we first saw it, we'd have got it for €500. All we did was go for a couple of coffees. If we buy it from you now for €700, those cups of coffee will have cost us €100 each. It's hardly fair, is it?'

An agonized expression crinkled the seller's eyes. Eventually, Andrew bought the Moulin Rouge for €800. I think I was right about the colours against the stone wall, but he's so devoted to the painting he doesn't care.

The Last Flight of Fancy

We planned a final trip to the flea market at Ahetze. I embarked on one last round of trying to persuade people to come with me for a truly spectacular day out, and recruited a new friend, Sue, who was waiting out the end of a career

with the NHS before planning to live in her pretty little
house next to the church in Burgaronne. Living in France, as
we have seen, can be hard on an English marriage, especially
when the wife speaks degree-level French and the husband
doesn't, so Sue was taking a break on her own and was glad
to have company and a new experience.

We took off in the morning with the mountains crystal
clear, the snow on the top slopes matching the white clouds
above. Strong winds were stripping the leaves from the
trees, and flocks of wild pigeons, called *palombes*, were wheel-
ing through the air above us. They were bang on time.
The *palombe* season runs from All Saints Day at the end of
October to St Martin's Day, 11 November. For this frantic
fortnight while the birds migrate south the hunters take to
the woods and set about enticing them within range of their
guns. Or, if they're determined to exterminate the species,
their nets.

Hunting has reduced the numbers of *palombes* so drasti-
cally that it is now rigorously controlled. Once, flocks of
thousands of birds darkened the sky every autumn, and they
were hunted as far north as the Gers. Baskets of them were
sent up to Paris every day. Now most of the old sites have
been abandoned, a mere trickle of birds fly past and it's
unusual to find them on a menu outside the region. The
hunters can only gather at a few designated sites, and only
use the traditional methods to catch them.

For two weeks, the *palombe*-spotters, called *paloumayres*,
spend all the hours of daylight up in their tree houses, on
the lookout for the flocks of birds. They climb up a long
ladder to little wooden cabins, pulling up their supplies – a
casserole, a bottle of wine and some water, the camping gas
and a coffee pot – in baskets after them. They also carry up
some tame pigeons in a wicker basket. The cabin has a
makeshift bed with a mattress of dry moss and a rough table

covered with oilcloth. They take turns to scan the sky for the tiny black dots of the *palombes* approaching from the north.

The tame pigeon, who spends the rest of the year at ease in a makeshift aviary erected next to his owner's chicken house, is taken out of his carrying basket and installed on a small wooden see-saw high in the branches. A light string attached to his leg ring stops him flying away. Another string runs from the free end of the see-saw to the hand of the *paloumayre*.

The *palombes* fly so fast that the hunters have only a few seconds to get their attention. Once a flock is spotted, the hunter tweaks the string attached to the see-saw, causing it to rock, which makes the tame bird flap its wings as it tries to balance on the moving plank. The wild birds, seeing the telltale flapping below them, assume that one of their number has found a good source of food. Unwarily, they bomb out of the sky – the *palombes* have a lovely tumbling motion in the air – and within range of the hunters' guns.

Ahetze was a picture postcard as ever, with the sun shining on the terracotta roofs, the ox-blood shutters, the white walls and the double bell tower of the church rising above the crammed stalls. A small flock of *palombes* was twisting and turning in the sky as we approached, and the shots of the *palombe* hunters echoed over the murmur of the market all morning.

We browsed for a couple of hours, then ate lunch on the tree-shaded terrace of the village restaurant. The dish of the day, of course, was *salmis de palombe*, much appreciated by the multinational Lovejoys, and by us. The *palombe* is a finer, more delicate meat than a woodpigeon; it's delicious, especially if simply roasted, but eating one is nowhere near as thrilling as watching the living birds spiralling through the crisp autumn air.

We lingered over a last coffee and headed back. By then the clouds had rolled in from the mountains, a giant grey duvet with cinnamon uplights at the horizon. I helped Sue clear up her garden, then we had a last glass of wine while a spectacular sunset took over the whole sky, turning gold, then teal blue, then bronze, then fading to rose before the darkness fell.

We talked about stray cats and complicated men, and how I felt about going back. I still had a long list of unrealized ambitions in the Béarn. There was still so much I wanted to do, so many places I wanted to explore, so many events I wanted to witness. Thanks to my injury, I had hardly been able to walk in the mountains at all. Margaret took me for a mercy stroll near the little village of Laruns for an afternoon, but my ankle wasn't strong enough for anything ambitious.

There were things I was distinctly looking forward to in London:

1. being in the same country as my daughter
2. my friends
3. my great big good-looking sofa
4. my own bed
5. people ringing up and saying they had theatre tickets and was I free?
6. fish and chips

That was it.

There were also many things I was dreading in London: the everyday violence and nastiness of the people, the vast ugliness of the city, the chaotic transport, the draining difficulty of accomplishing even a simple thing, the cynical, ignorant youth and the despised and despairing old, whose ranks I would inevitably join soon.

In London, I had happily passed days inside my house

because outside it I would find nothing but people spitting, swearing, abusing, attacking and exploiting each other. But a year of tranquillity had made me feel guilty. After all, I was not without talents, or influence. If my country was turning into a sewer, I could do something about it. I could not justify simply escaping to another country which had taken greater pains to maintain a good quality of life.

Besides, there were things I was not going to miss in France. I was longing to have a simple, casual conversation with someone who dared to think, whose conscience was still in working order and whose brain had not yet been overpowered by cheap booze. As if to make me feel good about leaving, I was invited to a dinner party from hell.

The table was dominated by a businessman, who suddenly announced that literature was all rubbish and that J. K. Rowling was all washed up and couldn't finish Harry Potter V. He didn't know Rowling, nor had he read any of her books. He didn't know anyone in publishing and couldn't remember who had told him the gossip he was passing on with such authority. He did know that I was an author, but obviously saw this as no reason to speak with caution.

I flexed my vocabulary, got ready with a magazine of 'effectivements' and 'de toutes façons', and pointed out that nothing is more difficult than to top a success, let alone a global-phenomenon-sized success. Think of Edmond Rostand, half-killed by the success of *Cyrano de Bergerac*. Furthermore, the Potter series was approaching the toughest part of the narrative cycle, so a hard time for the author was normal. The books were, in my opinion, a magnificent achievement, they thoroughly deserved their success. As the critics had said about *Cyrano*, it made you feel good just to know there was such a great talent in the world. Furthermore – this clinched it with the other women at the table, some of whom had been looking thoroughly alarmed – the author, having been a single mother for so long, was now enjoying the happiness of a new marriage and was about to have a baby. So possibly she had a few things besides writing on her mind.

My antagonist listened carefully, then reverted to his favourite topic, the pan-global Jewish conspiracy to take over the world. Didn't I realize that Tony Blair was Jewish? And Jack Straw? For a moment, I was happy to be going home. There are probably plenty of people in London with such objectionable attitudes, but it is much easier to avoid them.

A la Prochaine . . .

I gathered my final crop from the potager, the Jerusalem artichokes. By then, they were mighty plants with woody stems and wilting yellow flowers. I stuck a fork under the first one and levered it out of the ground, revealing a clutch of white racemes nestling in the root ball. These I arranged artistically on a spade for a Monty Don-style photograph, but in the chaos of packing I couldn't find the camera.

The owner of Maison Bergez hoped to rent it to a Danish couple who were looking for somewhere to stay while they were house-hunting for their retirement. There was no need to restore the knickknacks to their former homes. Amandine did a final clean-up, while I weeded the rest of the vegetable plot and tucked it up under a layer of black plastic for the winter. The first compost heap — by now I had two — was ready-rotted, and I could use some of its rich russet compost on the stony borders around the house.

On my last night, Annabel and Gerald took me to dinner at their favourite *auberge*, in a little village in the valley called Audax. *Garbure*, Jurançon, *confit*, a Béarnais last supper.

Gordon was going to drive for me. He wanted to go to Scotland to scatter his father's ashes near the place where he had been born. The urn, in its discreet travelling box, would join my computer in the back of the car. Since my ankle still wasn't strong enough for eight hours on the road, I was immensely grateful. I paid a last visit to Tarmac's grave, left a bag of biscuits and a bowl of water for Henri Cat, loaded Piglet and the Duchess into their baskets, locked the door of Maison Bergez and set off for the caravan in Bellocq.

The Pyrenees did their best to make me stay. On my last night they were grey silhouettes with a mother-of-pearl sky behind them, rounded shapes in the distance, a herd of fossilized dinosaurs, one humped dark back after another.

In the early morning there was mist in the valleys, so the peaks looked as if they were resting on pillows of silver silk. There was a strip of brilliance at the horizon, backlighting the whole chain. The second range, which is most often hidden in a haze, suddenly came clear, a series of steep, rounded hills, all a brilliant green, with wisps of mist lingering around their shoulders. By the time I was ready to go, the highest peak, the double-pointed Pic du Midi d'Ossau, was as clear as day and again I had the illusion that I could see every snow-covered stone.

The most haunting of all the Béarnais songs is 'Aqueras Montanhas', a local variation of a lament that is sung in all the provinces that made up the Pays d'Oc, the land of the troubadours. It is attributed to Gaston Fébus himself; somehow the melody evokes the sense of wonder which the mountains inspire, the longing to grasp an eternal mystery that lies up there somewhere in the mists and crags. That was the feeling that brought me here, and I still had it when I left. So of course I promised to come back.

Aqueras Montanhas

Aqueras montanhas,	These mountains
Qui tan hautas son,	They're so high
M'empachan de véder	They're hiding all my sweethearts
Mas amors ont son.	And everyone I love
Si sabi las véder	If I knew how to get to them
On las rencontrar	Where they could be found
Passeri l'augueta	Fear of drowning wouldn't stop me
Shens paur de'm negar.	Crossing the rivers
Aqueras montanhas	These mountains,
Be s'abaisharàn,	They're really going to fall
E mas amoretas	And I'll be able to see
Que pareisheràn.	All my sweethearts again
Devath ma frinèsta	Under my window
I a un auseron	There's a little bird
Total la nueit canta	It sings all night
Canta sa cançon	Singing its own song.

Epilogue

I looked different. It was hard to define exactly how, apart from the bad highlights done by a French hairdresser who'd sploshed on the bleach as if he was plastering bricks, but one of my friends said, 'There was a darkness in you and it's lifted.'

I felt lighter. I had more energy – that lasted about nine months. I could see that my face was softer, my eyes were brighter. I discovered a deep reservoir of serenity and a new capacity for patience. There is still a subtle sense of being centred, which allows me to make decisions about my life and work more calmly. They seem like better decisions than those I made before my year away, though of course only time will tell. But I care less. I seem to have acquired that sense of being in the moment, as my Buddhist friends would say.

Some of the qualities which I know that I used to have, before the long struggle of lone parenthood and the suffocating pressure of a semi-public life, seem to have reasserted themselves. I have a sense of fun, and of adventure, and of possibilities. The suspicion that life is completely futile doesn't seem well founded any more.

Some of my friendships are stronger, although I don't think Gill will ever forget how her sun-kissed summer holiday turned into a week of non-stop rain and no beaches. I'm still aware of the pressure on a friendship in a city. If you don't fancy a Carrie Bradshaw life, out in bars every night, it's hard to create another context of relaxation and shared experience. Some old friends have drifted away. I didn't fall over myself to pick up with the chaps – two of them – who rang me up in Orriule only once, to ask me how much I thought my London house was worth.

Before my year in France, I was sure that I didn't want to live there permanently, not least because I would be too far away from Chloe. She gained a year of unfettered independence while I was away, and enjoyed a lot of adventures in a new culture, but I suspect that I made the classic mistake of a baby-boom parent, and assumed my child was longing to be free of me when actually she was perfectly happy to have me around. She looks rosier now that I'm never far away, and seems to have more confidence. 'I'm gloriously happy that you're not in France,' she said. 'Why?' I asked. 'Because you're here,' she said.

Coming home was always the plan. Even a year ago, I had seen enough of ex-pat communities to know that full-time lotus-eating is not for me. One thing above all which I've always found scary is the degree to which these enclaves are so detached from reality that they are almost a parallel universe. Deliberately or not, people acquire fantasy identities. They lose the ability to discriminate between fantastic gossip and verifiable facts. Ridiculous vendettas take up all their attention, while important realities fade from their consciousness, so they suddenly wake up to find they've inadvertently broken the law or lost their savings.

Expatville is a fun place to visit but a bad place to live, especially for a writer. I'm a person who enjoys putting down roots, although it was good to be repotted for a year.

In my year in the Béarn, I met people who were third-generation ex-pats, people whose grandparents had moved abroad and whose families had never gone 'home'. Some spoke fluent French and had integrated quite far – but never fully – into their host community. Some spoke undiluted London English and were not fully literate in either language.

The crassness of some of the earlier immigrants was astonishing. Many of them had burned their boats financially, and could never afford to buy back into the British property market. These were the bitter ones. A surprising number spoke no French and had given up trying to learn. One of these was a woman who joked, 'My finger speaks French,' meaning that she could do her shopping by going into the market and pointing at what she wanted to buy.

All this is changing, very fast. There are, and always have been, good, brave, intelligent and curious people among the British in France. The balance is shifting rapidly towards them, as more and more cultural migrants arrive. Some of these are people buying retirement homes or holiday houses. Some of them make their living in the tourist industry, sharing their own delight in the country and its culture with short-term visitors.

Increasingly, however, people in the middle of their working lives are leaving their native countries for France. There are people like me, or like Andrew and Geoff, artists who can work anywhere. There are people who want to establish businesses, to farm, to make wine or cheese, to breed horses or to run restaurants. There are people with young families, who have looked long and hard at what they want for their children. This corner of 'old Europe' is becoming a New World for British settlers.

Most of these new immigrants are drawn by their love of rural France, and what it represents. In the case of the British they are also pushed by a growing horror of life in their own country. They want schools where their children will learn at least one language properly. They want streets that are safe, good roads, trains that run on time, clean hospitals, villages with living traditions, towns with vibrant centres, a flourishing countryside.

They're looking for all the infrastructure of a truly civilized country, which means everything that successive British governments have not considered worthy of adequate investment.

The French, who took the crucial decision to define themselves as a rural society, have provided this infrastructure for their own citizens as of right, at the cost of high taxation. How long they will be happy with their new settlers remains to be seen. Many a moribund French village is being revitalized by foreigners; sometimes the villagers are delighted, sometimes it is undeniable that they feel invaded and worry that their own culture will be smothered.

I miss my new friends and I miss our shared life of dropping in, passing by, sharing meals and setting off on explorations. I miss my garden; in London, I have a ten-foot patio; perhaps the most gorgeous patio in Hammersmith, but still a patio. I miss shopping being a pleasure and I miss having the time to cook. More than I could possibly have imagined, I miss the mountains.

I miss the paradoxical sense of freedom which came from living in a small community, in which the sense of personal safety is significant. On the night Gordon and I drove into London, two schoolgirls out trick-or-treating were raped in the local park. A few weeks later, a crack-head broke into my neighbour's house by throwing a brick through her sitting-room window and diving head-first after it. Since then, my chequebook and wallet, separately, have been stolen, my car has been broken into and my next-door neighbours have emigrated to Australia with their children, aged four and one.

Of course, more important things have happened in the world.

Andrew and Geoff restored their barn and James English France, their new company, was booked solid with photographers from the beginning of June 2003. They wanted to spend the next winter in Bordeaux, improving their French.

Roger painted a portrait of me, and included my profile in a mural in McGuire's Irish Pub in Saliès.

Every time he came out of hospital, Glynn Boyd Harte said he'd never felt so good and embroidered sparkling anecdotes about his adventures. In December 2003, at the private view of a new and wonderfully successful exhibition, he felt faint and returned home. A few days later, he died, at the age of fifty-five. The obituaries described his life as 'a vehicle of genius' and called him one of the most brilliant and influential artists of his time. I have a fond memory of him sitting by the fire in Maison Bergez and saying to Piglet, 'Do you realize you've got asymmetrical whiskers?'

In France, there is serious talk of abolishing the thirty-five-hour working week.

By order of President Chirac, on 29 November 2002 the remains of Alexandre Dumas were dug up from the small cemetery north of Paris where they had been for more than a century, placed in a coffin draped with velvet and emblazoned with the Musketeers' motto, *Tous Pour Un, Un Pour Tous*, and awarded a lying in state outside the Château de Monte-Cristo. This event was shown on television, with leading writers and actors standing vigil. Then, attended by Presidential Guards and four Musketeers dressed by the couturier Jean-Charles de Castelbajac, the coffin was transferred to central Paris and taken in procession from the Senate to the Panthéon, between cheering crowds who had been happy to obey the official suggestion that they should carry copies of Dumas's works. At the Panthéon, the remains of the great author were interred beside those of the rest of France's leading writers. In Saliès in 2003, fifty per cent of house sales were to British buyers.

Zoe and Matthieu were married in London just before Christmas. In April, they held a beautiful reception for two hundred people at the concert hall in Tilh, which began with a blessing from the Anglican vicar of Pau and ended with fireworks and dancing until dawn. They have bought a house in Laàs, and Zoe has opened a shop in London, to sell Basque linen and ceramics. She has called it Espadrille. It is in a part of Fulham where there are already so many shops, bars and delis selling French antiques, food and drink that people are calling it Little France.

Bibliography and Information

Literature and Biography

La Reine Margot. Alexandre Dumas, tr. Coward, Oxford University Press, 1997.

The Three Musketeers. Alexandre Dumas, tr. Sudley. Penguin, 1952.

Aspects of Love. David Garnett. Chatto & Windus, 1955.

Voyage en Espagne/España. Théophile Gautier. Folio Classique/Editions Gallimard, 1981.

Gaston Fébus: Prince Des Pyrénées. Pierre Tucoo-Chala. Editions Deucalion, 1993.

The First Bourbon: Henry IV of France and Navarre. Desmond Seward. Constable, 1971.

Eugénie: The Empress and her Empire. Desmond Seward. Sutton, 2004.

Cyrano de Bergerac. Edmund Rostand, tr. Burgess. Hutchinson, 1985.

The Man Who Was Cyrano: A life of Edmond Rostand. Sue Lloyd. Unlimited Publishing, US, 2003.

Magic. Edited by Sarah Brown and Gil McNeil. Bloomsbury, 2002.

History and Folklore

Lo Nouste Béarn. Hubert Dutech. Mon Hélios, 2003.

Le Béarn. Marcelin Berthelot. Lacour, 2000.

Proverbes du Pays de Béarn. V. Lespy. Lacour, 1992.

The Basque History of the World. Mark Kurlansky. Jonathan Cape, 1999.

Saliès-de-Béarn. Jean Labarthe. Les Amis De Vieux Saliès, 1996.

Légendes du Pays Basque – Les Pyrénées et Leurs Légendes. C Lacour. Editeur, 2002.

La France Secrète et Mysterieuse: Lieux et sources des légendes. Benoit Laudier. Guides Gallimard, 1996.

Contes de Gascogne. Jean-François Bladé, illustrated Jean-Claude Pertuzé.

Autrefois Le Pays Basque. Claude Bailhé. Editions Milan, 1999.

L'almanach du Pyrénéen. Gerard Bardon. Editions CPE, 2002.

Eleanor of Aquitaine. Alison Weir. Jonathan Cape, 1999.

Athenaïs: The Real Queen of France. Lisa Hilton. Little, Brown, 2002.

Cooking and Food

La Cuisine des Pyrénées. Francine Claustres. Editions Sud Ouest, 1994.

French Country Cooking. Elizabeth David. Penguin, 1966.

French Provincial Cooking. Elizabeth David. Penguin, 1968.

La Cuisine Gasconne. Guilou Giacomazzi. Lacour, 2001.

Cod: A Biography of the Fish that Changed the World. Mark Kurlansky. Jonathan Cape, 1998.

Memories of Gascony. Pierre Koffmann. Headline, 1991.

The Cooking of South-West France. Paula Wolfert. Dorling Kindersley, 1989.

Under the Sun. Caroline Conran. Pavilion, 2002.

Cuisine Grand-Mère. Marie-Pierre Moine. Ebury Press, 2001.

Tourism

Gascony & The Pyrenees. Cadogan Guides: Diana Facaros and Michael Pauls; updated Rosemary Bailey, 2001.

Bilbao & the Basque Lands. Cadogan Guides: Diana Facaros and Michael Pauls, 2001.

Pyrenees Aquitaine Côte Basque. Michelin.

Magazines and Periodicals

Pays Basque. Issue nos: 15, 16, 17, 18, 19, 20, 21, 22. Milan Presse, Toulouse.

Côte Ouest. 2002.

Maisons sud Ouest. 2002.

La Gazette des Ventes. Edition du Sud-Ouest,
   1 Route de Fajolles, 82100 Garganvillar.
   tel: 05 63 95 64 57*, fax: 05 63 95 64 57,
   email: michel.ferrer3@wanadoo.fr

The News. 3 Chemin de la Mounie, 24000 Perigueux.

Restaurants

This is a random and highly personal list of the restaurants which wormed their way into the story – sadly, in a year in a region justly famous for several great cuisines, I spent far too much time writing and not nearly enough on gastronomic research, so failing to get around even a quarter of the most distinguished establishments. For a more exhaustive listing, consult the Cadogan Guides (see above.)

Auberge du Forail, Place du Forail, St-Palais.
   tel: 05 59 65 73 22
Auberge de la Fontaine, Square de l'Église, 64390 Laàs.
   tel: 05 59 38 59 33

---

* **Telephone numbers** given are for dialling in France. If dialling from outside France, drop the initial zero and substitute the international code for France, 00 33. So the French number 05 59 38 11 18 would become the international number 00 33 5 59 38 11 18.

La Belle Auberge, 64270 Castagnède.
   tel: 05 59 38 15 28, fax: 05 59 65 03 57
Blue Cargo, Villa Itsasoan, Avenue Ilbarritz, 64200, Biarritz.
   tel: 05 59 24 36 30
Le Commerce/Chez Darracq, Amou. tel: 05 38 89 02,
   email: hotel-darracq-le-commerce-amout@wanadoo.fr
Chez Pantxoa, Port de Socoa, 64500 St-Jean-de-Luz.
   tel: 05 59 47 13 73
Chez Tante Ursule, Bas-Cambo. tel: 05 59 93 7575
Les Près d'Eugénie (gastronomic) and Auberge de la
   Ferme aux Grives (farmhouse) at Eugénie-les-Bains.
   tel: 05 58 05 06 07, fax 05 58 51 10 10.
   Website for the whole resort:
   www.ville-eugenie-les-bains.fr
La Terasse, 64370 Saliès-de-Béarn. tel: 05 59 38 09 83
Txamara, Port de Guéthary, 64210 Guéthary.
   tel: 05 59 26 51 44

Tourist Offices

Orthez: Office de Tourisme,
   Maison Jeanne d'Albret, 64300 Orthez.
   tel: 05 59 69 37 50, fax 05 59 69 12 00,
   email tourisme.orthez@wandoo.fr

Sauveterre-de-Béarn: Office de Tourisme,
   Place Royale, 64390 Sauveterre-de-Béarn.
   tel: 05 59 38 58 65, fax 05 59 38 94 82,
   email 0t.sauveterre@wanadoo.fr

Saliès-de-Béarn: Office de Tourisme,
   Rue des Bains, 64270 Saliès-de-Béarn.
   tel: 05 59 38 00 33, fax 05 59 38 02 95,
   email: Saliès-de-Béarn.tourisme@wanadoo.fr

Website: www.Béarn-gaves.com

Index of Recipes

Picture credits

Part titles November, February, March, May, June, July, September, October: Celia Brayfield. December: Editions Artpyr. January: Photo RMN 'G.F. Tournachon'. April: The Vanity Fair Print Company. August: Musée du second Empire, Picardy (portrait by Franz Xavier Winterhalter).

Plate section Maison Bergez; Squirly ironwork chairs; Lunch at Maysounabe; *Esprit de* Beverly Hills; Rock Pools at Biarritz; Saliès-de-Béarn townhouses; The Duchess; Piglet: Celia Brayfield. Andrew, out walking with Otto and a guest: Adrian Forster. Poster for Rostand's *Cyrano de Bergerac*: photo Marc Hauvette – Editions Lavielle. Saliès-de-Béarn, the bandstand: watercolour by Glynn Boyd Harte by kind permission of David Game (orientation as in the original). Detail from Roger Hallet's panorama of Saliès-de-Béarn, showing La Terrasse: by kind permission of the artist. Le lac de Bious-Artigues et l'Ossau: Jean Pascal Seyrat.